MATTERING PRESS

Mattering Press is an academic-led Open Access publisher that operates on a not-for-profit basis as a UK registered charity. It is committed to developing new publishing models that can widen the constituency of academic knowledge and provide authors with significant levels of support and feedback. All books are available to download for free or to purchase as hard copies. More at matteringpress.org.

The Press' work has been supported by: Centre for Invention and Social Process (Goldsmiths, University of London), European Association for the Study of Science and Technology, Hybrid Publishing Lab, infostreams, Institute for Social Futures (Lancaster University), OpenAIRE, Open Humanities Press, and Tetragon, as well as many other institutions and individuals that have supported individual book projects, both financially and in kind.

We are indebted to the ScholarLed community of Open Access, scholar-led publishers for their companionship and extend a special thanks to the Directory of Open Access Books and Project MUSE for cataloguing our titles.

MAKING THIS BOOK

Books contain multitudes. Mattering Press is keen to render more visible the unseen processes that go into the production of books. We would like to thank Joe Deville, who acted as the Press' coordinating editor for this book, the two reviewers Andrew Clement and Maxigas, Steven Lovatt for the copy editing, Jennifer Tomomitsu for the proof reading and work on the book production, Alex Billington and Tetragon for the typesetting, and Will Roscoe, Ed Akerboom, and infostreams for their contributions to the html versions of this book.

COVER

Cover art by Julien McHardy.

CONCEALING FOR FREEDOM

The Making of Encryption,
Secure Messaging and Digital Liberties

KSENIA ERMOSHINA
FRANCESCA MUSIANI

foreword by
LAURA DENARDIS

Mattering Press

First edition published by Mattering Press, Manchester.

ISBN: 978-1-912729-22-7 (ppk)
ISBN: 978-1-912729-23-4 (pdf)
ISBN: 978-1-912729-24-1 (epub)
ISBN: 978-1-912729-25-8 (html)
DOI: doi.org/10.28938/9781912729227

CONTENTS

List of figures   7

Authors   9

Foreword: The political life of encryption by Laura DeNardis   11

Preface: A note for readers   15

Acknowledgments   21

List of abbreviations and acronyms   27

0 · Introduction   31

1 · Concealing from whom? Threat modelling and
    risk as a relational concept   66

2 · Centralised architectures as informal standards
    for 'control by design'   89

3 · Peer-to-peer encryption and decentralised governance:
    A not-so-obvious pair   120

4 · Federation: Treading the line between technical compromise
    and ideological choice   148

5 · What is 'good' security? Categorising and evaluating
    encrypted messaging tools   183

6 · Conclusions: Encrypted communications as a site of
    social, political and technical controversy   210

Bibliography   241

Appendix: Interview selection process and ethical guidelines   257

Glossary   261

LIST OF FIGURES

FIG. 1.1 Digital security training observed in Kyiv, January 2017   72

FIG. 1.2 User representation of 'insecure communications'   76

FIG. 1.3 User representation of 'secure communications'   77

FIG. 1.4 Drawing collected during the interview on February 16, 2017   83

FIG. 3.1 A vision of 'safer Internet'.   123

FIG. 3.2 Adding a remote contact on Briar   141

FIG. 5.1 The Secure Messaging Scorecard, version 1.0   188

FIG. 5.2 Secure Messaging Scorecard main page between
August 2016 and its withdrawal in 2018   192

FIG. 5.3 Sample of 'user paths' on the SSD home page as of early 2017   202

AUTHORS

KSENIA ERMOSHINA and FRANCESCA MUSIANI are tenured researchers at the French National Centre for Scientific Research (CNRS). They are based at the Centre for Internet and Society, which Francesca co-founded and co-directs. From 2016 to 2018, Ksenia and Francesca worked within the H2020 project NEXTLEAP (NEXT-generation techno-social and Legal Encryption, Access and Privacy). Their research explores Internet infrastructures and architectures as tools of governance (and resistance) in today's digital world.

LAURA DENARDIS is a globally recognised Internet governance scholar and Professor in the School of Communication at American University in Washington, DC, where she also serves as Faculty Director of the Internet Governance Lab. With a background in information engineering and a doctorate in science and technology studies, she has published seven books and numerous articles on the political implications of Internet architecture and governance.

FOREWORD

THE POLITICAL LIFE OF ENCRYPTION

Laura DeNardis

WHAT HAPPENS IN CYBERSPACE NO LONGER STAYS IN CYBERSPACE. A ransomware attack on a fuel pipeline company leads to long lines at gas stations. A healthcare system data breach prevents people from receiving medical care. An infiltration into a home video security system leads to egregious violations of personal privacy. Foreign probing of digital voter rolls reduces trust in democracy. And security disruptions to cyber-physical industrial systems are also disruptions of our food supply, livelihoods and ability to function in daily life.

Being 'offline' is no longer a defence against the effects of any of these disruptions. People who have never even been on the Internet can be affected by, for example, a data breach of credit card information at their favourite retail store or be harmed by a security vulnerability in a telemedicine device. The complication of society's digital dependencies, with all of its undoubted upsides, is that the security of everything in life now depends upon strong cybersecurity. Hence, cybersecurity is a great human rights issue of our time. Democracy, financial transactions, consumer safety and the stability of all industrial sectors now depend upon it just as much as personal privacy does.

Strong encryption solves many of these concerns. Yet those who have invented the numerous ingenious encryption protocols over recent decades sometimes express surprise that widely available and strong encryption is not implemented everywhere in digital society. Is this merely because of the cost or processing power required for strong encryption, or something more complex?

Encryption is arguably the most politically charged of all Internet technologies. The ability of governments to apply encryption and break encryption has been at the core of diplomatic strategies, foreign intelligence, law enforcement and national security approaches for decades. The complication is that encryption – and especially encryption strength – is a site of contestation and tension between competing values, even within a single government. National security now requires strong cybersecurity around critical communication and industrial systems, and the digital economy. But at the same time, governments also have an interest in weak encryption for law enforcement and intelligence gathering purposes. Law enforcement personnel sometimes call this the 'going dark' problem, where encrypted messaging and encrypted devices become inaccessible for routine evidence gathering. The intelligence necessary for counter-terrorism similarly depends upon the ability to access encrypted communications.

Societal requirements for strong encryption – for securing financial transactions, defending infrastructure and protecting the right to privacy – are directly opposed to the societal requirement that law enforcement and intelligence agencies need access to encrypted information, or more authoritarian surveillance approaches that monitor and control the lives of citizens. This same tension exists between privacy and the invasive business models that rely upon personal data gathering in exchange for customised online ads. Many of the largest technology companies do not charge users for their services but they rank among the highest revenue generating institutions on the planet by collecting the personal data of users and converting this into revenue.

Responding to these tensions and the dynamic norms around the global intersection of security, privacy and social control, different governments have established diverse regulatory approaches to encryption technologies, ranging from banning some outright, to restricting exports to certain countries, to requiring licenses to use them. Because of the political stakes of encryption, it is not surprising that cryptography has sometimes been regulated under the same statutes as firearms and munitions.

In short, cryptography occupies a powerful place in modern society. It is a highly politicised lever of power balancing trust in the economy and democracy, national security, human safety, individual privacy, and law enforcement and intelligence gathering functions.

Considering the stakes, there has not been sufficient examination of encryption and secure messaging as a central lever of infrastructure politics. *Concealing for Freedom* is a much-needed book that cracks open the black box of encrypted secure messaging and discusses the consequences for freedom and online civil liberties. Secure messaging and tools are not just born when implemented into products or regulated by governments. They are created by design communities. And they are shaped by designers who make technical decisions that consider risk, threat models, business models, sociopolitical context and technical constraints. Decentralised versus centralised? Localisation versus globalisation? Anonymous or pseudonymous approaches? What counts as 'good' or 'desirable' security? The standardisation process itself, and design decisions about arrangements of architecture, are also arrangements of power.

Fundamental human rights such as personal privacy and free speech, and the right to trust in digital infrastructures and economies, are shaped by communication protocols. The tension in protocol design between security and privacy has a long history, but it came to the fore after American government contractor Edward Snowden's disclosures about the massive extent of National Security Agency (NSA) surveillance. Internet protocol designers immediately called for 'hardening the Internet' with more extensive end-to-end encryption. The Internet Engineering Task Force (IETF) published consensus documents suggesting that indiscriminate surveillance of either content or metadata was an assault on individual privacy that should prompt stronger encryption choices that make such surveillance either less possible or more expensive. These designers acknowledged both the importance of individual privacy and also the need to restore trust in the Internet. This wasn't the first-time protocol designers would push back against government surveillance.

The political and social stakes around encryption continue to rise as government and corporate surveillance approaches alike become more sophisticated, but also as new technologies emerge. As the Internet has leapt from two dimensional digital screens to the three-dimensional objects all around us – the Internet of Things – so the consequences for privacy and national security have become starker. There is also well-founded speculation about how rapid advancements in quantum computing power may intersect with encryption technologies, possibly cracking historically entrenched cryptography.

Considering the political pressure and the momentum of invasive and powerful emerging technologies, society may already be at a tipping point. We must design a world in which privacy and security are still possible.

PREFACE

A NOTE FOR READERS

THIS BOOK TELLS STORIES ABOUT ONLINE LIBERTIES SHAPED BY TECHNICAL architectures and infrastructures. It originates from a three-year research project called NEXTLEAP (nextleap.eu, NEXT-generation Techno-Social and Legal Encryption, Access and Privacy, funded by the European Commission in the frame of the H2020 Collective Awareness Platforms (CAPS) programme). The purpose of NEXTLEAP, which ran from 2016 to 2018, was to 'create, validate, and deploy communication and computation protocols that can serve as pillars for a secure, trust-worthy, annotable and privacy-respecting Internet[1] that ensures citizens' fundamental rights'[2]: as such, it was an interdisciplinary project at its core. Its consortium included computer scientists and social scientists working in close dialogue with one another in an attempt to build a protocol that 'actually works'. The project was founded in the immediate aftermath of the Snowden revelations, which made technical work surrounding encryption much more of a political issue than it had been in the past, even the fairly recent past, and showed the extent to which sociopolitical factors are crucial in assessing the worth of specific communication technologies vis-à-vis issues such as privacy protection and surveillance. Our role within the project, in close dialogue with technical partners, was to conduct an extensive sociological investigation of technical development processes and user adoption in the field of encrypted secure messaging.

Reflecting this interdisciplinary background, the book is somewhat of a hybrid object, as the research it is based upon was produced with different (albeit entwined) objectives, including to inform the very practical technical discussions among the project developers, to fuel interdisciplinary work in collaboration with computer scientists and to advance a science and technology studies (STS)- and sociology of innovation-oriented understanding of phenomena such as encryption and distributed architectures. We therefore thought it might be helpful to provide readers with some guidance about how to engage with the book, which might depend on their interests, backgrounds or even reading styles. Moreover, in order for the book to be as accessible as possible, a glossary has been included at the end of the book that provides definitions for the technical terms we use.[3] While some of these terms are especially crucial in the discourses and practices of developers, and as such will (also) be unpacked as the chapters unfold, we believe that a glossary can be useful as a general resource. We also provide a comprehensive list that explains the many abbreviations and acronyms that characterise this field. This is located before the book's Introduction. The book does not have an index, but as an Open Access text, e-book versions are freely available to download, so users can search for particular terms that interest them.

During our fieldwork we had the opportunity to meet and talk with many professionals, ranging from cryptographers to user experience and user interface (UI/UX) designers, trainers and users, who mentioned in our discussions (both recorded and off the record) the protocols and tools we focus on here. Moreover, as we continue to be engaged within the field of cryptographic tools and protocols ourselves, as usability researchers, we have been exposed to many ongoing debates in the community around such tools and protocols, and their implications for the field of encryption in secure messaging. This social science research, deeply embedded among technologists, and ultimately improving technology, is in our view one of the stand-out features of this book.

The book has two distinct but interrelated aims: first, to provide what we call an 'analytical portrait' of the state of the art of the highly complex and technical secure messaging field. While the field is changing rapidly and is becoming more of a matter of interest for the general public, it is in our view important to capture the details of how the different technologies and social practices that compose this field emerged, interact and currently operate. In this sense, one of the book's key contributions is to provide something akin to an analytical history of the present, creating a new record of a phenomenon that, even as it continues to develop, is changing the terrain of digital social life in myriad major ways. To make an analytical portrait, as we understand it, means to retrace the development of an artefact – in particular, moments of crises, debates, controversies – to try and understand the 'life' of a few selected encrypted messaging applications, from their creation to their appropriation and reconfigurations by users, to their becoming, in some instances, a subject of public debate, of governance and of lobbying.

The second, related aim is to conceptualise this phenomenon via tools and approaches that have been developed in the social sciences, with a particular focus on bringing to the field of secure messaging insights from STS. Indeed, encryption, the making of secure messaging tools that adopt it as its core principle, and the co-shaping of particular definitions of digital 'freedom', can be read through the lenses of questions and issues that have long been of concern to STS. These range from the effects of competing imaginaries and visions on the day-to-day enactment of technical innovation, to the performative effects that processes of categorisation and 'sorting things out' have on the structuration of a field. Writing with these issues in mind implies engaging in close dialogue with the established STS literature on socio-technical controversies, infrastructure- and architecture- embedded governance and the political value of 'mundane practices'. While the style of writing used when engaging with these questions may be unfamiliar to those outside the discipline, the intention is to advance the conceptualisation of encryption as an intimately 'socio-technical' phenomenon, a foremost example of why, today, digital communication technologies are controversial and contested, why they are both a target and tool of governance, and why they have assumed a fundamental place in the exercise of authority and power.

The book begins – in the introductory Chapter 0 and Chapter 1 – by introducing how a social science perspective can inform the understanding of very broad technical questions, such as encryption and decentralisation; it then progressively narrows its focus to issues specific to secure communications, such as the relationality of risk and the meaning of elaborating a threat model. In Chapters 2, 3 and 4 the book shifts to provide distinct analytical portraits of the field. It presents several case studies of secure messaging projects, including a real-time history of innovations in the making. The book then gradually shifts back in Chapters 5 and 6 to a more explicitly social science- and STS-informed mode of analysis, by examining issues such as sense-making and categorisation attempts in this field, and the implications of the 'making of' Internet freedoms via secure messaging for Internet governance.

As such, the different chapters in this book may 'matter' in different ways to different readers. Readers expecting higher levels of conceptualisation, drawing from STS traditions and the literature of technology and innovation in society, may be more immediately familiar with Chapters 0, 1 and 5, where notions such as 'translation' in an actor-network theory sense, Bowker and Star's 'sorting things out', as well as more recent STS-inspired notions of data justice and data activism are fundamental tools to analyse the fieldwork. However, these chapters should not be neglected by readers from more technical backgrounds, since they bring to light the relational and highly socially embedded nature of some tools that help users in their great diversity 'make sense' of the tools technologists build.

Admittedly, however, technologists will probably feel more at home in Chapters 2, 3 and 4, which focus more on technical analyses of the case studies and on how the technical architecture of different projects co-shapes development choices and user practices. Nevertheless, we would emphasise again that insights from STS inform these chapters in more ways than may appear at first sight. Indeed, by unveiling phenomena such as informal standardisation processes, controversies around different implementations of a particular protocol and trade-offs between usability and technical efficiency, the concepts and methods of STS are both inextricably entwined in shaping our perspectives and embedded in our writing.

While this book is likely to be of primary interest to the readerships described above, we hope that it may spark interest in wider readerships, including those categories of actors that have been so kind as to participate in our fieldwork – developers, activists, journalists, and, last but not least, users. For these groups of readers, we are hopeful that this book may prompt, or, perhaps more modestly, fuel, a series of 'taking stock' discussions on their practices with and around privacy-protecting communication tools. We also hope that regulators may find reasons to take pause and reflect upon our analysis. This is likely to happen most prominently in the concluding chapter, which is not simply the sum of the conclusions arrived at in previous chapters but a substantive discussion of, and overture towards, several pressing Internet governance issues of our time as they relate to the security of communications. This book has the not-so-concealed objective of being useful to these publics, at a time when encryption is as much, or ever more, a pressing societal concern as a technical one.

The field of encrypted messaging does not stand still. As we write this note, in November 2020 and in the context of a pandemic-driven increase in surveillance, we can observe new contributions that explore the links between civil liberties and encryption, such as UNICEF's working paper on children, encryption and privacy[4], alongside new threats to encryption, such as a resolution proposed by the Council of the European Union that controversially calls for a discussion of how to 'better balance' the two principles of 'security through encryption and security despite encryption'.[5] Such cases provide reminders – and there will certainly be more by the time this book is published – of the need for a technically-informed social and political analysis of what encrypted communications are 'made of', and of the definitions of freedom they co-produce. We hope that this book will be a lasting contribution towards this goal, and we look forward to it joining the debate.

NOTES

1 This introductory note is perhaps the best place to highlight the difference between the 'Internet' and the 'Web', although the two terms are all too often used interchangeably in day-to-day discourse. The Internet is the global system of interconnected computer networks that use a 'common language' – namely the Internet protocol suite – to communicate with one another. The Web, or World Wide Web (WWW), is a particular set of applications that is built on top of the Internet, one of the most widely used by end users (along with, e.g. file sharing and e-mail applications).

2 http://nextleap.eu.

3 Every time the first instance of a term included in the glossary occurs, it is highlighted in bold.

4 https://www.unicef-irc.org/publications/1152-encryption-privacy-and-childrens-right-to-protection-from-harm.html.

5 https://techcrunch.com/2020/11/09/whats-all-this-about-europe-wanting-crypto-backdoors.

ACKNOWLEDGMENTS

WHEN FINISHING A BOOK, THE TIME OF ACKNOWLEDGMENTS IS A PLEASURE and, to some extent, a surprise. It is at this moment that authors realise to what extent 'their own' work is actually the product of a collective endeavour – formal and informal interactions, moments of feedback and challenge, asking for help and taking stock, thanking and being grateful. To all the individuals and organisations listed below – and those we may have omitted by mistake – we are, indeed, deeply indebted for making this book what it is.

First of all, a heartfelt thank you to Mattering Press for taking this book project on board at the end of 2018, in a time-sensitive situation, and for following it carefully and benevolently ever since. Mattering is a wonderful experiment in researcher-led-and-owned, open publishing that we feel honoured to be a part of. Francesca had been hoping that a book project suitable for submission to MP would come along since she shared the 'keynote spotlight' with Julien McHardy at the 2014 meeting of the Spanish STS network (redCTS), and first heard about the promising nascent Press. She could not be happier that, seven years later, this 'declaration of intentions' which she made in a corner of her mind has come to fruition.

At Mattering Press, we wish to especially thank Joe Deville for the count-less, kind and patient hours of work on both the content and form of our book – despite the multiple disruptions in personal and professional lives that the Covid-19 pandemic has caused since early 2020. Thank you so much, Joe.

We wish to thank the team of the H2020 NEXTLEAP project: Jaya Klara Brekke, George Danezis, Giacomo Gilmozzi, Marios Isaakides, Nadim Kobeissi, Wouter Lueks, Vincent Puig, Carmela Troncoso and all the other colleagues who joined the team for shorter periods of time but whose contributions to the project were crucial for its success. A special thanks to NEXTLEAP coordinator Harry Halpin, who first suggested back in 2014 that we should embark on a project on decentralised architectures together and has been a stimulating colleague and co-author throughout the project. A very special thanks to Holger Krekel, head of Merlinux GmbH and lead developer of Delta Chat; we are grateful for numerous insightful and kind conversations during the project, and beyond, on the informatics and philosophy of federation, and for his support of our work. We remember fondly Bernard Stiegler, who prematurely left us on 5 August 2020. His insights permeate the project and its practical and academic outputs.

We also wish to thank the European Commission for funding the NEXTLEAP project via its innovative programme 'Collective Awareness Platforms for Sustainability and Social Innovation' (CAPS). Year after year, CAPS-funded projects have produced very stimulating work on sustainability and citizenship in the digital age, and we hope that this book is another 'brick in the wall' in this regard. Thank you to Fabrizio Sestini and Loretta Anania, EC Project Officers at DG CONNECT, for their attentive and kind spearheading of the project. We are also grateful to Francesca Bria, Maurizio De Cecco and Stefania Milan, who kindly reviewed our work at different stages.

Our heartfelt thanks also go to Laura DeNardis, who graciously agreed to dedicate some time from her extremely busy schedule as Dean of American University's School of Communication – and as one of the world's foremost Internet governance scholars – to write the preface for the book. Her words mean so much to us, as they position our book as a valuable contribution to the academic enterprise that analyses technical infrastructures and architectures as arrangements of power, and they stress the importance of encryption as a core Internet governance controversy of our times.

As this book was developing, a project of a different kind saw the light – the Centre for Internet and Society of CNRS, which Francesca co-founded, and which has been the 'professional home' for us both since January 2019. Thank you to the colleagues who started the adventure of this new research unit with us, this book would not be the same without our ongoing interactions and conversations: CIS co-founder and director Mélanie Dulong de Rosnay, Olivier Alexandre, Maria Castaldo, Jean-Marc Galan, Axel Meunier, Tommaso Venturini and Céline Vaslin. We also wish to acknowledge the interactions with colleagues of the *Groupement de recherche Internet, IA et Société*, that constitutes a vital dimension of CIS. Let us mention here, in particular, colleagues and friends Séverine Arsène, Anne Bellon, Romain Badouard, Lucien Castex, Marida Di Crosta, Clément Mabi, Cécile Méadel, Julien Rossi, Félix Tréguer, Valérie Schafer and Guillaume Sire. We are also indebted to our former research unit, the Institute for Communication Sciences (ISCC) of CNRS, and its director, Pascal Griset, who for three years provided a comfortable and stimulating working environment for the NEXTLEAP project.

Our ability to continue our work on the NEXTLEAP-born investigation on encrypted secure messaging, and on its outputs including this book, was greatly boosted by obtaining funding for a closely related project, *ResisTIC – The Net Resistants: Critique and Circumvention of Digital Coercion in Russia*. Our thanks go to the French national funding body, the Agence Nationale de la Recherche (that also previously funded Francesca's first substantial research project on decentralised architectures, ADAM, a predecessor to NEXTLEAP). We are also grateful to the ResisTIC team: Olga Bronnikova, Françoise Daucé, Fabrice Demarthon, Valéry Kossov, Benjamin Loveluck, Bella Ostromooukhova, Perrine Poupin and Anna Zaytseva, for the fruitful scientific exchanges and friendly conversations in the frame of the project and its seminars.

Over the years, a number of colleagues worldwide, beyond those already cited above, gave feedback on either the book proposal, on papers that eventually formed the basis of chapters or on draft chapters. Thank you, Sylvain Besençon, Nathalie Casemajor, Andrew Clement, Philip Di Salvo, Maxigas, Liudmila Sivetc, Sophie Toupin. Special acknowledgements go to Angela Sasse and Ruba Abu-Salma from UCL, who initiated us into usable security and kindly agreed to discuss our work at a very early stage.

During the writing of the book, Ksenia spent a year and a half at the Citizen Lab (University of Toronto, Canada) as a postdoctoral researcher, and wishes to thank its director Ronald Deibert as well as Masashi Crete-Nishihata, Jakob Dalek, John Scott-Railton, Bahr Abdul Razzak, Miles Kenyon, Lotus Ruan,

Adam Senft and all the team. We both wish to acknowledge the Centre for the Sociology of Innovation of MINES ParisTech, where we conducted our PhD theses in a wonderfully stimulating environment and Francesca still holds an associate researcher appointment. Francesca also wishes to thank the editorial team of the *Internet Policy Review,* as well as the Internet Governance Lab of American University, to which she owes a fruitful collaboration with Laura DeNardis, Derrick Cogburn and Nanette Levinson.

More broadly, our work was enriched by a number of academic communities of which we are members. Our thanks go to the International Conferences on Internet Science (INSCI), the Society for the Social Studies of Science (4S) and the European Association for the Study of Science and Technology (EASST), the Association of Internet Researchers (AoIR), the Global Internet Governance Academic Network (GigaNet), The Center for Science and Technology Studies of the European University at Saint-Petersburg, and last but not least, the International Association for Media and Communication Research (IAMCR). Within IAMCR, we wish to acknowledge our joint work with Aphra Kerr, Julia Pohle, Jeremy Shtern and Weiyu Zhang, who co-chair(ed) with Francesca the Communication Policy and Technology Section, and Sylvia Blake, Sibo Chen and Steph Hill, who co-chair(ed) with Ksenia the Emerging Scholars Network.

We write about technical issues that are deeply political, and we hope that our work can be useful to policy. In this regard, being able to interact closely with institutions and NGOs is invaluable. Francesca wishes to thank the French Parliament's Commission for Rights and Liberties in the Digital Age, the CSAlab and the Internet Society France for having engaged with the project and for involving her in their multi-stakeholder reflections on how to make the Internet more open, transparent and usable.

Last but not least, we wish to thank all the activist tech communities that have trusted us, assented to talk to us and assisted in arranging interviews with the most marginalised, at-risk user groups. A very special thanks goes to the Digital Security Lab Ukraine (namely Mykola Kostynyan, Vadym Hudyma, Iryna Chulivska, Maksim Lunochkin and others), Syster Servers collective, Campi Aperti project, Autistici, Riseup, Tails and Espiv. Very warm thanks to dkg, Samba, Vassilis and Spider Alex.

We could not finish these acknowledgments before thanking with all our hearts our families, for their love and support through thick and thin (as the first year of the Covid-19 pandemic concludes, this sentence stands for a whole lot of nuances). Chiara, Jean-Marc, Brune, Loïse, Marco, Patrizia, Carlo, Elena, Oksana, Sasha, Svetlana, Lerie and Timofey: this book is for you.

LIST OF ABBREVIATIONS
AND ACRONYMS

A separate glossary of technical definitions is also included at the end of the book.

CAPS	Collective Awareness Platforms
CEO	Chief Executive Officer
CIA	Central Intelligence Agency (United States of America)
CNNum	Conseil national du numérique (French Digital Council)
CTO	Chief Technology Officer
DNS	Domain Name System
DRM	Digital Rights Management
e2e	End-to-end
ECMA	European Computer Manufacturers Association
EDRi	European Digital Rights (organisation)
EFF	Electronic Frontier Foundation
ENISA	European Union Agency for Cybersecurity (maintained original acronym)
ETSI	European Telecommunications Standards Institute
EU	European Union
FBI	Federal Bureau of Investigation (United States of America)
FOSS or F/OSS	Free and Open-Source Software
FSB	Federal Security Service (Russian Federation)
GIF	Graphics Interchange Format
GitHub and GitLab	Platforms for collaboration between developers
GAIM (now Pidgin)	F/OSS Instant Messaging client
GCM	Google Cloud Messaging
GDPR	General Data Protection Regulation
GNU/Linux	Free software operating system

GPG (GnuPG) GNU	Privacy Guard (free-software replacement for PGP)
GPL	General Public License
HADOPI	Haute Autorité pour la Diffusion des Œuvres et la Protection des droits d'auteur sur Internet
HTML	HyperText Markup Language
I2P	Invisible Internet Project
IANA	Internet Assigned Numbers Authority
ICANN	Internet Corporation for Assigned Names and Numbers
ICTs	information and Communication Technologies
ID	Identifier
IETF	Internet Engineering Task Force
IG	Internet Governance
IM	Instant Messaging
IMAP	Internet Message Access Protocol
iOS	Mobile operating system developed by Apple, Inc.
IP	Internet Protocol
IRC	Internet Relay Chat
IRL	In Real Life
IRTF	Internet Research Task Force
ISO	International Standardization Organization
ISP	Internet Service Provider
ITU	International Telecommunications Union
LEAP	Encryption access project
MENA	Middle East and North Africa (region)
MIT	Massachusetts Institute of Technology
MTS	Telephone company, Russian Federation
MUAs	Mail User Agents
NEXTLEAP	NEXT-generation Techno-Social and Legal Encryption, Access and Privacy (H2020 project)
NIST	National Institute of Standards and Technology (United States of America)
NGO	Non-Governmental Organisation
NSA	National Security Agency (United States of America)

OMEMO	Multi-End Message and Object Encryption (recursive acronym)
OpenPGP	Open implementation of PGP
Opsec	Operational Security
OTR	Off-the-Record Messaging (see Glossary)
OWS	Open Whisper Systems
PGP	Pretty Good Privacy (see Glossary)
p2p	Peer-to-peer (system; see Glossary)
PRISM	Code name for NSA surveillance program begun in 2007
QR-code	Quick Response code
RfC	Request for Comments (IETF)
RightsCon	Summit on Human Rights in the digital age
RSA	Public-key encryption technology developed by RSA Data Security, Inc.
SD	Secure Digital
S/MIME	Secure/Multipurpose Internet Mail Extensions (cryptography norm)
SMS	Secure Messaging Scorecard
SMTP	Simple Mail Transfer Protocol
SNI	Server Name Indication
STS	Science and Technology Studies
TCP/IP	Transmission Control Protocol/Internet Protocol
TLS	Transport Layer Security
Tor or TOR	The Onion Router
UC	University of California
UDHR	Universal Declaration of Human Rights
UI/UX	User Experience and User Interface
UN	United Nations
UNICEF	United Nations International Children's Emergency Fund
USA	United States of America
USB	Universal Serial Bus (industry standard)
VPN	Virtual Private Network
W3C	World Wide Web Consortium
XMPP	Extensible Message and Presence Protocol
XML	Extensible Markup Language

0
INTRODUCTION

(F)or a time, I operated part of the US National Security Agency's global system of mass surveillance. In June 2013 I worked with journalists to reveal that system to a scandalised world. Without encryption I could not have written the story of how it all happened [...] and got the manuscript safely across borders that I myself can't cross (Snowden 2019a).

THUS WROTE EDWARD SNOWDEN, THE FORMER NSA CONTRACTOR TURNED into the world's most famous whistleblower for digital liberties, on 15 October 2019, shortly after the damning history of his revelations, and the process that led to them, was published under the title *Permanent Record* (Snowden 2019a, 2019b). According to Snowden, the current debates around encryption have fundamental implications for our individual liberties and collective presence on the Internet and attempts to undermine encryption amount to no less than making Internet users 'vulnerable by design'. Encryption has become one of the core battlegrounds of Internet governance.

Indeed, as can hardly be disputed anymore, Snowden's 2013 revelations have been a landmark event in the development of the field of secure communications. Encryption of communications on a large scale and in a usable manner has become a matter of public concern, with a new cryptographic imaginary taking hold, one which sees encryption as a necessary precondition for the formation of networked publics (Myers West 2018). Alongside turning encryption into a fully-fledged political issue, the Snowden revelations catalysed longstanding debates within the field of secure messaging **protocols**. The cryptography community (in particular, academic and free software collectives) renewed their efforts to create next-generation secure messaging protocols in order to overcome the limits of existing protocols, such as **PGP** (Pretty Good Privacy) and **OTR** (Off-the-Record Messaging). Protocols are a vital part of the Internet's functioning, providing its conceptual models as well as the set of specifications that explain how data should be regrouped into packets, addressed, transmitted, routed and received; as Laura DeNardis made clear in *Protocol Politics*, the selection and adoption of particular protocols carries important political and economic implications, as well as technical ones (DeNardis 2009).

With recent events such as the introduction of **end-to-end encryption** in WhatsApp, the most popular instant messaging platform, billions of users started protecting their communications by default and on an everyday basis, often without realising it. While the mantra 'I have nothing to hide' is still widespread among Internet users, interest in ways to secure and preserve online communications with means such as encryption is increasing, and this has important socio-technical consequences. While these consequences apply particularly to those whose lives depend on an accurate appreciation of the risks related to their own profession or political context, they are also ever more relevant to the 'ordinary citizen'.

In response to the increasingly widespread understanding of security in online communications as an important social and political issue, as well as a technical one, encrypted secure messaging is a vibrant field in the making. Developers remain in flux about how to implement security and privacy properties – despite a number of novel projects seeing the light – while users have not yet converged on a single application. For example, there is still debate about cryptographic properties such as **forward and future secrecy**, **group messaging** and **non-repudiation**. Furthermore, there is no clear standard to adopt for these properties. In terms of privacy, work is still immature; even the most popular secure messaging applications, such as Signal, expose users' metadata via the requirement to associate users with their phone number or, in the case of Wire, leak **social graphs** via a centralised contact book.

For all these reasons, next-generation secure messaging appears unstandardised and fragmented, leading to a state where secure messaging users exist in dozens of 'silos', unable to inter-operate (Sparrow and Halpin 2015). The 'silo effect' is considered among the most important obstacles to the adoption of secure messaging apps:

The common trend of creating new secure communication tools and assessing the usability of these tools is a significant obstacle to adoption due to creating fragmented user bases. Also, to reach their communication partners, participants needed to use tools that are interoperable (Abu-Salma et al. 2017a: 137).

This is in stark contrast to the model used for email, where any email service can openly communicate with another in a federated fashion, agreeing upon collective standards of operation. Thus, developers of modern secure messaging protocols are facing a number of trade-offs between various design issues, including security and privacy properties, the introduction of group support features, the degree of decentralisation of the application, standardisation attempts and choices related to the licenses under which they release their software. In the meantime, vibrant discussions are happening around adapting open federated protocols (e.g. XMPP) to integrate the most recent security features.[1] New initiatives, based on decentralised, federated or **peer-to-peer** protocols are emerging, yet still suffer from a number of limitations related to usability and scalability.

All these dynamics are relevant to this book's examination of developers' actions and their interactions with other stakeholders (users, security trainers, standardising bodies and funding organisations, for instance) and with the technical artefacts they develop, with a core common objective of creating tools that 'conceal for freedom' while differing in their intended technical architectures, their targeted user publics and their underlying values and business models.

As next-generation encryption is shaping the ways in which we can securely communicate, exchange and store content on the Internet, it is important to unveil the very recent, and sometimes less recent history of these protocols and their key applications, to understand how the opportunities and constraints they provide to Internet users came about, and how both developer communities and institutions are working towards making them available for the largest possible audience. Efforts towards this goal are built upon interwoven stories of technical development, of architectural choices, of community-building and of Internet governance and politics. This book is about these stories – exploring the *experience* of encryption in the variety of secure messaging protocols and tools existing today, and the implications of these endeavours for the '*making of* civil liberties on the Internet.

This book intends to provide two main empirical and theoretical contributions: firstly, it seeks to enrich a social sciences-informed understanding of encryption, including examining how its different solutions are created, developed, enacted and governed, and what this diverse experience of encryption, operating across many different sites, means for online civil liberties; secondly, it wishes to contribute to the understanding of the social and political implications of particular design choices when it comes to the technical architecture of digital networks, in particular their degree of (de-)centralisation.[2]

The first part of this introduction will discuss both of these perspectives. A second part will introduce our case studies, our methodology and approach to our fieldwork. In its final section, in order to facilitate navigation through the following chapters, we situate our case studies in a genealogy of the fundamental protocols in the encrypted messaging field, and we introduce relevant concepts and definitions that will be used in the following chapters, such as end-to-end encryption, centralisation, federation and peer-to-peer/decentralisation.

FOR A SOCIAL SCIENCES PERSPECTIVE ON ENCRYPTION

For quite a long time, 'encryption' as a research subject has mostly been the prerogative of computer scientists, with more 'social' issues concerning it often being confined to debates about usable security (i.e. discussions taking place within the computer scientist community, and based on survey-type studies that aim to find ways of making encrypted tools easier to use). As, since the Snowden revelations, encrypted communications and the goals of privacy and security they seek to enhance are becoming a matter of widespread public debate, it is important that the social sciences take up the challenge of investigating in depth how encrypted messaging tools are conceived and developed, how they are taken up by different user profiles – sometimes in unintended or unforeseen ways – how they inspire and are inspired by different imaginaries, and how they eventually become the target of governance. With this volume, and the three-year investigation it is based upon, we seek to contribute what is, to our knowledge, the first book-length endeavour focused on this subject that is grounded primarily in science and technology studies (STS) and more specifically in the sociology of innovation processes and technical development. First and foremost, our work exists in dialogue with contributions that have recently sought to apply some central concepts in the social sciences, in particular STS, to the study of encryption.

Encryption is a matter of competing imaginaries and of the visions, designs and implementations they co-shape, as Sarah Myers West has recently argued (2018). People think about encryption through cyphers (that transpose letters of an alphabet), and through codes (that replace words) in different social, cultural and political contexts. As Myers West notes, encryption has built its different meanings in the realm of national security and secrecy and in that of democratic systems, in each of which it enables private communication and makes it possible to avoid surveillance and potential social or political sanctions. Myers West's STS-driven investigation into encryption imaginaries is especially resonant with our research, as it illustrates how similar technologies may acquire different meanings and roles in different cultural settings. A particularly important insight is that these technologies should be understood not only in a technical sense but in the specific social, cultural and political contexts in which they are used. Myers West's conclusions are important to emphasise, as this book will provide numerous examples of how technologies (and technologists) do not determine universal solutions when it comes to the role and impact of encryption, with sociocultural contexts of use being paramount. The historical dimension of these sociocultural contexts and their evolution over time should also be taken into account, as Isadora Hellegren points out in her work – grounded in both discourse theory and an STS sensibility – that sees discourse as a contextual, structuring and performative process of meaning-making (Hellegren 2017). The multifaceted meaning of encryption evolves not only across communities of developers and users, but also across time, and understanding how various actors have constructed specific understandings of freedom with regard to technologies like encryption is significant to Internet historians, hackers, programmers and policymakers, as all of these actors are involved in constructing the form, function and meaning of Internet freedom, in particular when it comes to its relation to the state.

Encryption, and the debates around it, are the result of multiple public spheres and expert circles, embedded in broader Internet-and-society questions such as the control of networked media, surveillance and the protection of personal data. Linda Monsees' recent *Crypto-Politics* (2019) is an important contribution to the study of these aspects and more broadly to the development of a social sciences perspective on encryption, even if her primary focus is not the *making* of encryption for a specific use, but rather discourses on encryption as a whole as they unfold in traditional and less traditional political arenas. Monsees uses discourse analysis methods to examine post-Snowden debates related to encryption in both the United States and Germany and describes the landscape of media and specialist discussions as trying to make sense of today's 'diffuse security' – a context where 'security practices disperse multiple insecurities and threat images' (Monsees 2019: 5). Monsees develops the notion of 'publicness' to convey the idea that political controversies on encryption are often located outside established political institutions (although those that unfold in more traditional political arenas should not be neglected). In a way reminiscent of previous work on the performative role of controversies revolving around complex and open-ended sociotechnical phenomena, she concludes, echoing Hellegren, that 'encryption controversies entail specific ideas relating not only to what 'security' means but also how these conceptions rely on specific ideas about citizenship, statehood and privacy' (Monsees 2019: 10).

Beyond the dialogue with this nascent social science scholarship on encryption, our work further seeks to build on, and contribute to, the research of several scholars at the crossroads of media studies, sociology of technology and computer science. They have brought their conceptual and methodological lenses to the study of networked communication technologies and their implications for privacy, security and Internet governance.

The technical development of applications and protocols, and the set of choices involved in this development, critically contributes to making sense of what digital freedoms are, how they should be preserved and who are their adversaries. Anthropologist Gabriella Coleman has paved the way for scholars seeking to explore these questions. In particular, she has examined the role of hacker culture,[3] exploring what hackers mean by freedom and how they enact it as a form of self-determination that considers unrestricted access to knowledge a necessary precondition for the evolution of their 'technical art' (Coleman 2005). Furthermore, Coleman's work is of particular relevance for a social sciences-based study of encryption. Together with Alex Golub, Coleman has defined 'crypto-freedom' as a particular form of hacker practice, grounded in an understanding of freedom that positions the state as the main adversary in the battle for online privacy. This practice is derived from the particular historical and cultural context of liberalism in the United States and grounded in the belief that this freedom should primarily be preserved and fostered on the Internet through the development and use of encryption technology (Coleman and Golub 2008).

Since the Snowden revelations, several authors have tackled the question of what it means to be online as an individual, a citizen and a consumer in a world that is now broadly aware of the extent to which we are being surveilled. Within this realm, they have focused on the issue of the role played by the technical development of the architectures and infrastructures of online communication.

As explored by the work of Stefania Milan and colleagues (e.g. Milan and van der Velden 2018), we are bearing witness to an increasing variety of 'data activism' practices – a set of socio-technical tactics, resistances and mobilisations that adopt a critical approach towards datafication, mass data collection and pervasive surveillance. Data activism, as Milan conceptualises it, can be understood as a contemporary evolution of phenomena such as those analysed by Coleman (as well as Milan herself in previous works, e.g. 2013), like radical tech activism and hacktivism. Data activism is meant to represent the 'next step' in these forms of activism. It is both designed for the digital and shaped by the digital, inasmuch as it 'explicitly engages with the new forms (that) information and knowledge take today as well as their modes of production, challenging dominant understandings of datafication' (Milan and van der Velden 2018). Interestingly, the proponents of the concept point out that, given that datafication and the uses of ICTs for different political purposes are so widespread and pervasive, data activism might progressively acquire an appeal for more diverse communities of concerned citizens. This might extend beyond previous forms of tech activist engagement that seemed (self-)restricted to a niche of experts and technologists (ibid. 2018). Broadening the frame of, and interest in, tech activism is a widely discussed concern in a number of the most recent encryption projects, including some we will analyse more closely as this book unfolds.

Also relevant to our research, and key to understanding several of the dynamics described in the following chapters, is work that explores what it means to be a 'digital citizen' of the post-Snowden Internet. The conceptual lens of 'data justice' has been proposed by Arne Hintz, Lina Dencik and Karin Wahl-Jorgensen (2019) to illustrate that not only is citizenship and the possibility of citizen agency in today's Internet profoundly shaped by phenomena such as massive data collection and commodification, but also that user rights and practices concerning online privacy and surveillance are today conceived of in highly individualised terms. According to these authors, these individualising dynamics engender or at least maintain a context of inequality, as they transfer the responsibility to 'engage and negotiate citizenship in a digital age onto individuals' (Gangneux 2019).

As our case studies will illustrate, this issue is important in relation to encryption technologies and their mass adoption because the target audience of secure messaging applications either born or substantially developed post-Snowden is far from being limited to tech-savvy and activist groups: several projects are aimed at widespread use. This is a major change in the field, as for a long time, a majority of the technical crypto community considered that greater user-friendliness and usability could realise in practice their desire for large-scale adoption, while simultaneously considering ease of use and comfort a secondary issue to the soundness of the technology. Scholars have previously suggested that the comparatively little attention given to this issue by developers implies a 'forced responsibilisation' of users, as it places all the burden of 'getting up to speed' on them: it is up to users to acquire the competencies to compensate for the technical artefact's lack of usability. It has been further argued that this is to the detriment of the development of resilient collective digital security strategies (Kazansky 2015) and that it 'delegates' technical matters to 'progressive techies' despite a widespread societal desire to develop technologies for social justice (Aouragh et al. 2015).

Finally, we have found a particularly useful set of concepts within STS-focused studies of Internet governance (see e.g. Epstein, Katzenbach and Musiani 2016). Complementary to the predominantly institutional approaches that set the agenda for Internet Governance (IG) research in its early days – and which remain one of its preeminent features – STS approaches invite a consideration of the agency of technology designers, policymakers and users as they interact, in a distributed fashion, with technologies, rules and regulations. These, in turn, lead to consequences with systemic effects that may, at times, be unintended. Following these approaches, social and political ordering is understood as a set of ongoing and contested processes, which translates into a growing attention to the mundane practices of all those involved in providing and maintaining, hacking and undermining, developing and testing, or merely using the network of networks (Musiani 2015). Conceptually, STS-informed IG research relies on understanding governance as a normative 'system of systems' and it acknowledges the agency, often discrete yet pervasive, of both human and non-human actors and infrastructures. Particular attention is paid to the processes by which norms – technical or otherwise – are created, negotiated, put to the test and re-aligned, and also how they raise conflicts. These processes are understood to be as important as the stabilised norms themselves, if not more so. These are conceptual contributions that will be particularly relevant in the central chapters of the book, where we introduce the variety of architectural models that different projects choose to adopt initially and which they subsequently have to 'tinker with' due to factors including early user adoption, changes in the developers' teams and efforts to find suitable business models.

STS also provides crucial conceptual resources to enable the understanding of encryption as a site of controversy and contestation, in particular with the notion of sociotechnical controversy. On the one hand, since the very early days of the Internet, being on and managing the network of networks has been about exercising control over particular functions that provide specific actors with the power and opportunity to act to their advantage. On the other hand, there is very rarely a single way to implement these functions or a single actor capable of controlling them. Thus, the Internet is controversial and contested, both a target and an instrument of governance, and the object of interest of a myriad of actors: from the most powerful and centralised to the 'simple' Internet user (Epstein, Katzenbach and Musiani 2016). Infrastructural and architectural arrangements, the development and implementation of particular protocols, can be understood as a fundamental place to exercise economic and political power, as we have examined elsewhere (e.g. DeNardis and Musiani 2016).

The Internet exhibits an increasing number of sites of contestation. These include the interconnection agreements between Internet service providers (Meier-Hahn 2015), the debate around net neutrality (Marsden 2017), the use of deep-packet-inspection (Mueller, Kuehn and Santoso 2012), the deployment of content filtering technologies (Deibert and Crete-Nishihata 2012), ubiquitous surveillance measures and the use of DNS for regulatory aims (DeNardis and Hackl 2015), prediction of people's online behaviours via algorithmic governance (Ziewitz 2016) and the shaping of the visibility and hierarchies of search engine results (Mager 2012). Furthermore, contentious politics, activism and citizen-led protest are often embedded in the Internet and its applications. This is illustrated, for example, by Milan and ten Oever's (2017) work on civil society engagement within ICANN (which operates the Internet's Domain Name System), aimed at 'encoding' human rights into Internet infrastructures. Another illustration is our previous research on the shaping and use of citizen- and activist-oriented mobile and Web applications, and how the design of these tools shapes citizen participation and citizen-state interaction (Ermoshina 2016). Among all these examples, encryption technologies for online communications are becoming one of the core sites of 'governance by architecture', rife with controversies that concern, in turn, the development of these technologies, their implementation, their (sometimes surprising) appropriation by users and the attempts to regulate them.

Interestingly in this regard, Snowden's disclosures of 2013, and the subsequent widening of mass-surveillance-related debates, not only revealed a need for further legal reform of intelligence and surveillance systems but have also highlighted 'a variety of changing practices, policies and discourses that can (...) be related to post-Snowden contentions' (Pohle and Van Audenhove

2017: 2–3). A number of sociotechnical controversies can be related to this. A notable example was the FBI vs Apple controversy that spanned 2015 and 2016, when Apple Inc. received several orders by district courts in the United States to assist ongoing criminal investigations by extracting data from iPhones with extensive cryptographic security protections. Apple itself could not break this encryption unless it wrote specific new software to enable authorities to bypass such barriers. This debate notably questioned whether – and if yes to what extent – judicial or governmental authorities could compel technical manufacturers to provide assistance in unlocking devices protected by encryption systems (see also Schulze 2017). Controversies such as this have contributed to unveil facets of the *experience* of encryption in today's Internet and suggest that the most pressing issues of our time related to encryption may be not only legal and technical, but also social.

FOR A SOCIAL SCIENCES PERSPECTIVE ON (DE-)CENTRALISATION

As previously mentioned, the second core empirical and theoretical contribution of this book is intended to be the understanding of the social and political implications of particular design choices when it comes to the technical architecture of digital networks, in particular their degree of decentralisation (or lack of it). This issue, which has permeated the debates of both scholars and practitioners of networked technologies since their early days, in fact goes even further back in time. Indeed, the struggle between centralised, profit-driven systems and decentralised, user-controlled, user-innovated architectures is one that appears in many infrastructures and has been a longstanding concern of sociologists and historians of technology (see e.g. Edwards et al. 2007). In the early days of the telephone, people living in rural areas sometimes put together their own phone networks using barbed-wire fences as transmission lines; they were shared, distributed resources (Fischer 1987). The grand battle between trucking and rail in the United States was a duel between huge centralised systems (the railways) and independent entrepreneurs, often individuals, who used trucks to offer point-to-point (rather than station-to-station) delivery, and ultimately won by turning a publicly funded infrastructure (state and federal roads) towards a private purpose. Off-grid solar power installations as an alternative means of producing electricity outside standard circuits, and institutional resistance to these, are another case in point (Turner 2010). It is of little surprise, then, that the tension between different degrees of centralisation of technical architecture may also be found in the Internet, and in the different protocols and applications populating it – a tension that has been evident since its beginnings.

Indeed, in the history of Internet-based services, the concurrent push towards different types of design choice, in particular design based on peer-to-peer versus **client/server** architecture,[4] has for quite some time been a source of compromises and tension – including social, technical, political, economic and legal tensions (see Musiani 2015b). In a client/server architecture, having information stored not on a user's machine but a separate server, possibly one managed by a third party, greatly complicates resistance to censorship because it provides an obvious control point (DeNardis 2014) for authorities. On the other hand, without such a server, communication between users who are not permanently digitally connected becomes much more difficult. This is why core Internet services such as email usually resort to intermediaries that are able to ensure the ongoing functioning of the service but can also potentially stop it, limit it, block it, and read what passes through the servers they depend on (on the liability of Internet intermediaries for these actions see Riordan 2016).

Efforts aimed at developing decentralised systems date back to the early Internet (Minar and Hedlund 2001). They were generally built as ad-hoc strategic responses to specific threats of shutdown. The file-sharing system BitTorrent, for example, was developed as a response to the shutdown of Napster, in order to make legal prosecution for breach of IP in file sharing networks much more complicated (Izal et al. 2004). Napster had a peer-to-peer component in file search but was in fact being run by a small group of people. This implied that the system was fully dependent on these individuals, technically as well as legally. As a consequence, such systems can be effectively neutralised by turning off servers or seizing the equipment or the people in charge of them (Ku 2016). In contrast, decentralised systems do not have any central servers, and the functioning of the system involves many peers (people, and the computing resources at their disposal) who do not, or may not, even know each other. If any particular node is unavailable to the system, it continues to run regardless. Thus, the logic behind the creation of a decentralised system is usually to be resilient to targeting by authorities, and such systems are accordingly often deemed by technical and political actors in need of such resilience to be superior to proprietary, closed, more centralised systems, because they value long-term robustness over cost-effective commercial expedience (Oram 2001).

Decentralised systems have been subject to 'waves' of interest in the last twenty years, starting with the early 2000s file sharing frenzy and the hailing of peer-to-peer as a 'disruptive technology' (Oram 2001). In recent years there has been an even greater interest in and uptake of decentralisation. In the process, the motivations for adopting decentralised technologies have broadened from a particular strategy of opposition to specific companies or pieces of regulation, to proposals of an alternative 'vision' of what corporate, legal and state institutions should be. Two main dynamics have driven this tendency: the first is the emergence of blockchain technology (in particular with Bitcoin technology, as a response to the 2008 financial crisis; see Campbell-Verduyn 2017 and Brunton 2019), and the second was spurred by Edward Snowden's revelations of mass surveillance operations facilitated by a number of telecommunications companies and Silicon Valley giants, on behalf of the US National Security Agency (see Pohle and Van Audenhove 2017). These events greatly raised the general public's awareness of the surveillance-based, and personal data-based, business models of near-monopoly tech companies, and their 'dangerous liaisons' with state security agencies (Musiani 2013).

As a consequence of these dynamics, 'both decentralisation and the notion of authority took on broader meaning and decentralisation became a technical, political, economic and social aim in and of itself, reaching outside the 'hacker' circles of the early p2p systems' (Brekke & Isakiidis 2019). However, this larger appreciation of decentralisation as a principle and a vision is not devoid of side effects; most notably, often decentralisation has become an objective in and of itself, with little understanding of intent or assessment of actual effects. As information studies scholar and Internet pioneer Philip Agre said in 2003, 'architecture is politics, but should not be understood as a substitute for politics'; decentralised protocols are too readily assumed, because of their technical qualities, to bring about decentralised political, social and economic outcomes. By choosing to structure the central part of this book around the different degrees of centralisation of the technical architecture for the examined secure messaging systems, we intend to take Agre's lesson seriously, and assess in detail the extent to which economic, social, legal (and last but not least technical) factors complicate the picture of a linear 'translation' from a peer-to-peer technical architecture into a successful decentralised socioeconomic system, or from a centralised technical model to a top-down sociopolitical structure.

CASE STUDY SELECTION

The core of this book is an in-depth understanding of three different end-to-end encrypted mail and messaging applications. After a preliminary survey of thirty cases of encrypted messaging applications,[5] we proceeded to select a few of them for more detailed study. These three applications were selected based on their underlying protocols, and because of the relative accessibility of the developer communities for interviews and observations. The three applications originally selected were Signal (a centralised end-to-end encrypted instant messaging application), LEAP/Pixelated (a federated end-to-end encrypted asynchronous messaging protocol and client) and Briar (a peer-to-peer end-to-end encrypted messaging application for resilient communication using **network-layer protection**, such as Tor hidden services).

These three cases offered the possibility to address various research questions, such as the motivations behind:

- particular architectural choices (centralised, federated or peer-to-peer);
- specific choices of licensing, **UI/UX** design, relations between the underlying protocols and the application level;[6]
- solutions to privacy properties (such as metadata protection);
- design choices for group communication;

– various approaches to security properties (forward and future secrecy; **server-side archives**; **cryptographic deniability**; ephemeral or disappearing messaging).

However, when in September 2016 we started our fieldwork on the three selected projects, we quickly understood that these projects could hardly be treated as discrete given their connections with other initiatives in the field of encrypted messaging and email. In fact, the underlying protocols used by these three projects gave birth to a number of **client-side implementations**, forked or actively interacted with various applications in the field. Thus, we decided to 'follow' the three projects as they grew and transformed and use them as our 'threads of Ariadne', respecting the loops and knots that these threads were naturally forming on their way. During our fieldwork we had the opportunity to meet and talk with a large number of professionals, ranging from cryptographers to UI/UX designers, trainers and users, about the protocols and tools we focus on here (in discussions both recorded and off the record).

The research work subtending this book was and is thus an attempt to tell the complex story of protocols and communities, and eventually, to approach questions of governance of encryption protocols. Through a comparative analysis of centralised and decentralised protocols and their implementations, we address here several important and broader questions: What are the architectural patterns of successful centralised and decentralised systems? How do developers go about building scalable and high-performing privacy-preserving decentralised architectures? Can decentralisation help deliver privacy and anonymity? What are the motivations, values and characteristics of user communities that lead to the success or failure of certain (de-)centralised systems?

A NOTE ON METHODOLOGY

Grounded in the different strands of literature from STS and the other disciplines we introduced above, our approach can be described as a multi-sited ethnography, inasmuch as we have undertaken research in, and between, several online and offline locations as part of our study, and we have also explicitly conceived specific technical protocols and systems as 'part of a larger context that exceeds the boundaries of the field site' (Muir 2011: 1015; see also a reflection on the method by its first proponent, George Marcus, who points out that multi-sited ethnography has been 'most creative, critical, and interesting where it has been involved with the [STS] study of distributed knowledge systems, (Marcus 2012: 27).

We analyse the development of the architectures and the interfaces of messaging apps as 'meeting points' between the intentional goals of developers and the needs of users (Oudshoorn and Pinch 2005), In doing so, we aim to provide a fieldwork-driven explanation of emerging systems and communities of practice through 'analytical thick descriptions' (for a recent treatment of the concept, first introduced by anthropologist Clifford Geertz, see Ponterotto 2006) of events, artefacts and organisations. In particular, we pay attention to moments of crisis, debate and controversy – to try and understand the life of a technical artefact, from its creation to its appropriation and reconfigurations by users, to its becoming a subject of public debate, of governance, of lobbying. The primary methodology to achieve this goal has been to observe, for relatively prolonged periods of time, specific case-study groups or communities, while on the side conducting in-depth interviews with their members and reading appropriate documentation such as release notes and accounts of working sessions.

Just as we seek a nuanced understanding of developers' motivations and the representations they have of users and their needs, in the tradition of 'user studies' developed within STS (see Oudshoorn and Pinch 2005 or, in the French tradition, Jouët 2000), we understand users not as a homogeneous and passive group, but as active participants in innovation and co-shaping technologies. In software development, this is possible via routes such as bug reporting, **pull requests** on code, mailing list comments and in-person contact between users and developers.

Among our interview subjects, developers were mostly selected on the basis of pre-existing personal relationships that the NEXTLEAP research team members had with the cryptographic research community. For projects with which research team members did not have any previous personal connections, we also reached out to developers via the GitLab and GitHub pages of the projects (e.g. Ricochet, Conversations). In contrast, user studies tended to be conducted with individuals selected through their attendance at training events in their local environments (both high-risk, in the case of Ukraine and Russia, and low risk in the case of France, Germany, Austria and the United Kingdom).[7] Our selection of events and conferences to attend was driven primarily by our interest in speaking to users from high-risk contexts. Indeed, while the inclusion of high-risk individuals was important for the project (as Chapter 1 will show), due to the level of repression these users face in their native environment, it would have been difficult if not impossible to interview them there, since they would be unable to speak openly. This was the case for users from Egypt, Turkey, Kenya and Iran, where the interviews took place in March 2017 at the Internet Freedom Festival and at RightsCon. All interviews were conducted between autumn 2016 and the late summer of 2018, with 63 interviews in total. At several of these gatherings and training events, we also asked our respondents to take a moment to provide us with a drawing or a graphical representation of what/ who they considered to be their security threat or adversary when it comes to digital communications. These images proved to be a very fruitful addition to our fieldwork materials, as Chapter 1, in particular, will show.

Throughout our research, and due to the sensitive nature of our subject vis-à-vis online civil liberties, it was important to keep questioning the modalities of our access to fieldwork, and to be continually reflexive about our core assumptions and the ethical guidelines we as researchers were working with – questions that have been identified as particularly relevant when issues of secrecy, privacy and security are at play (Barbosa and Milan 2019; De Goede et al. 2019; see also the Appendix to this book).

Being the 'useful sociologist' in a team of technologists

The fieldwork behind this book was a journey through disciplines, fields of expertise, methodologies and communities – an experience of professional and sometimes personal transformation for us as researchers, that led to a redefinition of our role as sociologists within a tech-oriented project. The NEXTLEAP team was a consortium of six partners: four were research teams based at academic institutions (three in computer science, one – the authors of this book – in sociology), one was a research centre whose activities include a mix of philosophy-inspired action research and outreach to civil society and institutions, and one was a software development firm. Thus, the team was far from being exclusively composed of academics, and STS academics were a definite minority.

We, the authors of this book, come from what is often considered as 'the temple of actor-network theory':[8] the Center for Sociology of Innovation, based at the MINES ParisTech school of engineering in Paris We therefore initially approached our research on secure messaging as a challenge for STS. Our initial academic desire was to target the work of technical actors – developers and protocol designers – and the encryption protocols themselves. However, after we delivered the first state-of-the-art description of end-to-end encrypted messaging applications and protocols, we faced a clear demand from other members of the research team: 'focus on users'. The following months of fieldwork were marked by several interactions between us and the technologists in the team, and ultimately led to an important redesign of our interview guide. At times we were also asked to revise our research questions and priorities to include a clearer focus on insights from user-oriented interviews. Eventually, we came to understand how we looked to the rest of the team: when software development cycles include a non-technical role, this role is usually that of the 'usability researcher', a place that had been, somehow, automatically reserved for us.

Thus, the story behind this book is also a story of two STS researchers defining their own role within an interdisciplinary team, not without a certain amount of tension. The attempts to convey to the technologists what our STS approach was, and how it could actually be useful for them and their development process, despite not being straightforward user studies, eventually led us to develop our own 'circumvention techniques' to make collaborative work possible.

Embodying the 'useful sociologist' in a team of technologists, we found ourselves between fields, something that is also reflected in our previous publications related to the project. We found ourselves presenting our work at conferences on usable security, publishing our works in computer science reviews focusing on usability studies, side-by-side with usability researchers. However, we maintained a connection with the STS world through a thin but, we believe, robust thread of reflexivity, as we developed a critical attitude to our own usability alter-ego and managed to use it as a key that helped us penetrate the otherwise quite hermetic world of crypto protocol design. While, by consortium design, our interactions and collaborations with our primarily technical colleagues were frequent and close, this book is most definitely, in retrospect, a way to tell the story of our three-year investigation that is intimately our own, departing when necessary, from the compromises needed throughout the project to produce results and publications driven by the conventions of both computer science and the social sciences.

The first step in this process was perhaps the Autocrypt[9] gathering in Berlin, in December 2016, where Ksenia was invited to talk about 'user needs and desires' for encrypted email and messaging and develop 'use-cases' that could potentially be helpful in the design of the new specifications for email encryption. This event became the true starting point for our fieldwork – a gathering of some of the most advanced cryptographers and developers, working on projects such as Matrix.org, Enigmail, Wire, Secure Scuttlebutt, LEAP, Riseup and others. At the end of the day, the rest of the NEXTLEAP research team's 'hunt for the user' had finally brought us to the heart of ongoing development and protocol design work.

Thus, this book is an occasion to reflect upon our work as an example of embedded real-time STS, where researchers are active participants in techno-scientific work involving multiple stakeholders and contingencies. Throughout our case studies, we describe several examples of how our research fits into protocol design work, and occasionally reflect upon tensions within the research team. Ultimately, the desire to 'meet the user', that shows through the work of our technical colleagues, tells us something about the evolution of encrypted messaging towards a more human-centric design, reflected in recent developments among certain Internet governance standardisation bodies, such as the IETF (Internet Engineering Task Force) and its research branch IRTF (Internet Research Task Force), that seek to include human rights considerations in protocol design (see ten Oever 2021).

Before we present the structure of the book, and in order to facilitate navigation through the chapters that follow, the last part of our introduction will present a genealogy of the fundamental protocols in the encrypted messaging field; in it, we introduce relevant concepts and definitions that will be used in the following chapters.

Encrypted messaging protocols: The short genealogy of a 'feedback loop'

The most recent generation of tools for secure communications (appearing in the 2010s, in particular post-Snowden) marked the rise of encrypted secure messaging 'for the masses'.[10] Yet despite this recent success vis-à-vis the general public, encrypted messaging is an unstandardised and fragmented field, as developers remain in a state of flux about how to implement security and privacy properties. In particular, developers face a number of trade-offs between various design issues, including security and privacy properties, the introduction of group support features, the degree of decentralisation of the application, and standardisation and licensing attempts. To attempt an initial systematisation of this complicated landscape, our first step was an in-depth survey of thirty email and chat applications offering end-to-end encryption.[11] As part of this, we analysed their architectural and protocol choices, as well as their interfaces and business models (see also Ermoshina, Musiani and Halpin 2016). As an introduction and contextualisation of our research subject, this section provides a historical look at the development of email and secure messaging protocols in the light of cryptographic and usability problems that these protocols have sought to solve, while introducing relevant concepts and definitions that will be used in the following chapters. This brief, non-linear history of protocols and applications that have recently built the field of secure messaging is also a first look at an issue which we will further develop in the coming chapters: the technical and organisational choices made by protocol designers and app developers are, in fact, enacting various forms of freedom, both for users and developers.

End-to-end encrypted messaging is increasingly prominent, with its adoption by large proprietary applications such as WhatsApp and Facebook Messenger. In 'end-to-end' encrypted messaging, the server that hosts messages for a user or any third-party adversary that intercepts data as the message is *en route* cannot read the message content due to the use of encryption. The 'end' in 'end-to-end' encryption therefore refers to the 'endpoint', which in the case of messaging is the client device of the user rather than the server.

After the Snowden revelations, the academic cryptographic community has, with renewed impetus, sought to rigorously engage with the '**untrusted server**' problem. This is an issue that until recently had felt, as suggested by Phillip Rogaway, 'almost intentionally pushed aside', although it is perhaps 'the most fundamental privacy problem in cryptography: how can parties communicate in such a way that nobody knows who said what' (Rogaway 2015). The so-called 'new generation secure messaging protocols', such as Signal's **Double Ratchet**, seek to address these issues and provide a remedy for the security and privacy flaws identified in older protocols, such as OTR or PGP. The success of the Signal protocol, widely forked and adopted by many secure messaging projects, has catalysed debates within cryptographic communities, and led to the revival and renewal of older protocols, creating a 'feedback loop' effect. Thus, the genealogy presented here challenges linear histories of secure messaging protocols, as it unveils dynamic iterations between recent and older protocols, as well as between what was considered 'synchronous' versus 'asynchronous' protocols.

Email encryption

Historically, email has been considered a form of asynchronous messaging, where a user does not have to be online to receive the message, while chat is considered to be a form of asynchronous messaging, where a user has to be online to receive the message. However, these distinctions are increasingly blurring now that popular chat protocols generally support asynchronous messaging, and the email protocol is more and more often used for instant messaging, with the rapidly evolving galaxy of **chat-over-email** projects (see Chapter 4). Email is now considered a possible infrastructural solution for projects seeking not only privacy and security but also **interoperability** and some resistance to censorship.

Email is based on standardised and open protocols that allow interoperability between different email servers, so that, for example, a Microsoft server can send email to a Google server. SMTP (Simple Mail Transfer Protocol) is the protocol originally used for transferring email and as such is one of the oldest standards for asynchronous messaging, first defined in 1982 by the IETF[12] (Unger et al. 2015) and by default not including provision for content confidentiality. Classically, as the NSA's PRISM program has eloquently revealed, email is sent unencrypted and so the server has full access to the content of email messages. The federated nature of email infrastructure makes this even more problematic, as trust in service providers within decentralised systems is hard to guarantee. Thus, developers have for a long time made clear their intention to progress towards usable methods of end-to-end encryption for email.

To add end-to-end encryption capabilities to email, the PGP (Pretty Good Privacy) protocol was created in 1991 by Phil Zimmerman, as an ambitious technosocial attempt to 'preserve democracy' and let people 'take privacy in their hands.[13] Due both to pressure from the US government and patent claims by RSA Corporation, Zimmerman pushed PGP to become an IETF standard. The OpenPGP set of standards was finally defined in 1997, to allow the open implementation of PGP. GPG (GnuGPG) is a free software implementation of the OpenPGP standards developed by Free Software Foundation in 1999 and compliant with the OpenPGP standard specifications, serving as the free software foundation for most modern PGP-enabled applications.

OpenPGP is implemented in both desktop and mobile email apps, including Outlook, Apple Mail and Thunderbird through plug-ins. An alternative standard for encrypted email, called S/MIME,[14] is also supported via plug-ins by most major email clients. The main difference between OpenPGP and S/MIME is that the latter requires the installation of certificates provisioned by centralised certificate authorities. In contrast to PGP, which is based on a decentralised 'Web of Trust' between users who accept and sign each other's keys (and therefore delegates the responsibility of the complexity of **key management** to the end-user), S/MIME uses a centralised **public key infrastructure** to manage keys. Thus, while it has been adopted by some large, centralised institutions, it has been much less frequently adopted by the general public. In contrast to centralised approaches, OpenPGP offloads the key management to the users via a decentralised 'Web of Trust' model.

OpenPGP and S/MIME also work on mobile devices, such as PGPMail, but as OpenPGP binds the key to the particular device, there have often been concerns about how to securely transport any long-term private key material between devices, and so mobile adoption of encrypted email is considered to be low among users and problematic in terms of security. Although the challenges of using PGP on mobile platforms are well known, mobile PGP has not been subject to usability studies in the same manner that PGP itself has. S/MIME has been tested in some usability studies and in general demonstrates better usability than PGP, insofar as key management does not have to be maintained by the end-user, but users still have trouble understanding the interface.

In general, PGP was considered to have poor usability as users could not understand key management and judge how cryptographic keys establish trust relationships, or even understand the interface. These problems extend to security: if an adversary compromises a user's private key, this allows all encrypted messages to be read. While there has been a resurgence of interest in OpenPGP since 2013, it has not been deployed to any great extent by ordinary users due to the aforementioned issues. In 2015, the IETF reopened the OpenPGP Working Group[15] in order to allow the fundamental algorithms to be upgraded and to use more modern cryptographic **primitives** (for example, support for new algorithms).

The underlying PGP protocol presents a number of well recognised flaws. First, PGP tends to allow any and every combination of uses of encryption and signatures based on user preference, but does not offer authentication of the **headers** (i.e. the 'to' and 'from' fields). This allows messages to be surreptitiously forwarded and otherwise redirected. In general, PGP has been considered an open standard that has serious problems in terms of both security and usability, and this prompted the rise of a generation of competing technologies such as Off the Record Messaging. However, recently, the email community has been quite active and has developed a number of initiatives that have sought to renew PGP and to 'make email encryption great again', as Delta Chat's lead developer and former NEXTLEAP member, Holger Krekel, summarised during a conversation with us. The result is that, since 2016, the PGP community has experienced a definite revival through the introduction of new solutions such as Autocrypt, which automates both secret and public key management by adding an Autocrypt-specific mail header to outgoing mails which contains, among other information, the sender's public key.[16]

Instant messaging encryption

Unlike email, which started as a high-**latency** and asynchronous messaging system, chat protocols began as low-latency synchronous messaging, although recently the line has become increasingly blurred as many chat protocols allow asynchronous message delivery. The user patterns of chat apps have also become increasingly varied in recent years, questioning the distinction between social media and messaging platforms ('messaging is the new social media [...] families use WhatsApp groups instead of Facebook'; Balive 2015).

The development of encryption for chat apps corresponded to changes in the contexts of usage (notably the move from desktop to smartphone technologies) and the spread of mobile Internet. The first encryption protocol for instant messaging, called OTR (2004), presumed a synchronous setting with both contacts being online at the same time. The birth of the second important protocol for end-to-end encryption protocols (Axolotl, started in 2013, now called Signal protocol) corresponded to the rise of instant messengers (in 2013, chat apps surpassed short message services in global message volume for the first time; see eMarketer 2015) and to the Snowden revelations.

The most widely used standardised chat protocol is called **XMPP** (Extensible Message and Presence Protocol) and it became an IETF standard in 2004. XMPP is a federated standard that 'provides a technology for the asynchronous, end-to-end exchange of structured data [...] among a distributed network of globally addressable, presence-aware clients and servers' (Borisov et al. 2004). There are many implementations of the XMPP specifications, with the XMPP Foundation giving a list of 35 clients, 12 servers and 15 libraries using the XMPP protocol.[17] XMPP traffic and content are not encrypted by default, although network-level encryption security using **TLS** has been built into the core. In addition, according to the XMPP foundation, a team of developers is working on an upgrade of the standard to support end-to-end encryption.[18]

The OTR (Off-the-Record) protocol, released in 2004, is an extension to XMPP to provide end-to-end encryption. In their paper with the iconic title 'Off-the-Record Communication, or, Why Not to Use PGP', the creators of OTR, Borisov and Goldberg, describe their protocol as a security upgrade of PGP, at least insofar as it does not have long-term public keys that can be compromised. OTR also provides deniable authentication for users, unlike PGP messages, the latter of which can be later 'used as a verifiable record of the communication event and the identities of the participants' (Borisov et al., 2004). The first OTR implementation was a popular Linux IM client, GAIM. At the present moment it is said to be used by 14 instant messaging clients,[19] including earlier versions of Cryptocat (in-browser Javascript client), Jitsi, and ChatSecure (XMPP client for Android and iOS). However, the first versions of OTR were designed for synchronous messaging between two people, and so did not work for group messaging or asynchronous messaging.[20]

The Signal Protocol, the non-federated protocol developed in 2013 by Open Whisper Systems, is said to have evolved in response to the flaws and limits of OTR. Moxie Marlinspike, the co-author of Signal, was inspired by some features of OTR, such as the idea of **ephemeral key exchange** (Marlinspike 2013), but also added additional security features such as future and forward secrecy, support for asynchronous messaging and group messaging, going a step further than OTR by allowing clients to be offline. The Signal Protocol is used in mobile messaging applications such as the homonymous Signal (formerly TextSecure and RedPhone) and WhatsApp, while its forks are used in Wire and Riot. Silent Circle, a Washington, DC-based encrypted communications firm founded in 2011, has used a version of the Signal Protocol since 2015 in its Silent Phone. In 2016 Facebook announced the implementation of Signal Protocol for Facebook Messenger.[21]

Regardless of these multiple re-usages and forks, the Signal Protocol remains unstandardised, as we will explore in Chapter 2. However, the first step towards 'standardisation' of parts of the Signal Protocol has begun with the creation of **OMEMO** (a recursive acronym for 'OMEMO Multi-End Message and Object

Encryption'). OMEMO is a new encrypted extension of the XMPP protocol developed in 2015 that effectively copies the Signal Protocol and adopts it to XMPP. It was presented to the XMPP Standards Foundation in 2015 but is still in its experimental phase.[22] OMEMO builds upon the work of the Signal Protocol, responding to the flaws of both OTR and PGP, due to OTR's 'inter-client mobility problems' and the absence of forward secrecy of OpenPGP and its vulnerability to so-called replay attacks. The software implementations of OMEMO are growing, and include Conversations, an open-source application for Android that counts over 50000 downloads via Google Play Market, and an unknown number of installs via F-Droid.

Network-level anonymity

End-to-end encryption does not usually allow a user to be anonymous to the server or a third party without additional network-level encryption. Thus, network-level initiatives, such as P2P routing services or anonymous remailers, which can add supplementary privacy properties to end-to-end encrypted messaging, are worth mentioning here. Metadata protection and traffic obfuscation is still an area of active research, stimulating experiments with standards and architectures (e.g. Vuvuzela's usage of 'noise' to obfuscate metadata, discussed in Van den Hooff et al. 2015). There seem to be no functional standards on this level yet; however, some solutions, such as Tor or I2P, tend to serve as references or *de facto* standards for different projects.

The Tor hidden service protocol offers a platform to develop decentralised and encrypted instant messenger servers. Tor (the name is derived from the acronym of the original software project, 'The Onion Router'), is software that directs Internet traffic through a network of volunteers, globally dispersed, which act as relays to conceal a user's location and usage, essentially making it more difficult for a third party to trace Internet activity to a particular user. Tor's success and fame mostly relies on its ability to provide privacy and anonymity to vulnerable Internet users. It is used as a default by projects such as the Tor Messenger, Pond and Ricochet. Another example is the decentralised and end-to-end encrypted mobile messenger Briar, which relies on the Tor network when available, but could also work over Bluetooth in case of emergency off-the-grid situations. Briar is described in more detail in Chapter 3.

Tor only provides anonymity for network addresses, but not metadata such as the sender, recipient and time of message, which are kept in the email header at the time of email or can be deduced by the server. Historically, work has been carried out on anonymous high-latency remailers to fix these transport metadata leaks in federated messaging, these falling under three types: Cypherpunk Anonymous Remailer, Mixmaster and Mixminion. The last of these is not currently active, according to the project's website.[23]

A number of experimental network-level tools, while not guaranteeing anonymity, provide some level of encryption. Zero Tier One is an end-to-end encrypted, peer-to-peer virtual network that provides static network addresses which remain stable even if the user changes physical WiFi/networks. CJDNS implements a virtual **IPv6** network in which all packets are encrypted to the final recipient, using **public key cryptography** for network address allocation and a distributed hash table for routing.[24]

A fragmented yet vibrant field

As we observed in previous mapping research on P2P services (Méadel and Musiani 2015), part of the reason why there is such great diversity and complexity in this field is the relatively short lifespan of several projects. While our mapping of thirty end-to-end encrypted messaging and email apps covered only projects that are currently active (with one exception, Pond, 'in stasis', albeit not deactivated), our preliminary research revealed countless others that, after two or three years of pre-beta phase, and sometimes less, stopped development with no evident explanation. While in more than a few cases, the motives behind this are primarily related to technical experiments that did not deliver as hoped or expected, a number of additional factors may also be responsible, including the failure to develop an economic model, the internal governance of FOSS development groups, and the inability to rally a critical mass of users around the app (possibly due to a lack of ease-of-use, as discussed below).

Despite the prevalence of free and open-source software projects, proprietary software is not absent in this landscape, revealing both a potentially fruitful 'business-to-business' market for end-to-end encryption and a lack of open-source and standards adoption by mainstream applications. Open source itself is multi-layered and sometimes hybrid, with the code on the client side being open source and the server side being proprietary. Perhaps unsurprisingly, the proprietary features are more important in applications destined for business-to-business use. Free and open-source software is predominant for tools adopted or designed to be used by activists and tech-savvy users. The transparency of code and encryption protocols used by open-source software is aimed not only at improving the project, but also at producing communities of peer reviewers, experts, beta-testers and advanced users who participate in a collective reflection on the future of privacy-enhancing technologies.

The target audience of the applications is far from being limited to tech-savvy and activist groups; several projects are intended for widespread use, and user-friendliness appears to be the main issue that stands between this wish and its realisation. A look at visual aspects connected to applications – the design of interfaces, for example, or the design of diagrams and graphics to explain the functioning of the applications – also reveals the different publics targeted by applications and how the developers perceive them. General public-oriented systems use very 'politically neutral' imagery, resorting to the very classical 'Alice and Bob' models[25] while stressing that their tools are for 'everyone' (e.g. for 'sharing holiday photos'), while tools meant for companies emphasise in both visuals and words a focus on security. Other narratives refer to fictional anarchist leaders or real-life activists (e.g. 'Nestor Makhno' or 'Vera Zassulitch'), figures likely to resonate with the target audience. Interestingly, in some instances where user feedback is visible on the App Store or Google Play, it shows that end-to-end encryption is perceived as problematic because both sender and receiver have to install the app for encryption to take place, which complicates usage.

Several secure messaging projects propose solutions to the problem of data storage. Indeed, despite the guarantees of 'no personal data collection', some projects still store key data on the servers (such as usage statistics, device infor-mation, keys, usernames or friend relations). Developers tend to explain such practices by reference to technical requirements (e.g. proposing a better user experience based on the usage statistics collected) but many developers remain keen to seek alternatives that involve minimal data storage and use stronger forms of decentralisation.

A related issue is a powerful 'double' narrative about end-to-end encryption. If on the one hand, it is associated with a very strong discourse on empower- ment and the better protection of fundamental civil liberties, several projects show in parallel a desire/need to defend themselves from associations with criminal activity and allegations such as 'encryption is used by jihadists' (Sanger and Perlroth 2015). Such narratives are fuelled by previous and current ones about decentralised technologies and peer-to-peer, with their history of alleged 'empowering-yet-illegal' tools. These issues in turn connect to the broader context of discussions about governance by infrastructure and civil liberties (Musiani et al. 2016), some of them particularly related to encryption (or the breaking of it), such as the Apple vs FBI case[26] and WhatsApp using, since April 2016, encryption by default. Thus, the present research hints at something that we will address in the following chapters – something a large majority of the projects need to take into account, and indeed are already taking into account: architecture is politics, but not a substitute for politics (Agre 2003).

Given the range of debates, controversies and emergent publics around encryption and secure messaging, we hope to have begun to show why a social perspective is necessary for the design and refinement of technical protocols. This includes the necessity to understand how and whether users understand and value the various security properties of the protocols. For example, how do users understand what is a 'key' or what is 'forward secrecy'? Often, protocol designers make assumptions about whether or not 'ordinary users' can under- stand the security and privacy properties of their protocols. For example, almost all protocols from PGP to Signal use methods such as 'out-of-band fingerprint verification' to determine whether or not the recipient of their message really is who they think they are. Our research shows that users rarely actually use these techniques to verify the identity of their contacts.

Another example that has been debated in the technical community is deniable authentication. While a protocol may be technically deniable, would this cryptographic deniability be able to stand the test of society, for example in a court of law? Answering these kinds of questions influences the kinds of protocols that can be designed by the research community. Lastly, why do only some protocols enable decentralisation via **open standards**? Do only specific groups of users (tech-savvy and activists) have a strong preference for peer-to-peer or federated solutions over centralised services? This book hopes to address these and other related questions.

STRUCTURE OF THE BOOK

Over the course of the next six chapters, the overall objective of the book is to provide an analytical portrait of the field of encrypted secure messaging, in order to explore the experience of encryption in today's variety of secure messaging protocols and tools, and their implications for the making of digital liberties.

The field of encrypted messaging offers many solutions designed to conceal, obfuscate and disguise private communications and other online activities. These solutions are tailored to protect against specific 'adversaries'. The security and privacy features worked into different protocols offer various degrees of protection and let users conceal different parts of their online identities. To illustrate this, Chapter 1 shows how instruments such as 'threat modelling' and risk assessment are deployed during the development of tools in order to either identify from whom a user needs to hide or to analyse the possibility or chance of a threat being realised. Also, it becomes important not only to know who to conceal from, but also to evaluate the chances of actually 'meeting' this adversary. In fact, users perceive themselves as having, not a single identity, but rather a set of profiles or personas: daughter, journalist, lover, activist, colleague... Each role, according to users, may require a specific form of digital self-care or a specific set of tools. Each persona implies a specific pattern of online behaviour, thus creating what is called 'security by compartmentalisation'. A consequence, as we argue in Chapter 1, is that when applied to online privacy and security, risk is a relational and socially defined concept, as it greatly depends on the user's social graphs and communicative contexts.

Chapter 2 moves into the more empirically focused part of the book, by examining the case of a centralised application – Signal – and its underlying eponymous protocol. The Signal protocol is now considered to embody 'best practice' in the field of encrypted messaging and has become a trend-setter for other projects in terms of privacy and security features. Currently, Signal is centralised, as a single server mediates the setup of the protocol in its most widespread deployments. A new means of 'quasi-standardisation' or 'standardisation by running code' is being practised around this protocol. In this process, a quasi-standard is defined as 'something that works' and is iterated and redeployed by others. Centralisation has allowed Signal developers to update the protocol rapidly enough in response to research and bugs, and to limit concerns about the technical competence of having third-party developers potentially adapting their protocol to other applications than their in-house one. However, the 'bottleneck' of centralisation also implies that difficulties and tensions have arisen in connection with some attempts to reimplement the Signal protocol, due to the lack of clear guidelines and specifications in order to do so. Chapter 2 discusses centralisation as a 'control by design' model – in particular, control over changes in the protocol, so as to respond quickly to technical challenges. Here the chapter draws on two other cases alongside Signal: Telegram and Wire.

Chapter 3 examines peer-to-peer based secure messaging applications. Particular populations of users, especially those living in 'high-risk' environments, show interest towards these decentralised systems, as they see an alignment between their own favoured political and economic models – based on the principles of horizontal connections, mutual assistance, self-governance, participation – and the technical architecture of distributed networks. Peer-to-peer, as with previous recent instances, also promises less control by both governments and private corporations. However, peer-to-peer encrypted messaging faces a number of technical challenges, including a 'vicious circle' between adoption barriers and a dependency on a critical mass of users, the difficulty of managing users' reputations and identities (identities are unique but users usually find them hard to memorise due to the form they are presented in), placing trust in the client (which presents many advantages censorship-wise but may present risks for users living in authoritarian regimes, where the main threat model remains physical pressure and device seizure). By discussing, in particular, the case of the application Briar and its underlying protocol, this chapter analyses both the potential and the challenges of decentralised architectures as applied to encrypted messaging.

Chapter 4 completes the analysis of different architectural choices and their impact on the configuration of encryption tools by examining systems based on federative models. When it comes to communities of developers debating online, the tensions between centralisation and more distributed architectural forms, such as federation, go hand-in-hand with debates over standards. Federation can help alleviate and distribute the very high degree of personal responsibility held by a centralised service provider and favours the freedom of users to choose between different solutions. On the other hand, it can present problems in terms of security, as it is harder to audit all the different implementations of a federated protocol and ensure correct updates. Drawing on the examples of Conversations (and its underlying OMEMO protocol), Matrix.org, and LEAP/Pixelated, Chapter 4 retraces the debates on federation in encrypted messaging, and analyses how federation takes shape in these debates as both an infrastructural configuration and a social experiment, in each case seeking a compromise between more distributed architectures and high levels of security.

Given the great variety of encrypted messaging solutions, how is one – a user, an NGO, a professional – to make sense of them? Chapter 5 tells the story of one such attempt. Classifications and categorisations are, to put it in Bowker and Star's (1999) words, 'powerful technologies', whose architecture is simultaneously informatic and moral and which can become relatively invisible as they progressively stabilise while at the same time not losing their power. Thus, categorisation systems should be acknowledged as a significant site of political, ethical and cultural work. This chapter examines such work as it relates to encrypted messaging tools, by examining, in particular, one of the most prominent initiatives in this regard: the Electronic Frontier Foundation's 2014 release of the Secure Messaging Scorecard (SMS). A particular focus is on the debates it sparked, and its subsequent re-evaluation and evolutions. We show how the different versions of the SMS, as they move from an approach centred on the tools and their technical features to one that gives priority to users and their contexts of use, actively participate in the co-shaping of specific definitions of privacy, security and encryption that put users at the core of the categorisation system and entrust them with new responsibilities.

Finally, the concluding chapter of the book ties together insights from the previous chapters to reflect on encryption as a site of social, political and technical controversy. Issues related to encryption and its adoption in messaging systems are inextricably entangled with issues of standardisation (formal/informal), the political economy of software development and adoption, and choices of technical architecture. This concluding chapter will offer some reflections on these different aspects as they have been informed by our fieldwork and will then tie the diverse ways in which political effects can be achieved through technological choices to broader political concerns related to privacy, examining in particular how they can interact with recent supra-national legal instruments such as the General Data Protection Regulation (GDPR). Finally, we will comment on the implications of our study and of cognate research for the development of social studies of encryption and for its interactions with Internet governance research, in particular of STS inspiration.

We now move into the first chapter of this book, written from the standpoint of users and security trainers – encrypted messaging experts working in an intermediary zone between developers and users. We will follow them as they deploy various strategies to make sense of the complex and moving ecosystem of end-to-end encrypted messengers.

NOTES

1 For example, future secrecy, which we will address in detail later in the book.
2 Following up on previous work by the authors (e.g. Musiani 2015b).
3 Scholarly and non-scholarly debates about the term 'hacker' are ongoing. For the purpose of this book, and given that several projects and tools examined in it do not necessarily refer to an imaginary of subversion, we follow Hellegren's (2017) definition of a hacker as a member of a community that unites with like-minded members 'in their practices of developing and modifying internet-specific technologies'.

4 Many Internet protocols are client/server, which means that the machines that communicate are not equivalent: one is a server, permanently on and waiting for connections; the others are clients, who connect when they have something to ask. This is a logical mode of operation, for example, in the case of the Web: when you visit a website, you are a reader, and the entity which manages the website produces the content you seek to read. But not all uses of the Internet fit into this model; they include direct sending of messages, or file exchanges – not a one-way communication but a peer-to-peer one, with two machines or two humans communicating directly.

5 This work is available as deliverable 3.1 of the NEXTLEAP project.

6 The three cases develop both a user-facing client application and a protocol that can potentially be separated from it (Signal protocol, LEAP and Bramble respectively).

7 We will come back to the high-risk/low-risk distinction, its opportunities and shortcomings, in Chapter 1.

8 We frequently get this type of remark from STS conference attendees.

9 Autocrypt will be extensively presented in Chapter 4 as an example of a federated-architecture encrypted messaging system.

10 A previous version of this section was published as Ermoshina, K., F. Musiani & H. Halpin, 'End-to-end encrypted messaging protocols: An overview', in Franco Bagnoli et al., eds, *Internet science. Third international conference, INSCI 2016, Florence, Italy, September 12–14, 2016, Proceedings*, Springer, p. 244–254.

11 The thirty applications we examined are: Briar, Caliopen, ChatSecure, CoverMe, CryptoCat, Equalit.ie, GData, i2P, Jitsi, Mailpile, Mailvelope, ParanoiaWorks, Patchwork, Pidgin, Pixelated, Pond, Protonmail, qTOX, Ricochet, Scramble, Signal, SilentCircle, SureSpot, Teem/SwellRT, Telegram, Threema, Tor Messenger, Vuvuzela, Wickr, Wire.

12 https://tools.ietf.org/html/rfc821.

13 https://www.philzimmermann.com/EN/essays/WhyIWrotePGP.html.

14 See, e.g., https://docs.microsoft.com/en-us/microsoft-365/security/office-365-security/s-mime-for-message-signing-and-encryption?view=o365-worldwide.

15 https://datatracker.ietf.org/wg/openpgp/charter.

16 See Chapter 4. Also, https://autocrypt.org/level1.html#autocrypt-level-1-enabling-encryption-avoiding-annoyances.

17 https://xmpp.org/software.

18 http://xmpp.org/about/technology-overview.html.

19 https://otr.cypherpunks.ca/software.php.

20 The latest version of OTR (v4) aims at supporting asynchronous messaging and out-of-order delivery.

21 https://whispersystems.org/blog/facebook-messenger.

22 https://xmpp.org/extensions/xep-0384.html#top.

23 http://mixminion.net.

24 https://github.com/cjdelisle/cjdns/blob/master/doc/Whitepaper.md.

25 'Alice and Bob' are fictional characters used as placeholder names in cryptology and other computer science/engineering literature to lay out a scenario where there are several participants in a thought experiment or a model.

26 The Apple vs FBI dispute was a landmark controversy about whether courts can compel communication technology manufacturers to assist in unlocking phones whose data are encrypted. The controversy was spurred by orders issued by US District Courts to Apple in 2015 and 2016.

I

CONCEALING FROM WHOM? THREAT MODELLING AND RISK AS A RELATIONAL CONCEPT

NOWADAYS, THE FIELD OF ENCRYPTED MESSAGING PROPOSES A LARGE variety of solutions for concealing, obfuscating and disguising private communications and other online activities, tailored to enable protection against specific 'adversaries'. Security and privacy features worked into different protocols offer various degrees of protection and let users conceal different parts of their online identities. As a prelude to the more detailed analysis of how some of these systems are created, developed and used – which will be the objective of Chapters 2 to 4 – this chapter seeks to discuss how instruments such as 'threat modelling' and risk assessment are deployed during the development of encrypted messaging systems, in order to identify from whom a user needs to hide, or to analyse the possibility of an impending threat. It is not only important to know who to hide from, but also to evaluate the chances of actually 'meeting' this adversary. In fact, users perceive themselves, not as having a single identity, but rather as possessing a set of 'profiles' or 'personas', and every role may require particular patterns of digital self-care, served by specific sets of tools. These different personas imply a specific online behaviour pattern, thus creating what is called 'security by compartmentalisation'. This chapter explores how, when applied to digital security, risk is a relational and socially defined concept, as it greatly depends on a user's social graphs and communicative contexts.[1]

CREATING AND CONCEALING AN ONLINE PRESENCE

In response to the recent increasing variety of use-cases for encrypted secure messaging, a number of privacy-enhancing tools offer several different solutions to conceal private communications or other online exchanges. From the more popular centralised solutions such as Wire, Telegram, Signal and WhatsApp to less widely used decentralised platforms such as Ricochet or Briar – some of which will be the subject of the following chapters – and email clients supporting PGP encryption, these solutions are tailored to protect against specific 'adversaries'. Security and privacy features worked into different protocols offer various degrees of protection and let users 'hide' different parts of their online identities.

The great variety of concealing devices that are being developed for our communicative tools is a response to the increasingly complex relationship between Internet users and the circulation of their personal data online. Indeed, our online traces are multi-layered and embedded in the material infrastructure of the Internet. Our identity can be disclosed not only by the content of our messages, but also by the unique identifiers of our hardware devices (such as **MAC addresses**), our **IP addresses** and other related metadata, thus contributing to the 'turn to infrastructure' in privacy and its governance (Musiani et al. 2016). This raises questions such as which of our multiple online identifiers can be considered as personal, which data should we hide, and from whom, and – to invoke David Pozen's 'mosaic theory' (2005) – when does a combination of several items of *a priori* non-identifying information construct a degree of personalisation sufficient to de-anonymise a user?

Drawing upon previous work such as the anthropology of spam filters (Kockelman 2013), we understand cryptographic systems as sieves that separate items of information that have to be hidden from items that can be shown. Encryption algorithms appear as inverses or shadows of the information they sort. In fact, designing privacy-enhancing tools requires imagining the 'worst of all possible worlds', being constructed through various scenarios implying risk, uncertainty and flaws in security. Identification of a threat model serves as a way of agreeing upon an appropriate threshold of anonymity and confidentiality for a particular context of usage. Thus, different users may define in different ways who their adversary is, may disagree (or in any case, have to find grounds to agree) on which types of data should be concealed, and make a choice about which tools are more likely to give them the level of protection they need. Depending on different use-cases, from 'nothing-to-hide' low-risk situations, to high-risk scenarios in war zones or in authoritarian contexts, users, trainers and developers co-construct threat models and decide which data to conceal and on the ways in which to do it, which sometimes relies on a variety of *arts de faire* deployed by users to 'hijack' (Callon 1986) existing encryption tools and develop their own ways to conceal themselves.

To understand how threat models are constructed, it is useful to recall the interdisciplinary work that, in the last fifteen years, has explored the 'collective' dimension of privacy and the extent to which protecting it requires the interdependence of multiple factors and actors. For instance, Daniel Solove has described the ways in which the contours of online social representation are gradually identified as a result of the informational traces left behind by different interactions, dispersed across a variety of databases and networks (Solove 2006). These traces are at the core of states' and corporations' attempts to track and profile citizens and users, as well as central to activists' strategies to expose corporate and state malfeasance. Successfully preserving one's privacy in the connected world is thus about managing visibilities (Flyverbom et al. 2016). Along the same lines, emphasising the ways in which users can be active creators of their own privacy, Antonio Casilli has shown how the right to privacy has turned into a 'collective negotiation' whose main objective is to master one's projection of self in social interactions with others (Casilli 2015). Paul Dourish and Ken Anderson nicely summarise the core message put forward by this approach to privacy and security when they suggest that these are 'difficult concepts to manage from a technical perspective precisely because they are caught up in larger collective rhetorics and practices of risk, danger, secrecy, trust, morality, identity, and more. As an alternative, they argue that we should move 'toward a holistic view of situated and collective information practice' (Dourish and Anderson 2006).

Surveillance studies have also paid specific attention to the collective and relational dimensions of surveillance, privacy and security. Authors interested in exploring the concept of resistance have underlined the algorithmic and 'rhizomatic' nature of new surveillance practices and the responses needed to counter them (Martin et al. 2009); others show how a traditional conceptualisation of surveillance, involving an exclusive relationship between the surveillant and his object, does not properly take into account the 'surveillant assemblages' (including those that seek to respond to surveillance) that are currently on display in networked media, and are transforming the targets and the hierarchies of surveillance activities, while at the same time reconfiguring the notion of privacy (Haggerty and Erickson 2000).

Some contributions by scholars of online surveillance and privacy, while grounded in research that demonstrates the pervasiveness of digital surveillance and echoes the conceptualisation of surveillance as 'assemblage', are explicitly aimed at providing practical 'guides' for users. This is the case with Finn Brunton and Helen Nissenbaum's *Obfuscation,* which aims to provide both a rationale and a set of tools aimed at the 'deliberate use of ambiguous, confusing, or misleading information to interfere with surveillance and data collection projects'; these strategies may include noncompliance and sabotage (Brunton and Nissenbaum 2015). The work of Lex Gill and colleagues, with a particular focus on the Canadian context, also seeks to provide a 'field guide' to the debates on encryption and offer hands-on suggestions for 'policymakers, legal professionals, academics, journalists, and advocates who are trying to navigate the complex implications of this technology' (Gill et al. 2018). The increasing frequency of this type of contribution – the provision by scholars of hands-on guides in this field – is interesting to acknowledge in the context of this book. Such texts create hybrids that operate somewhere between scholarly contributions, on the one hand, and, on the other, practical guides meant to act as companions to the proliferation of tools and possible use-cases. Thus, such texts – and possibly, to some extent, the present book – contribute to concretely co-shaping users' responses to surveillance and actions aimed at protecting privacy.

'KNOW YOUR ENEMY': THREAT MODELLING AS A TOOL FOR TRAINERS

In design studies and software engineering, threat modelling is considered an inherent part of the normal design cycle where 'security needs' are understood as yet another facet of the complex design process: 'We must consider security needs throughout the design process, just as we do with performance, usability, localizability, serviceability, or any other facet' (Torr 2005). When applied to the software development process, threat modelling is defined as a 'formal process of identifying, documenting and mitigating security threats to a software system' (Oladimeji et al. 2006). Threat modelling enables development teams to examine the application 'through the eyes of a potential adversary' in order to identify major security risks. However, threat modelling processes and techniques are also applied to human agents, in order to find security flaws in user behaviour patterns (both online and offline), identify sensitive information 'to be protected', determine potential adversaries, and evaluate their capacities and propose solutions for risk mitigation and protection.

The idea of threat modelling applied to users instead of informational systems is related to the difficulty – rather, the impossibility – of 'hiding from everyone'. As the Electronic Frontier Foundation, a leading NGO in the digital security sphere, puts it:

> It's impossible to protect against every kind of trick or attacker, so you should concentrate on which people might want your data, what they might want from it, and how they might get it. Coming up with a set of possible attacks you plan to protect against is called threat modelling.[2]

Threat modelling is linked to another instrument called risk assessment. While threat modelling means identifying from whom a user needs to hide, risk assessment is a tool that trainers and digital security organisations use in order to analyse the chance of a threat being realised. It becomes important not only to know who to hide from, but also to evaluate the actual chances of coming face-to-face with one's adversary. While risk has been described as a cultural 'translation' of danger (Douglas and Wildavsky 1982; Vaz and Bruno 2006), risk assessment is a 'quantification of uncertainty' (Hong 2017), that produces risk as something that can be 'known, mitigated, increased and decreased, calculated' (Porter 1995).

For the digital security trainers, we interviewed over the course of this research, threat modelling and risk assessment have become powerful instruments for narrowing down and structuring their training sessions. Several training sessions that we have observed in Ukraine and Russia used different threat modelling techniques. For example, the 'Digital security for activists' session that took place in Saint-Petersburg, Russia, on 10 April 2016, started with P., the trainer, offering the following introduction:

> Before we start, we need to decide from whom we are protecting. First, the state. In just the last year 200 court cases have been opened because of online publications, comments and so on. Second, we should be protecting ourselves from corporations. It may be naive to say so, but it is clear that different corporations are accumulating information, and a lot of useful services that are given to us for free, however in exchange these companies are appropriating information about us. Third – there are other malicious agents who would like to get access to our online wallets or to hack us just for fun (translation from Russian by the authors).

This division between three categories of adversary was not just used rhetorically to introduce the training session: it was subsequently used throughout the three-hour workshop, in order to group various privacy-enhancing tools that people might need, around the three big categories of adversaries. Structuring training around a specific adversary means identifying not just the technical resources the adversary possesses, but also the extra-technical parameters – the legal context, for example.

Another way of structuring a training session was experimented with by Ukrainian trainers V. and M., both of whom specialised in high-risk users likely to face powerful, state-level adversaries, or maybe even physical threats. The training, held on 15 January 2017 in Kyiv, involved using a spreadsheet for both participants and trainers to complete (Figure 1.1).

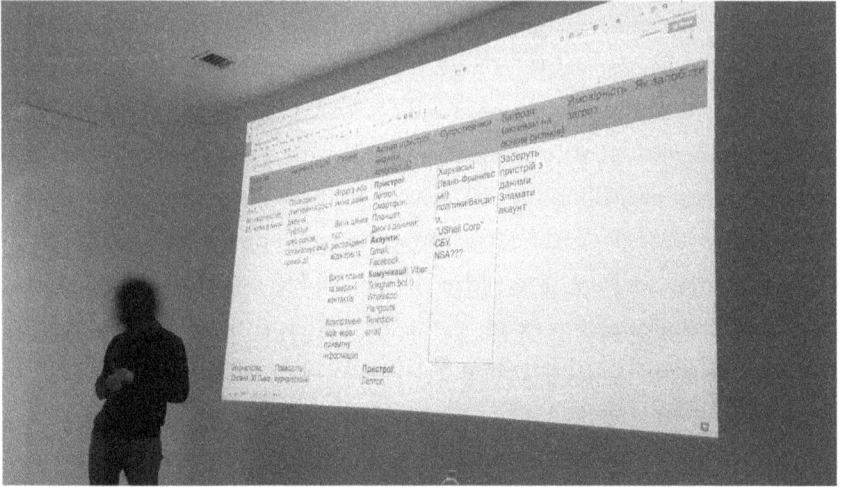

FIG. 1.1 Digital security training observed in Kyiv, January 2017. The table includes the following columns (from left to right): Description of a person, its functions and activities, risks, 'assets' (devices, accounts, types of communications used), adversaries, threats (applied to the assets based on risks), possibility of a threat to happen, how to avoid risks (photograph by the authors).

The training was organised around a collaborative construction of several fictional profiles (for example: Anya, 25 years old, ecological activist; Oksana, 30 years old, journalist, etc.) and the identification of corresponding assets, adversaries and threats. In this way, trainers were focused not on enumerating existing privacy-enhancing tools, but on explaining a precise methodology of personalised threat modelling. For trainers, a user's ability to analyse a very concrete situation and context is more important than their possessing sophisticated knowledge of multiple tools. Though some of the observed training sessions were nonetheless centred around demonstrations of particular tools, the majority of trainers are largely critical of tool-centred approaches and insist instead on tailored, threat-model-based forms of training:

> Very often trainings turn into tool-trainings. But in our work tools are not our primary and even not secondary concerns. What's primary is the evaluation of what participants need, what they already use. And only after we think of what we can suggest them to use, and again, without any hard

recommendations 'you need only this tool and that's all' (M., informational security trainer, Ukraine).

The digital security community is highly reflexive about its own training practices and the evaluation criteria used to assess secure messaging applications and mail clients. In recent years, the transition from a tool-centred approach to a user-centred one has been something of a paradigm shift among trainers and experts, where the user's capacities to evaluate their own threat model are seen as increasingly crucial. As the famous EFF guide 'Surveillance Self-Defense' puts it,

> Trying to protect all your data from everyone all the time is impractical and exhausting. But, do not fear! Security is a process, and through thoughtful planning, you can assess what's right for you. Security isn't about the tools you use or the software you download. It begins with understanding the unique threats you face and how you can counter those threats.[3]

This 'tailored approach' to threat models during security training sessions is also important because developers in the secure messaging field are currently discussing a number of unsolved cryptography problems, such as metadata storage, the vulnerabilities of centralised infrastructures, the usage of telephone numbers as identifiers and so on. In the absence of the 'perfect tool' in all these respects, trainers recommend patchworks of different tools and operational security practices ('physical security') that aim to minimise the drawbacks of existing tools and offer different features, from encryption 'in transit' to encryption 'at rest', metadata obfuscation, and so on. Threat modelling is a practice that helps to fix, and in some ways compensate for, some of these unsolved technical problems.

It is also important to note that, for a specific threat model, extra-cryptographic factors such as a particular tool having a low learning curve before it can be used, peer pressure or network effect (first-time users joining a tool because a critical mass of individuals already uses it) may be more important than the technical efficiency of a cryptographic protocol. Thus, a trainer in Ukraine would – seemingly counter-intuitively but, from their standpoint, ultimately logically – often advise their high-risk users to use WhatsApp and Gmail instead of Signal or a PGP-encrypted form of email, as 'everyone already uses it and knows how it works'. In other words, the adoption of these tools will happen quicker and result in fewer mistakes. Thus, time and learning curve become additional factors affecting the recommendation of a specific tool.

'NOTHING TO HIDE' OR 'TINFOIL HAT FREAKS'? A CONTINUUM OF RISK LEVELS

Away from trainers and digital security experts, users develop their own methods to evaluate their risks, and invent specific *ad hoc* practices of digital self-defence. However, even after the Snowden revelations, a significant proportion of European citizens share the idea that they have 'nothing to hide', sometimes considering the mere fact of concealing online traces as a potential indication of criminal activity. A recent study has revealed a certain state of public apathy: 'though online users are concerned and feel unease about the mass collection of their personal data, the lack of understanding as to how such data is collected as well as a sense of powerlessness leads to the public's resignation and apathy' (Hintz and Dencik 2017).

The 'nothing to hide' argument has, famously, been widely criticised by the security community, resulting in the production of a variety of cultural content and online tutorials aimed at increasing the awareness of the general public about digital security.[4] These contributions fuel the ongoing debate about the thin line separating both targeted surveillance from mass surveillance and high-risk from low-risk users. The demarcation between hiding from governments and hiding from corporations is also increasingly blurred, with the image of the 'adversary' becoming much more complex and hybrid (Musiani 2013).

While the vast majority of user studies in **usable security** – the field of study that evaluates the usability of digital security – have been conducted with subjects from the 'general population' (in fact, usually, university students), our research provides slightly different results regarding users' awareness of and concerns about privacy. We classified our interviewed population against two axes: individuals' knowledge about technologies and their risk situation. This resulted in four groups that we will examine in turn in the remainder of this chapter – although, as we will further explore later, while we found this distinction operationally useful, it also had its limits.

For profiles with a low-level risk situation but possessing a high degree of technical knowledge, the awareness of privacy and security related risks was very high; however, the generally adopted user behaviour was not holistically secure: a large number of tech developers or trainers were using unencrypted email and text messaging applications. For example, despite recent usability research showing that Telegram was suffering from a number of important usability and security problems (Abu-Salma et al. 2017a), with encryption for group chat being very basic, Pirate Party activists – themselves software developers, system administrators and/or hosting providers – use Telegram on a daily basis (for example, the group of Pirate Party Russia on Telegram counts 469 users as of 24 November 2019). However, other tactics of self-defence are used, such as self-censorship (avoiding talking about specific topics) and pseudonymisation (avoiding real profile photos and usernames).

Surprisingly, there is no strict correlation, at least in our interviews, between users' threat models, level of technical knowledge, the security features of a tool – such as key length or key generation algorithm – and the dynamics of tool adoption. Instead, other extra-cryptographic and extra-security features can become arguments for the adoption of a specific tool. In the case of Telegram, it is interesting to observe how the actual cryptographic protocol and security and privacy properties lose their importance for users, compared to the features of the interface and to the reputation of the app's creator. The trust in Telegram, according to our interviews, is not located in the technology, but in the person using the technology and their political position:

> User1: 'Maybe you should not discuss that over Telegram?'
> User2: 'Why not? Pashka Durov will never give away any of our data, he does not care about Russian police' (from online discussion in a group chat 'Soprotivlenie' [Resistance], posted on 11 June 2017; translation from Russian by the authors).

Within high-risk and low-knowledge populations, however, the awareness of risks regarding privacy issues (such as the necessity of using privacy-preserving browser plug-ins) was not absolute, with behaviour related to email and messaging estimated as being more important. Even if these users could not always clearly describe possible attack vectors, they had a highly multi-faceted and complex image of who their adversary was. This was clearly expressed in the drawings collected during interviews and observed workshops, which respondents drew when asked by us to illustrate who or what they considered to be their adversary (Figure 1.2).

'Low-knowledge, high-risk' users, for their part, deploy specific, often unique and personal, methods to protect their communications and information, resulting in an assemblage of different tools and practices, both in their offline (social engineering, operational security or 'opsec') and online behaviour (Figure 1.3).

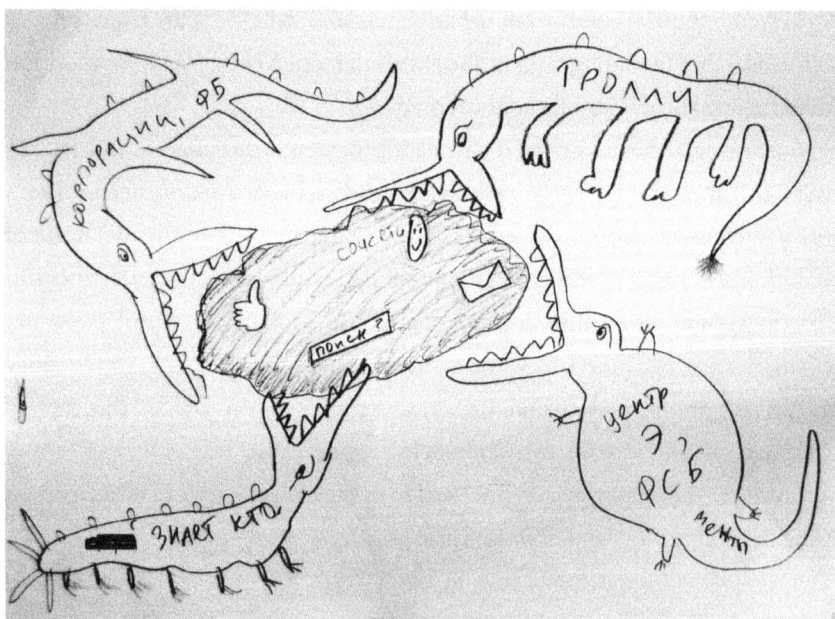

FIG. 1.2 User representation of 'insecure communications'. Drawing collected during a digital security workshop in Saint-Petersburg, April 2017. By a female activist of a feminist collective. The 'crocodiles' are labelled (from left top clockwise): 'Corporations, Facebook'; 'Trolls'; 'Center against extremism, FSB, police'; 'Who the f**k knows'. On the cloud: 'Search'; 'Social networks'.

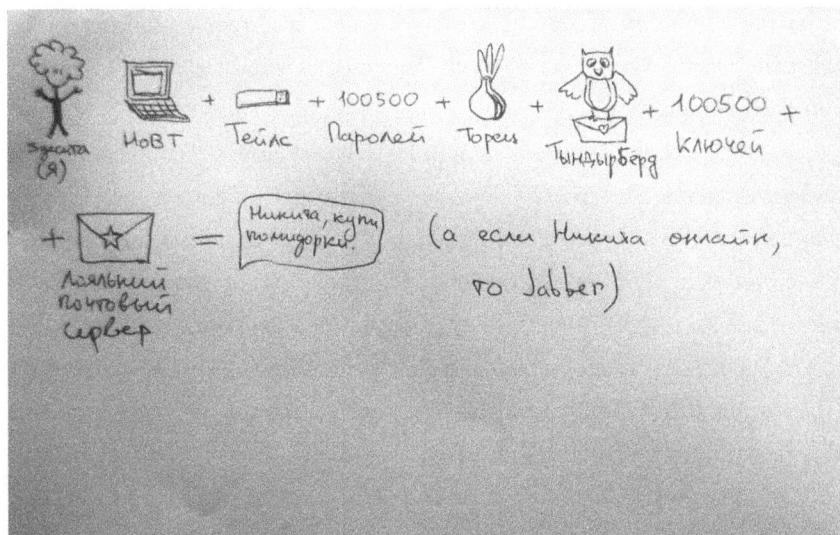

FIG. 1.3 User representation of 'secure communications'. Drawing collected during a digital security workshop in Saint-Petersburg, April 2017. Female, antifascist activist. From the left: 'Me: laptop + Tails + 100500 passwords + Tor + Thunderbird + 100500 keys + trusted email provider = message "Nikita, could you buy some tomatoes please?" (And if Nikita is online, then Jabber)'

For instance, high-risk users in Russia and Ukraine – namely left-wing activists who face police threats and targeted surveillance – are widely using the so-called 'one-time secrets', special web-based **pastebins** or pads that claim to destroy messages once read.[5] These users describe the main threat they face as being the seizure of their devices. Thus, they suggest, a self-destroying link is the most secure way to communicate, even though the links to these locations are often sent via unsecured channels, such as Facebook Messenger. The flip side of these practices is that applications that are *a priori* more specifically targeted to activists become infrequent choices for these high-risk users.

SECURITY BY COMPARTMENTALISATION AND 'RELATIONAL' RISK

As these examples show, the multitude of messaging apps echoes the variety of user behaviour and risk assessment practices. In fact, users perceive themselves as having a plurality of identities, each of which may require specific digital self-care practices and sets of tools. This creates what we call 'security by compartmentalisation'.

Users select different messaging apps for different groups of contacts, according to the perceived level of risk. Even some of our high-risk interviewees report that they use WhatsApp or Facebook Messenger for work and family relations, while preferring PGP-encrypted email, Signal or Privnote for activist-related contacts. Some prefer to move all the communications to a single application, but report having a hard time convincing relatives to change their online behaviour (the so-called 'digital migration problem') or face compatibility problems (for example, older phones cannot run Signal).

As a consequence, when applied to digital security, risk is a relational concept, as it greatly depends on the user's social graphs and contexts of communication. A high-risk user from Ukraine, involved in a collective for the support of political prisoners, explains:

> My risk is always connected to the risk of other people. I do not want to use my mobile phone to connect to my activist account, as it will be possible to connect the two. And even if I think that I have not done anything, other people have reasons to hide themselves. And finally… I never know when someone comes after me. Predicting future is not wise. Khodorkovsky just before his arrest also said that no one was interested in him.

In this sense, even though using axes to categorise users can serve practical ends – making it easier, for example, to apply statistical treatments to our data, something that the technologists in the NEXTLEAP team very much appreciated, which resulted in a few collaborative papers – the difference between low-risk and high-risk users is actually highly context-dependent, and always shifting: a low-risk person in contact with high-risk ones has to increase their level of security and may themself become high risk. As a user from Austria, a festival organiser self-identifying as a low-risk person, puts it:

> I work on a festival which is all about generating outreach. And I adapt to the
> people I invite or strategize projects with. So the risk of my communication
> is related to the risk taken by the people I am talking to. So for example with
> [X], [Y][6] or others I always encrypt everything of course and I also always
> check if a guest I am inviting has a public key on a keyserver so I start com-
> munication encrypted [...] Enemy? Lots of my guest speakers have serious
> enemies; so I again adapt to that.

This 'compartmentalisation' approach to security also results in some hardware-
based user bricolages or tinkering, ranging from the more popular practice
of 'dual-booting' (combining an 'activist' and a 'normal' operating system on
the same machine), to more sophisticated hiding places or concealed operating systems. These user behaviours and user-driven practices of security by
compartmentalisation have been recently incorporated *by design* in a project
named Qubes. This is an operational system based on a multitude of virtual
machines creating isolated working environments that let users coordinate
and manage different 'parts' of their online identities with different needs and
security requirements.

However, risks and threat models also evolve over time. Not only are these
dependent on users' relational networks, but also on the supposed reactions
and behaviours of the adversary. Thus, for this high-risk and high-knowledge
user from Greece, it is important to constantly reinvent their everyday security
practices:

> According to the act or what I do I have a specific OPSEC. I remember the
> main steps by heart, though I don't use the same practices every time as
> once used a specific methodology then it's burned. Depending on the place
> I try to masquerade to the common practices of this area rather than blindly
> improvise. The adversary is always learning from me and from trusted people
> or friends that are not careful enough.

If the distinction between high risk and low risk needs to be taken with a grain
of salt, so too do the definitions of sensitive and insensitive data. Religion,

morality and gender become important parameters in influencing the definition of what 'sensitive information' is. Our interviews with Middle Eastern users, for example, show that one of the most important adversaries from whom Muslim women have to hide is their own partner or family member. As one of our interviewees, a twenty-seven-year-old Iranian woman, explains, photos of a non-religious wedding can become as sensitive as an instance of political critique, and can present significant levels of risk to the person sharing the photos. It is not, therefore, the type of information itself that defines the category of 'high risk', but the user's broader context: threat models and risk levels thus can be gender and culture dependent.

'IF YOU USE THAT TOOL, YOU HAVE SOMETHING TO HIDE': PARADOXES OF THE MASS ADOPTION OF ENCRYPTION

According to our fieldwork, open-source and licensing choices are covered less in high-risk training sessions, as high-risk users do not always associate open source with security. Open source was perceived as a less important criterion in the context of an immediate physical threat: if a proprietary but 'efficient' and 'easy to explain' solution exists, trainers will give it priority. For example, in Ukraine, WhatsApp is the most recommended application, because it is considered easy to install. Trainers consider WhatsApp's proprietary license and collaboration with Facebook (notably in relation to metadata sharing) as less important than users' perceptions around security. The primary task in high-risk contexts with low-knowledge users is to help them quickly abandon unencrypted tools, as well as tools whose creators may be collaborating with their adversaries.

> Since WhatsApp adopted end-to-end encryption, we usually do not spend that much time on instant messaging encryption [during trainings] and recommend to stay with WhatsApp if people already use it. So they can still communicate with all of their friends, and also... it looks familiar, and it does not shock them. And people say [during trainings] if they use WhatsApp it's less suspicious than if they use a special app for activists (I., female informational security trainer, Ukraine).

This quote raises an important concern addressed by a number of our user interviewees and observed during both cryptoparties and informational security trainings: *does the very fact of using an activist-targeted app constitute a threat in itself?* This refers to Ethan Zuckerman's (2008) famous 'Cute Cat Theory of Digital Activism', according to which it is safer and easier for activists to use the same mainstream platforms as those used for sharing 'lolcats' pictures, whereas using a tool marked as 'activist' may put users under targeted (and thus, easier and cheaper) surveillance.

This concern reveals a shared (but often underexplored) anxiety among users about specific kinds of metadata (even though this particular term is not always used explicitly), e.g. data about their installation of particular apps. In interviews, we were often confronted by an extensive critique of all the existing tools by both informational security trainers and non-technical users. This echoes the findings of another recent usability study of end-to-end encryption tools, which concluded that 'most participants did not believe secure tools could offer protection against powerful or knowledgeable adversaries' (Abu-Salma et al. 2017b: 2). Many users mentioned as a reason for not adopting encryption the fact that their social graphs and 'activist' lifestyle would be exposed to adversaries by using specific tools. A Russian user also mentioned the opposite effect – using an activist-targeted tool as means of 'earning trust' – recounting the story of an undercover police officer who used a @riseup.net email account as a way of penetrating a student movement mailing list during the 2011–12 mass protests.

The quintessence of this 'tool-scepticism' can be illustrated with a drawing (Figure 1.4) authored by one of our respondents – a European high-risk war correspondent working in the Middle East – when asked to draw a representation of his adversary.

The adoption of encryption by mainstream messaging applications (as opposed to applications designed more specifically for activists) leads to a peculiar effect that one of our respondents summarised as 'fish in the sea' (used in the sense of being 'one among many similar entities' in a wide-open space that offers mutual protection via mutual concealment):

> Imagine if I have nothing to hide, but I still use an end-to-end encrypted app, then people who need to hide themselves... like whistleblowers for example... it will be easier for them, say, to disappear in this big flow of cat photos or love messages. So I feel like I am helping someone when I use encryption all the time for all of my communications (Female, low-risk user, tech-journalist, Austria).

An interesting phenomenon of 'shared responsibility' arises from this mass adoption of encryption: the more users opt for end-to-end encryption tools, the more secure it becomes for everyone to use these tools, but specifically for those users whose life and freedom depend on them. As we will see in the following chapters, while in the mass adoption of distributed or peer-to-peer applications there is a real technical correlation between the number of users and the level of privacy protection, for centralised applications (like Signal and WhatsApp) or for email encryption, the consequences of mass adoption are often described as increasing the difficulty, human and technical, for the adversary to achieve its surveillance objectives:

> The more people use encryption, the more expensive it will be for the governments to read everything. It's not about reaching 100% security... This simply does not exist! It's about making them waste their time and money to decrypt our stuff and in the end they are reading something like 'Let's go eat pizza tonight'... (male, informational security trainer, Ukraine)

Even though the collaboration of Signal's head developer, Moxie Marlinspike, with WhatsApp and Facebook was controversial and subject to critiques within a number of tech-savvy circles – in particular in the **F/OSS** (Free and Open-Source Software) communities – mass adoption of end-to-end encryption had an important impact on Internet governance. With applications such as WhatsApp bringing strong cryptography into the mainstream, the thesis of 'encryption as a human right' and the demand for 'equal access to encryption' have become more widespread. Among recent initiatives, a 2017 letter signed by 65 privacy-focused NGOs (including Privacy Now, EFF and Article 19) and addressed to the UN,

FIG. 1.4 Drawing collected during the interview on February 16, 2017. The user commented on the drawing as follows: 'In the case of a truly secure communication I say something, but no one knows what I said and to whom [...] I could have just given you a blank sheet of paper, it would have meant that no traces of a communication act are visible. But as soon as you asked me to draw you something...' (C, male, journalist, high risk).

demanded the decriminalisation of users of privacy-enhancing technologies and digital security trainers (see IFEX, 2017). Two years earlier, privacy and the right to conceal were presented by the United Nations Special Rapporteur on Human Rights as a core component of freedom of opinion and expression:

> Discussions of encryption and anonymity have all too often focused only on their potential use for criminal purposes in times of terrorism. But emergency situations do not relieve States of the obligation to ensure respect for international human rights law [...] General debate should highlight the protection that encryption and anonymity provide, especially to the groups most at risk of unlawful interferences (Kaye 2015).

In our interviews, developers and information security trainers underlined the urgency of finding a reliable solution to the problem of **metadata** collection. As we have already implied, this is a key area where debates around encryption become relevant. Metadata are data that describe or provide information about other data, such as social media discussions, email exchanges or online transactions. Devices and systems that are connected to the Internet (or support its operation), including messaging and other online communication systems, collect this 'information about information' that, when aggregated, can account for a user's daily Internet activities, but also for real life activities and activities of other users. The collection of metadata is, or can be, especially problematic because it happens in the background and for a variety of purposes, and users can usually gain access to a mere fraction of the metadata collected about them. Controversies around metadata collection are numerous, including the presence of informed consent, the level of clarity concerning use or sharing, the existence of retention policies (documents stipulating how long an entity will store metadata) and the legal possibility of bulk or warrantless collection, in particular by governmental agencies (Piscitello 2016). Ultimately, developers and trainers appear to share a consensus that there is currently no solution in the field of end-to-end encrypted instant messaging apps that offers good metadata protection. Developers and trainers associate the leaking of metadata with centralisation:

> Metadata connects you weirdly with other people, and there's more sense in the metadata than in the data itself for technological reasons [...] No one from the messaging apps is trying to solve that. Instead they suggest to sync your address books so they know exactly who you're talking to even though you trust them to somehow make it into **hashes** or whatever. That's the issue we are not solving with the apps, we make it worse. We now have centralised servers that become honeypots, and it's not about the data, it's about the metadata (Peter S., Heml.is).

'ACTUALLY, IN GOOGLE WE TRUST': QUESTIONING THE PRIVACY-SECURITY DICHOTOMY

When we first attempted to interpret our fieldwork, our hypothesis was that very distinct threat models could be associated with distinct types of users, grouped according to their risk status – 'high' or 'low'. As already noted, this hypothesis was operationally useful, especially for our joint work with computer scientists more familiar with usability studies. However, our fieldwork showed the limits of this opposition, demonstrating the relativity of two binary visions: users could be categorised not only as high risk vs low risk, but also according to their concern about privacy vs security. These two concerns, and the defensive practices they give rise to, are in fact interpenetrating, as the remainder of this section will further demonstrate.

Indeed, among our interviewees, citizens of supposedly 'low-risk' countries (Western countries led by long-term democratic regimes) were more concerned with privacy-related issues, while individuals 'at high risk' (i.e. belonging to particular socio-demographic groups that placed them in the spotlight of authoritarian regimes) focused on urgent needs and life-and-death situations, often adopting technical solutions that are easier to install and use, even if they do not, in fact, provide strong levels of privacy protection (WhatsApp, for example). This difference can be exemplified by the different attitudes towards tech giants, such as Google, Apple, Facebook, Amazon and Microsoft. Criticism of these companies mostly comes from Western users who have a high degree of knowledge about information technology and its socio-economy. Several 'high-risk' users, by contrast, shared the idea that centralised and quasi-monopolistic services like Gmail, for example, offer a better security-usability ratio. In a context of risk and urgency, there tends to be a compromise between user-friendliness and security, while technically experienced low-risk users often focus more on developing genuinely complex and multi-layered privacy and security preserving toolkits.

However, some of the criticisms of the practices of tech giants that have originated within the F/OSS community have touched larger, non-technical populations in high-risk countries. An example is the controversy about Signal's dependence upon Google Play and Google Services,[7] which originated within free software circles with the launch – and subsequent rapid shutdown – of the project LibreSignal.[8] Signal's dependence upon Google became a problem for a specific privacy-aware and tech-savvy user community, who opt for decentralised alternatives to the communication tools provided by Net giants. In this context, the choice of a 'Google-free' messenger can also be perceived as a 'lifestyle' choice. This choice often coexists with alternative choices of hardware (e.g. a

Linux phone, a Fair Phone, Copperhead OS, or other privacy enhancing tools). As one tech-savvy user put it, 'If I don't like mainstream in media, if I don't like mainstream in music – why would I like mainstream on my computer?' [Daniel, mail service provider, festival organiser].

However, according to our interviews, Signal's dependencies on Google Play had an important impact not only on tech-savvy users from *a priori* low-risk environments, but also on users in problematic settings and with little technical knowledge. For example, in Syria, the country-wide blocking of Google Play meant that low-knowledge users no longer had comfortable and immediate access to the Signal app, yet they lacked the competencies to look for alternative routes to acquire it. Technical decisions made by developers of privacy-enhancing technologies – such as dependencies on third-party libraries and their licensing and protocol choices – are not only a preference or lifestyle issue for users but may also impact their security in life-and-death contexts.

Users in 'high-risk' type settings also mentioned as important for their threat models the issue of decentralised networks, once considered an overwhelmingly 'high-tech, low-risk' concern. For example, our recent exchanges with Russian and Ukrainian left-wing activists revealed a growing desire among these populations to run their own file storage and decentralised communication infrastructures.

CONCLUSIONS: RISK IS RELATIONAL, THREAT MODELLING IS CRUCIAL

By providing a number of examples related to contexts of use, users' perceived needs and selection of possibly appropriate tools, this chapter has shown that in the field of online communications, and more particularly secure messaging, risk is relational, and threat modelling is crucial for choosing the right tool to protect one's communications. For example, if a user's primary objective is to conceal from one's own government, this objective is inextricably entangled with changes in consumer habits and migrating from closed-source platforms with business models based on user data. In this context, the 'adversary' resembles a constantly evolving, fluid network connecting with both private and institutional infrastructures, rather than a single entity with well-defined capacities and a predetermined set of surveillance and attack techniques and tools.

Trainers and digital security organisations are shifting towards a user-centred approach and user-tailored training sessions. At the same time, they increasingly face the challenge of communicating to their trainees that privacy-preserving and privacy-enhancing tools do not guarantee, in and by themselves, absolute security. Unsolved cryptographic challenges, such as how to build usable metadata-preserving solutions, are somehow 'compensated for' by a patchwork of operational security techniques and combination of tools that users invent and constantly modify. Thus, the identification of 'who we must conceal from' – threat modelling and risk assessment – is a constantly changing process that depends upon a large set of often non-technical or non-cryptographic parameters, such as a user's social graph, gender, religious or ethical norms, profession, geopolitical situation/the political regime, or the reputation and charisma of app creators. Indeed, encrypted communication is the product of, and sometimes the catalyst for changing, a vast network including institutions (or actors positioning themselves in opposition or resistance to them) and of course, myriad infrastructures and technical devices in which concepts such as security and privacy are embedded (see our previous discussion about 'doing Internet governance' in the introduction).

The very distinction between high risk and low risk, while useful operationally for the researcher as a practical methodological tool in order to build a diverse sample of users for interviews, shows its limits, mainly due to the 'relational' nature of risk we have introduced in this chapter. If a low-risk user has at least one high-risk user in her social graph, she may adopt a higher level of protection and even install a specific tool for communicating with this contact – and inversely, in specific sociopolitical contexts, what is usually understood as low-risk/non-sensitive data may in fact place its owners in higher risk categories. Indeed, if designing privacy-enhancing tools requires imagining the 'worst of all possible worlds', this may well be the world of an individual among our contacts: the person who is most in need of concealing. The following chapters explore how developers seeking to respond to the ongoing turn to 'mass encryption' take this into account, as they explore different architectural configurations for encrypted secure messaging tools and cope with their constraints and opportunities.

NOTES

1 An earlier version of this chapter was published as Ermoshina, K. and F. Musiani, 'Hiding from Whom? Threat Models and In-the-Making Encryption Technologies', *Intermédialités: Histoire et théorie des arts, des lettres et des techniques*, 32 (2019), special issue Cacher/Concealing. It was also presented and discussed at the annual conference of the International Association for Media and Communication Research in Eugene, Oregon, 7–11 July 2018. We are grateful to the French Privacy and Data Protection Commission (CNIL) and Inria for selecting this work as a runner-up to the 2019 CNIL-Inria Privacy Protection Prize.

2 https://ssd.eff.org/en/glossary/threat-model.

3 See, https://ssd.eff.org/en/playlist/academic-researcher#assessing-your-risks; we will analyse in Chapter 6 how this shift entails a change of methodology used to rank, evaluate and recommend secure communication tools.

4 Among recent initiatives, the documentary *Nothing to Hide*: http://www.allocine. fr/video/player_gen_cmedia=19571391&cfilm=253027.htm.

5 The most popular services are One Time Secret (https://onetimesecret.com) and Privnote (https://privnote.com).

6 Mentioning two important and well-known tech and human rights activists.

7 https://github.com/WhisperSystems/Signal-Android/issues/127.

8 https://github.com/LibreSignal/LibreSignal; see Chapter 3.

2

CENTRALISED ARCHITECTURES AS INFORMAL STANDARDS FOR 'CONTROL BY DESIGN'

THIS CHAPTER IS THE FIRST OF A SERIES, CONSTITUTING THE CENTRAL PART of the book, that is best read as a triptych. Together, these three chapters are meant to provide an analysis of different architectural choices and their impact on the configuration – social and economic as well as technical – of encrypted messaging tools. Evaluating the consequences of these choices is important, in our view, for the reasons expressed in the introductory discussion of the contributions social sciences can make to the study of encryption and decentralisation. We saw some of this at work in Chapter 1: every technical choice made by developers of secure messaging tools is not about reaching a perfect model, but about implementing, in practice, a series of compromises that are about technical performance, but also about community-building, standard-setting and finding suitable governance and organisational models. It is also about business models and reaching specific publics. Illustrating this interweaving of dynamics has been the core aim of this triptych of chapters.

Furthermore, we understand our review of the three types of architecture as a discussion of different ways to practise specific visions of online freedom: freedom to control the implementation of the technical solution, freedom proposed to users to choose their infrastructure to a more or less large extent, freedom to do without intermediaries or to configure them in specific ways, etc. Indeed, throughout these chapters, the overarching, central concept for this book – 'concealing for freedom' – is fleshed out, not as a fixed value, but as something that is performed differently in different settings and defined by the field(s) within which it operates.

This chapter discusses centralisation, as defined in the Introduction, as a 'control by design' model for secure messaging protocols and applications. In particular, we discuss the dynamics of centralisation-as-control deployed as a means to respond quickly to technical challenges in a situation of uncertainty. To do so, we explore Signal as a central case study, but we also touch upon the cases of Telegram and Wire. This chapter shows how 'concealing for freedom' dynamics unfold for both developers and users in the case of centralised architectures. While centralised tools can offer users suitable solutions to protect their freedom 'from' particular adversaries, their stance vis-à-vis active freedoms, such as the freedom 'of' choice – of particular incarnations of a protocol, of specific interface elements – is much more problematic. On the developers' side, centralised architectures can restrict the freedom 'to' reuse and implement code in different applications subtending the same protocol (Nyman and Lindman 2013). As Nyman (2015: 116) points out, quoting Raymond (1999), closed source licensing, made easier by centralised arrangements, erects a number of artificial technical, legal or institutional barriers that prevent 'good solutions from being re-used'. In this case, a certain level of standardisation – be it formal or informal, as we will analyse below – can become a factor of freedom for developers.

As seminal secure messaging protocols such as PGP and OTR started showing their age in terms of security and usability, cryptographers, unsurprisingly, wanted to develop new and better protocols in the wake of the Snowden revelations. Open-source developers started to deploy efforts to create a next-generation secure messaging protocol. The most advanced and popular protocol in this regard is the Signal protocol, used by applications such as Signal (formerly TextSecure).

The Signal protocol is now considered the 'best practice' in the field of encrypted messaging and has become a trendsetter for other projects in terms of privacy and security features. Currently, Signal is centralised, as a single server mediates the setup of the protocol in most widespread deployments (e.g. WhatsApp, Google Allo, Facebook Messenger, Wire). A new means of *'quasi-standardisation'* or 'standardisation by running code' is being practised around this protocol. In this process, a quasi-standard is defined as 'something that works' and that has been iterated and redeployed by others. Centralisation has allowed Signal developers to swiftly update the protocol in response to research and bugs, and to limit concerns about the technical competence of third-party developers standardising their protocol. However, the 'bottleneck' of centralisation also implies that difficulties and tensions have arisen in connection with some attempts to reimplement the Signal protocol, due to the lack of specifications. This chapter will examine how these attempts to 'control by design' play out in the context of the development of secure messaging's foremost protocols and applications, paying particular attention to attempts at informal standardisation as a way to 'open up' the protocol.[1]

FROM AXOLOTL TO SIGNAL: BETWEEN INNOVATION AND CONTINUITY

As we mentioned in the Introduction to this book, many actors in the field of secure messaging share a tacit agreement that the Signal protocol's Double Ratchet is currently the leading protocol for instant messaging. In order to better understand how the Signal protocol interacts with previous and potential future developments of encryption protocols, it is useful to recall briefly the historical debates around two major protocols that dominated the ecosystem for many years before Snowden: OTR and PGP.

The main problems with PGP discussed in the cryptographic community, and shared by advanced users, could be summarised according to two main issues: complex key management and lack of repudiation and forward secrecy. The crisis of 'public key infrastructures' and of the very concept of cryptographic keys and signatures was also highlighted by digital security trainer communities and international NGOs promoting privacy-enhancing technologies, such as Tactical Tech and the Electronic Frontier Foundation (Musiani and Ermoshina 2017). While still offering one of the most cryptographically robust solutions, PGP clearly faces usability challenges.

The OTR protocol started as a research project at UC Berkeley in 2002 and was first released in 2004. OTR developer Ian Goldberg described himself, in our interview with him, as a very early PGP user and mostly an 'email person'; it was his student, Nikita Borisov, who drew Goldberg's attention to the growing field of social networking and instant messaging, thus identifying a new security gap to be filled. Ian's description of the mission behind OTR relates this protocol to pre-existing technologies, as a way to respond to challenges that were not properly addressed by PGP:

> Your choices at that time were either completely unprotected communication neither encrypted nor authenticated, or PGP in which case it's confidential and authenticated unless your key leaks in which it's not confidential and the authentication with digital signatures leads to non-repudiation (Interview with Ian Goldberg, May 2018).

While OTR's solution of using per-conversation keys offered good repudiation and forward secrecy, it did not permit group chat encryption as, in Goldberg's words, 'that was how instant communication worked back then: you had to be online at the same time': OTR's design was inspired by existing tools that required synchrony (e.g. Aim). However, while popular in high-risk activist communities, OTR-based applications (such as Jabber) were widely criticised for their lack of multi-device support and other usability problems.

These shared concerns were at the core of the efforts subtending the Signal protocol, which successfully managed to address them, according to Goldberg: 'Text Secure, and later Signal, basically took OTR protocol and added basic features to it to make it work in an asynchronous setting'. Using per-conversation key material in a similar manner to OTR, it did not force complex key management on users. It maintained properties of repudiation and forward secrecy by virtue of the Axolotl Diffie-Hellman key ratchet, but added 'future secrecy' so that messages could not be read at any point in the future in the case of a key material compromise (Cohn-Gordon et al. 2016). It also solved the asynchronous messaging problem by allowing longer-term pre-keys managed by the Signal server and offered group messaging implemented as point-to-point messaging. The Signal protocol uses the 'Axolotl' key ratchet for initial key exchange and the ongoing renewal and maintenance of short-lived session keys, so there is no long-term key that can be compromised. This provides forward secrecy so that the compromise of a short-term key does not compromise past keys (which would enable an adversary to decrypt past messages).

As the Signal protocol initiated a dialogue with the previous crypto protocol 'tradition' (mainly by addressing the aforementioned limits of OTR and PGP), it quickly attracted the attention of the academic cryptographic community, and only minor flaws were found (Frosch et al. 2016). Although alternative approaches were developed and widely deployed, like MTProto by Telegram, these protocols developed their own cryptographic primitives and so received less attention from the academic community; additionally, a number of bugs and usability problems were revealed (Jakobsen and Orlandi 2016; Abu-Salma et al. 2017a). Interestingly, while Signal has deeply influenced the crypto protocol field, it did not depart from previous efforts, but drew from their well-known flaws: it is this continuity that can partly account for the interest from crypto experts.

With minor variants implemented in the vastly popular WhatsApp messenger, the core Signal protocol seems well on its way to replacing the use of XMPP+OTR and to becoming a competitive, if somewhat 'boutique', feature for mainstream messaging services (as shown by the adoption of the Signal protocol as an option by both Google Allo and Facebook Messenger). Encrypted messaging applications like WhatsApp, Telegram, and Signal[2] are now the default application of this kind for users who consider themselves high risk. Usability studies have shown that although Signal, like OTR, is relatively easy to set up and use, even highly skilled users fail to use verification correctly. Signal is centralised, as a single server mediates the setup of the protocol in most widespread deployments (WhatsApp, Google Allo, Facebook Messenger, Wire).

There are also open-source alternatives that claim to use the Signal protocol or its forks, such as Wire, another centralised application, that uses a fork of Axolotl protocol called Proteus. Parts of the Signal protocol were copied by a draft XMPP-Foundation standard called OMEMO, for use by applications such as Conversations and ChatSecure, which led to usage of Signal's double ratchet in federated projects. Another decentralised project, called Matrix, has reused parts of the Signal protocol to integrate them into their own cryptographic library, called Olm. While Signal appears to be widely adopted and considered an improvement over both OTR and PGP, the core Signal protocol remains officially unstandardised, even though the protocol's creators Trevor Perrin and Moxie Marlinspike have produced an informal draft after considerable 'community pressure' (in the words of Matrix.org's lead developer).

A 'QUASI-STANDARDISATION' PROCESS

While most users we have interviewed, including high-risk users, do not appear to have standardisation as an explicit priority, developers care deeply about standards as 'something they would eventually be working on', to increase the 'dialogue' between applications and reduce the silo effect: 'In the long term I am not opposed to the idea of standardising, it's great to have a reference for interoperability' (Briar lead developer).

Standardisation is understood as a *reference* and thus as an important communication or mediation instrument, that helps members of the security community understand each other and build a ground for common knowledge (such as cryptographic libraries); it also guarantees a smoother development of new applications on top of standardised protocols. Yet a widespread discontent with existing standards bodies is expressed by developers, for several reasons. Developers underline recent transformations of these organisations, referring to a previous 'golden age' of standardising bodies, when their mode of existence was closer to that of FOSS communities. Our respondents note the growing importance of private actors as stakeholders within standardising bodies:

> My impression of the IETF is that it's not the same beast it was in the early days. There was a time when it was a group of enthusiastic people who would come to the IETF with an idea that was sort of halfway finished and they'd say look I wanna let everybody know about this, let's knock it into shape and we'll all build on it. I think it's become a much slower moving and more adversarial environment. This area of technologies has attracted more money and more corporate participation and therefore, conflicts of interest (Briar lead developer).

This institutionalisation of standardising bodies and their progressive removal from coding communities creates an environment that is less suitable for experiments and unfinished projects:

> I think that [an automated, periodical clearing out of message history] is something that we will implement, it just probably will not be standardised because the XMPP community is very conservative. I don't think... they don't fully get it. It's something that users want... so why?... I don't know. They end up in that old school stuff (ChatSecure developer).

As Callon (1986) would put it, standardisation implies the 'translation' of a protocol as a sociotechnical experiment into a pre-standard, able to 'enroll' and convince various agents within evaluation bodies. Standardisation involves collective work that opens up the core-set of protocol authors to include external experts from standardising organisations, some of them being far from users' experiences and needs, and from the 'real' economy of the encrypted messaging field – a process that is hardly appealing to some developers, as it is seen as time-consuming in the early stages of project development:

> I wouldn't really think about submitting something to the IETF on an early stage these days because I think that would probably involve a lot of work to convince other people to allow it to become a standard... and obviously everybody would have their own thoughts of how better to work (Briar lead developer).

Instead, most developers share the philosophy that they would build the application first, and then focus on standardisation and decentralisation via the use of open standards:

> I used to work with W3C a long time ago and I am very aware of how they work and that they may have some limitations. We want to get Matrix as mature enough and solid and stable enough, then we can pass it over to a proper governance organization but right now it's still evolving very rapidly (Matrix.org lead developer).

In the case of secure messaging, it is still felt that more development is needed on the code, and standardisation would only slow down existing development efforts. Indeed, a new way of 'quasi-standardisation' or 'standardisation by running code' is being practised in the field of end-to-end encrypted messaging applications, around the Signal protocol. In this process, a quasi-standard is defined as something that has been previously iterated and redeployed by others with success. In this sense, all of the various Signal protocol deployments (e.g. Wire, WhatsApp and OMEMO-based apps such as Conversations and ChatSecure) work as crash-tests for the protocol, where the protocol gets forged by usage:

> I think the direction to take is [the one] Signal is taking, when you kind of build a system for a while, you iterate a bit until you think you have something that works well and then you start to document it and if other people wanna interoperate, you talk to them about standardizing on that stage, on a much later stage [...] I wonder whether they [Signal] will think about standardizing at some point, maybe the idea is about delaying it to a later stage of the project, and not about avoiding it (Briar lead developer).

The Signal protocol, characterised by the double Diffie-Hellman ratchet, is now considered the best practice in the field and has become a trend-setter for other projects in terms of privacy and security features (e.g. forward secrecy and future secrecy for example). Developers, even those working in federated (e.g. Conversations) or peer-to-peer (e.g. Briar) projects – which will be explored in Chapters 3 and 4 – see the Signal solution as one of the best designs available, despite its lack of formal standardisation – and, maybe, precisely because its standardisation is happening informally, in the 'mundane practices' and multiple implementations taking place in different projects.

SIGNAL'S MULTIPLE IMPLEMENTATIONS: 'SNOWDEN MEETS THE MARKET'

The field of instant messaging applications has been deeply transformed by the different implementations of the Signal protocol, but also because of the growing popularity of other secure messaging tools, such as Telegram, Threema or Wickr that use their own protocols. The turn to encryption has modified the market and brought considerable changes at the governance level, engaging important private sector players in the game:

> What is happening in the last two years [interview was done in 2016] is fantastic, with a number of messengers popping up and also greater publicity around Axolotl or Signal... Snowden also talking about it... So this is really good for the industry. And we've seen it's triggered even the big ones who started using encryption (Alan, Wire CTO).

Post-Snowden, one of the most important manifestations of the 'turn to encryption' in messaging applications has been WhatsApp's – one of the 'big ones', in Alan's words – implementation of end-to-end encryption, which became operational in April 2016 (Metz 2016). However, according to former Pirate Bay founder Peter Sunde – creator of Heml.is, an end-to-end encrypted IM application – the adoption of end-to-end encryption by WhatsApp happened for much more 'financial' reasons. Before being purchased by Facebook, WhatsApp's value was estimated at 19 billion dollars. After an unfruitful attempt to purchase Sunde's protocol, they turned to Signal and acquired the Signal protocol for 1 million dollars. After the implementation of end-to-end encryption in WhatsApp, the app was sold to Facebook for a better price of 21 billion dollars. Peter Sunde recalls:

> [WhatsApp's CEO] was upset that I and other guys [from Heml.is team] were talking about ideology and politics because he was not interested in politics. He was more interested in the government staying out of his life, and not touching him so much and so on. And he did not wanna call that ideology, which was probably the first problem we had between us. And then he said encryption is not something people care about because no one is interested in what people talk about on WhatsApp because there was nothing important. For him it was more like we need to have something because people are complaining in the media, rather than it's actually about

> privacy… It was just a business thing. He has no clue what people are using his app for… I don't think he was in touch with his user base, he was more interested in user growth (Peter Sunde, Heml.is core developer).

The element of 'political ideology' raised by Peter in the above citation is another important factor that influences interactions and collaborations among different instant messaging and cryptographic projects. Our fieldwork within developer communities shows that common ideological grounds may become a crucial factor for the decision whether to adopt specific protocol choices and design decisions. We will show later in the chapter how, in the case of Wire, the importance of specific values cement F/OSS communities, and their influence on fundamental development choices.

However, in the case of Signal's cooperation with WhatsApp (and, as a consequence, with Facebook), reflections on the social consequences of the adoption of end-to-end encryption are used to justify this controversial deal, that became one of the most important collaborations in the recent history of instant messaging. Several of our respondents underline the ultimately positive consequences of WhatsApp's turn to encryption, that, according to them, has solved major problems related to its adoption costs by users. Let us recall the Ukrainian security trainer pointing out, in the previous chapter, that since WhatsApp's adoption of end-to-end encryption she recommended users to 'stay with it' if they already used it, and also high-risk users pointing out how a generalist, centralised application such as WhatsApp could in fact make activists less conspicuous than if they used an activist-targeted app.

FORKING THE SIGNAL PROTOCOL: NON-STANDARDISATION AS A BUSINESS-MODEL

One of the most well-known and popular **forks** of the Signal protocol is called Proteus and is used by the application Wire. Wire was launched by ex-Skype developers, who desired, according to its CTO, to respond to 'one of the biggest gaps that was missing on the market, related to privacy and security'. Wire's primary targeted user group is identified as privacy-aware consumers:

> Our users in the first phase are primarily consumers, who care about privacy. […] I like to compare passive smoking with rising awareness about privacy when people understand how information can be misused. It's something that needs to be spread more (Alan, Wire CTO).

As Wire is not aimed at activists or at a tech-savvy audience, but at the average user, one of its main concerns is to build a usable interface and integrate new features that will distinguish it from other end-to-end encrypted messengers. Thus, Wire supports drawings, GIF exchange, large end-to-end encrypted group chats, multiple-participant group video calls, disappearing timed messages, file transfer, and so on. A number of our interviewees have underlined the aesthetic aspect of Wire's user interface as an advantage, favouring Wire's widespread adoption as opposed to Signal. Another of Wire's selling arguments is the quality and encryption of its voice calls, as it offers end-to-end encrypted voice calls using a specific protocol based on **constant bit rate encoding**.

The underlying Wire encryption protocol, called Proteus, is a fork of Axolotl with 'pieces that were needed to have support for the multiple devices as a standalone' [Wire CTO]. However, difficulties and tensions have been observed around Wire's attempts to reimplement the Signal protocol. Some of these difficulties are connected with the lack of specifications – the set of documented requirements that a product must satisfy, often considered as a first form of standardisation.[3] A draft specification[4] was produced in 2016 – as our respondents explain, not without pressure from other developer communities:

> OWS [Open Whisper Systems, the company managing Signal until 2018, now Signal Messenger LLC] did not prioritize standardizing [the protocol] both because it gave them flexibility to change it as well as allow it to be more valuable to them as intellectual property. However, they have just finished standardizing a lot of it, […] and I think to some extent that was because of the pressure coming from community like us (Matrix.org lead developer).

So, this lack of specification obliges developers to re-code from scratch sometimes using other programming languages:

There was, I would even say on purpose, not enough available documentation. But if you wanted to develop your own implementation, you were pushed or bullied that you have copied their implementation. [...] I was very naive and went to Moxie last year in June and asked him to review our implementation and we would pay him very good money for that. Instead he said you can pay 1,5 million, and I will keep your binaries and will help you to get the implementation going. And then I was like ... yeah, exactly... [A legal dispute happened.] And then it was just settled. He dropped his charges, we dropped our charges and we are using Axolotl the way we do and how we would like (Alan, Wire CTO).

One of ChatSecure's developers explains this conflict as a consequence of a specific licensing politics that led to tampering and modifications in the legal terms and agreements between the Signal team and other implementers:

The Signal protocol is open source under the GPL, that means you can't integrate it into a commercial product; that's why OWS were getting large licensing agreements from Facebook and Google and WhatsApp to integrate without opening up all of their source code. Part of that was incompatibilities with GPL and AppStore specifically. So we needed to get some of the legal language exempted [...] Moxie needs to protect his revenue. Part of his arguments with Wire was that they [Signal] hadn't documented Signal protocol, so there was no open specification, so if you wanted to write a compatible reimplementation, you would have to read the source code which would create a derivative work, which would not allow you to use it commercially because he would argue he still has copyright of the majority of the work (ChatSecure developer).

The Signal developers, for their part, argue that they are concerned about the technical competence of having third-party developers standardise or deploy forks of their protocol ('Moxie is a very good coder, and his standards are very high'). They are also preoccupied with maintaining the prerogative of updating the protocol rapidly enough in response to research and bugs. This makes it possible to use the non-standardisation of the protocol as part of Signal's business model, where the expertise and specification necessary for a proper deployment of the protocol can be offered by the Signal team as a service:

> You can say OK, we will license this technology, which is not something I am interested in because I would like it to remain free software. But you can also say 'we are the people who understand this technology, it makes sense to hire us if you want to deploy it'. If people build systems on top of it, then they pay somebody to contribute changes down into that codebase (Briar lead developer).

As our interviews with users and observation of security training sessions have revealed, open source and licensing choices are less covered in sessions destined for high-risk users, as they do not always associate open source with security. Open source is often perceived as a less important criterion in the context of an immediate physical threat; when a proprietary, centralised, but 'efficient' and 'easy to explain' solution exists, trainers will give it priority. The primary task for trainers in high-risk contexts with low-knowledge users is to help them quickly abandon unencrypted tools as well as tools that collaborate with their adversaries. However, users do care about sources of funding and business models of end-to-end encrypted messaging applications, and particularly of centralised systems, due to the great authority the architecture accords to their creators. This was, and is, the case with Signal, as well; in particular, questions about business models are very frequent on the different chats about cybersecurity that we have been observing since September 2016. Users ask for transparency of funding but at the same time show a certain scepticism regarding crowdfunding models (donations) that seem not sustainable enough for an application to be properly maintained. Recent critiques addressed to Signal concern its dependence on US government funding:

> Signal was created by the same spooky regime change outfits that fund the Tor Project. The money primarily comes through the federal government's premier Internet Freedom venture capital outfit: Open Technology Fund,

which works closely with the State Department's regime change arm and is funded through several layers of Cold War CIA cutouts — including Radio Free Asia and the Broadcasting Board of Governors (Levine 2016).

Telegram creator Pavel Durov's critique of Signal goes in the same direction, stressing that no US-government funded application can be trusted.

Beyond Signal's 'non-standardisation as a business model', centralised end-to-end encrypted secure messaging applications propose different business models, though it seems that no ideal solution has yet been found. Wire's project is to propose paid services to users for supplementary storage space (encrypted Cloud services). Wire also proposes business solutions for end-to-end encryption of the Internet of Things. Threema, one of the few end-to-end encrypted applications requiring a financial subscription from users, asks for a $2 contribution per user. Some users underline that as an advantage: 'All of us use Threema [...] I prefer to pay, at least I am sure that I am not the product' (Cryptoparty organiser, male, Austria).

As in previous histories of software development, for Signal and the ecosystem of applications using variations of the Signal protocol, the licensing, business-model and open/closed source choices turn out to be complex sociotechnical processes that are embedded in both community-related interactions, economic context and legal arrangements.

CENTRALISATION CALLS FOR CENTRALISATION? SIGNAL'S 'DEPENDENCIES' CRITIQUED

Though the Signal protocol has enjoyed extensive attention from academics and has been formally verified, with only minor flaws found, several users and tech-savvy communities have critiqued the tool – critiques that were high-lighted during our interviews. Interestingly, some of these critiques do not concern cryptographic properties of the protocol per se, but are focused on the application's UI/UX, privacy features and the particular architectural design choices that bind Signal to other applications and protocols that are, in their turn, under scrutiny by particular communities because of their centralised and/or proprietary structures.

De-Googling Signal: The LibreSignal controversy

First of all, tech-savvy users – especially crypto trainers from low-risk countries such as Austria, Germany and France – have pointed out Signal's dependence on Google services. They see it as a negative from the standpoints of both open-source community ethics and privacy, the two main points of controversy being Signal's relationship with Google Cloud Messaging (GCM) services and its reliance on Google Play. As a consequence, two initiatives were launched in order to 'decentralise' or 'de-Googlise' Signal: The F-Droid repository,[5] which aimed to distribute Signal outside the Google Play Store; and a Github repository, which aimed at completely removing the Google components of Signal, even from the server side. This second project was called 'LibreSignal'. Open-source client used the Signal protocol and was lauded as 'The truly private and Google-Free messenger for Android'.

LibreSignal's authors stated on their GitHub page that the problem of Signal relying on GCM 'is only an issue for people who use a custom Android ROM without Google Play Services. For the vast majority of people who do have Google Play on their phone, this issue is completely irrelevant'.[6] Thus, the Google dependencies of Signal are problematic only for a very specific user community, both privacy-aware and tech-savvy (those who, like the mail service provider cited in Chapter 1, 'do not like mainstream on [their] computer'), who opt for decentralised communication tools explicitly designed to be alternatives to those developed by the Silicon Valley tech giants. In this context, the choice of a 'Google-free' messenger can be perceived and defined as a 'lifestyle' choice. During our interviews, we noticed that this choice often coexists with alternative hardware choices (Linux phone, Fair Phone, CopperheadOS and others), or customised versions of the Android operating system, in particular versions free of Google Play.

LibreSignal was launched in 2015 but its development was stopped in November 2016 after a long online discussion between the LibreSignal team and Moxie Marlinspike. LibreSignal started as a fork of TextSecure,[7] that several open-source contributors forked by integrating an alternative to Google Cloud Messaging, called WebSocket.

LibreSignal published a **build** on F-Droid, the community-maintained software repository for Android, similar to Google Play but containing only free and open-source apps. However, in the course of a discussion on the GitHub repository of the project, Moxie Marlinspike controversially demanded that the name of the fork be changed (not referring to TextSecure or Signal), and that it should not use Open Whisper System servers. He also insisted that no distribution of Signal via FDroid was possible.[8] The debate between LibreSignal and OWS raised several issues that are important for the overall understanding of the sociotechnical and legal problems related to the debate about centralisation in secure messaging, and its relationship with projects focused on federated architectures (see also Chapter 4). A first argument concerned the server infrastructure needed for federated projects, which seemed complicated to set up and maintain, compared to the 'forking' of the client-side code. The latter does not, as the former does, demand coordination efforts between different agents: developers are able to fork and experiment on their own without having to care for the server infrastructure. However, the process of publishing a build on any of the app repositories – the open-source oriented F-Droid or the proprietary GooglePlay – demands a greater coordination and enrolment of a multitude of actors, as well as adherence to a number of legal and technical standards. This problem of federated protocols, as opposed to centralised ones, which we will come back to in Chapter 4, was also underlined in our interviews:

> Obviously, I think that federation is good otherwise I wouldn't be doing
> Conversations or using XMPP. But of course it's more challenging to do.
> Because you have to coordinate with a lot of different vendor (ChatSecure
> developer).

In the case of Signal, the problems of forking and federating the protocol – as LibreSignal intended to do – turned out to be legal (disputes concerning the use of the Signal trademark), technical (the quality of LibreSignal builds, questioned by OWS), and financial (the costs of running servers).[9] Ultimately, the enflamed debate about the LibreSignal GitHub page led Moxie Marlinspike to publish his standpoint on federation and centralisation in a blog post, 'The Ecosystem is Moving', which would become a landmark intervention in the controversy surrounding architectural choices in secure messaging (Marlinspike 2016). The Signal team was accused of not being 'truly' open source because of their refusal to draw upon open federated protocols. Comments such as 'The problem is that Moxie and OWS don't want Signal to be 100% free/libre software (it is not important for them …)' or 'They are not interested in removing the Google GCM dependencies […] Moxie has been quite explicit on this point, several times' were commonplace.[10]

Starting from 21 February 2017, Signal could be used without dependencies upon Google services. As Elijah Sparrow, the creator of LEAP (see Chapter 4) explains, the long process of 'degooglising' Signal is related to an important technical problem, that of notifications, that demanded infrastructure investment:

> LibreSignal was an attempt to avoid the Google services push. The problem with push on mobile is that it's a very difficult problem to be able to push events to mobile devices without burning the battery and without setting up a complex infrastructure for that. So you can rely on Google infrastructure for that, it's more efficient and they do it for free. But it's controversial […] mostly because it requires to install all Google services on your device, which means you basically have to turn your device over to Google that always finds ways to gather your data so you couldn't run Signal on a Google-free device. That's recently changed, Signal very recently supports push notifications without Google services [although] Moxie still insists that no one should distribute the Signal application outside the Google Play market because he wants to get bug reports and data who's running and how they are running it when it's crushing (LEAP lead developer).

The problem of Google Cloud Messaging dependency and push notifications was addressed by other projects that found different solutions to this problem. For example, ChatSecure uses its own system for push notifications – a complex system, based on randomised tokens – that claims to have better privacy properties than the one used in Signal. For its part, Wire claims to be 'pretty much Google-free'; however, it relies on another 'net giant', Amazon, for push notifications and analytics. Wire's CTO describes the transition from Google services as a long evolution, marked by a dependency on Google's 'reputation' privacy-wise:

> [Being free of Google] took time… It wasn't easy. As you know maybe, when we started Wire 3+ years ago, Google was already under suspicion but there were some people in the company who were Google fans, now they are completely disillusioned [, nonetheless] it took us some time to take away all of the Google stuff (Alan, Wire CTO).

'ID'D BY PHONE NUMBER': THE PRIVACY WEAKNESS OF CENTRALISED APPLICATIONS?

The second important controversy focused on Signal concerned the usage of phone numbers as identification mechanisms. Although the Signal protocol provides confidentiality, it involves exposing phone numbers to the server and so allows the server – despite efforts by Signal, acknowledged by the tech-savvy public, to minimise logs – or a passive adversary to capture all the metadata, including the social graph of users. This phenomenon is not specific to Signal, but common to the majority of popular IM apps that are based on centralised architectures. As a consequence, having users' phone numbers as an identification mechanism is considered one of the central problems of post-Snowden end-to-end encrypted secure messaging.

The developer of Heml.is and Pirate Bay, Peter Sunde, as well as Wire's CTO, Alan, argue that identification via phone numbers and the possibility of sharing a user's phone contacts are important for contact discovery: they help users to build their network of contacts, and to rapidly find other users in their phonebook who use the same messaging app. An easy contact discovery is important, according to Alan, to build contacts and stabilise users' relationship with a new messaging app:

> In the beginning we didn't have a possibility to have your phone number to register, we wanted to have just emails. But then we had an amazing two days with hundreds of thousands of downloads, even millions [however] we could not build a good network effect. People were just downloading it individually and not connecting to each other. So we went towards [having] your address book uploaded so it will help you to have some contacts established, and then once people have contacts, they stick with Wire (Alan, Wire CTO).[11]

Here Alan raises an important issue, also underlined by several users in our interviews, which we call the 'migration problem': how do we migrate our contacts from one IM to another? Or inversely, how do we 'stick with' a new IM if no one from our social group is using it? A significant number of our respondents among non-tech savvy users explain the weak adoption of PGP and Signal with reference to the unpopularity of these tools among their peer groups ('no one uses it). Moxie Marlinspike also underlines how secure messaging tools are far from being immune to the network externalities effect, well-known and documented for social networks (e.g. Zhang et al. 2017):

> Social networks have value proportional to their size, so participants aren't motivated to join new social networks which aren't already large. It's a paradox where if people haven't already joined, people aren't motivated to join (Marlinspike 2014).

This effect also becomes an important factor for advising on IMs choices during security training sessions. For example, several Ukrainian trainers whom we interviewed tended to recommend WhatsApp and Gmail over Signal, and PGP over Thunderbird, partly because users already have some of their contacts using these tools, and the transition/adoption costs are lower (see also Chapter 1).

Eventually, Wire decided to move away from the use of phone numbers as an authentication method, and to give users the option of signing up only with an email address. On 25 May 2017, Wire added to its system the option to delete a previously registered phone number and adopt email-only authentication. This design solution was partly influenced by the critiques addressed to Signal, and as a 'selling argument' means of distinguishing itself from the latter. Wire largely promoted this new feature on social media and published a guide on the specific subject of 'staying anonymous on Wire'. Anonymisation became one of the app's core features – giving users the possibility to subscribe using a fake email account, over VPN or Tor, providing almost no personal information (Wire 2017). In general discussions, this feature also became a popular argument in favour of adopting Wire over Signal, as could be inferred both from our interviews and from social media and press analysis. Eventually, Edward Snowden came to recommend Wire as an alternative to Signal for those users wishing to stay within the realm of centralised applications.[12]

As the controversy unfolded, the use of phone numbers as an identification mechanism appeared to be related to the centralised architecture as such, making it more complicated to consider a transition towards federated systems. This issue was closely linked to the critique of telecom operators, perceived by several developers as fundamentally driven by a proprietary culture, and untrustworthy in terms of privacy. Using phone numbers as an authentication method is seen as linked to the increase in metadata collection (see the following section), and as opposed to alternative methods of identification, used in federated systems:

> With Signal it's impossible to create a decentralised system because phone numbers aren't decentralised. With XMPP it's like an email address. Even users who aren't technologically savvy can understand: this is my user ID, and this is my server. We have no idea what server you use and what's your ID. It's on the client side, and we don't need it for pushing messages (ChatSecure developer).

The lack of confidence in telephone numbers as a means of authentication is grounded in specific episodes of digital infrastructure-based attempts at state control in collaboration with the private sector (Musiani 2013). For example, in Russia, the use of phone numbers as IDs has been a source of important leaks and attacks on Telegram, another widely used centralised secure messaging app. On 29 April 2016, the accounts of two opposition activists from Moscow were seized by the Russian government: in collaboration with the telephone company MTS – which both activists subscribed to for their mobile communications – the government deactivated the SMS delivery service for the two users, and reclaimed recovery codes for their Telegram accounts. When these codes reached the MTS servers, the police could intercept them and use them to access the activists' accounts. Pavel Durov, the creator and core developer of Telegram, highly recommended using **two-factor authentication** in order to prevent this kind of attack – a method that is also recommended during cryptoparties – and to reinforce protection of accounts on centralised end-to-end encrypted messengers.

Overall, our research demonstrated that high-risk, tech-savvy and privacy-concerned users are aware of and preoccupied by the possibility of their phone numbers being used for identification. Similarly, the usage of existing users' social graphs – especially using third-party authorisation mechanisms, such as Twitter, Gmail or Facebook authentication services – was widely criticised. Wire's introduction of a 'matching' feature, suggesting new contacts based on a particular user's Wire contact list, was also attacked as 'creepy' by some of our respondents (tech-savvy security trainers from Austria and Germany). Ultimately, the 'phone numbers as IDs' controversy suggests that – among specific communities of users and developers in particular, but post-Snowden, more widely among the general public – there is a strong need for an alternative contact discovery mechanism that would give users better control over their social graphs.

Metadata collection: A misunderstood and unsolved issue for centralised applications

Some secure messaging solutions, like the experimental Ricochet,[13] attempted to use Tor to hide the IP address of their users. However, none of the popular

Signal-based messengers hide metadata, even though its users often believe that Signal indeed protects metadata and keeps their conversations anonymous. Although Signal does not log metadata (besides the last time a user installed the application and the time of her latest connection), it has been argued by one of our developer respondents that a real-world adversary could simply watch the encrypted messages going in and out of the Signal server in order to capture, to a large degree, the social graph of its users.

Even more easily, the physical seizure of a device would reveal the phone numbers of all other Signal contacts. Although applications such as Ricochet attempted to achieve protection against this kind of threat – which is a particular worry for users living in authoritarian countries – high-risk users are in general much more aware of the existence of Signal and find it easy to use, while all interviewed users were unaware of attempts at possible alternatives, such as the anonymised Ricochet application. In short, the issue of metadata collection (see Chapter 1) is one of the most controversial in the field of secure messaging today, as on the one hand, developers recognise that there is currently no satisfactory way to limit it or prevent it altogether, and on the other hand, it is an issue largely misunderstood or misinterpreted by users – even users who are informed and concerned about the problem – who believe they are completely anonymous when in fact they are far from it.

In the absence of solutions that prevent metadata collection, 'selling arguments' by different IM services have focused on its minimisation. Wire, for example, claims to reduce metadata storage of its messages to 72 hours, and this only to follow up on abuse or for troubleshooting reasons. In this sense, the minimisation of metadata collection is meant to single Wire out with respect to other IM applications:[14]

[For Wire] what was important was end-to-end encryption as a first step. But besides, there is a whole new dynamic that needs to happen, related to all of the metadata and what, how, it is used for. So the first step is to absolutely minimize all of the metadata. This is the part we are currently heavily working on, and some of the metadata we have was here for historic reasons. When you launch an application first without end-to-end encryption and then you upgrade it to support end-to-end encryption there is still some stuff left from the previous implementation. This is something that we are cleaning up (Alan, Wire CTO).

Based on our interviews, it's clear that most developers have come to consider the improvement of privacy via the minimisation of metadata collection to be the second most important feature in IM after the development of end-to-end encryption itself. Yet interestingly, developers themselves sometimes misinterpret the issue of metadata collection, confusing whether or not a third-party adversary could be passively monitoring the communication – and thus collecting metadata – with whether or not *they*, as developers, personally collect data – as exemplified by one developer who candidly stated, 'I do not have anything in my code that would let me know how many people are watching the app right now'. Other developers – a majority – declare their full awareness that they do have to collect some metadata in order to interoperate with features such as push notifications of arriving messages; however, they try to limit the collection as much as possible, to minimise harm:

> With push messaging, it's the first time we're exposed to possible metadata. But we don't log anything, we don't know who is talking to who, we don't log any information. We designed it specifically to be as harmless as possible [and] I think we're going to enable server operators to run additional components that reduce exposures as well. There's now some level of registration with our servers but it's optional. It's required to use push-messaging, but if you use an account with TOR, we disable this information (ChatSecure lead developer).

Most developers who are aware of third-party data collection of metadata declared themselves supportive of using Tor and disabling the collection of phone numbers in particular, but they lacked a comprehensive plan to minimise the collection of data as such. High-risk and low-risk users alike generally supported reducing data collection and increasing privacy, although often, non-trained users assumed that end-to-end encryption in itself could hide metadata. Thus, as the reader may recall from Chapter 1, developers and information security trainers underline the urgency to find a reliable solution to the metadata collection problem and state that, at present, nothing in the field of end-to-end encrypted instant messaging apps offers good metadata protection. Furthermore, developers and trainers associated the leaking of metadata with centralised servers – which, as Peter Sunde mentioned in a previously-cited interview, become 'honeypots'.

POLITICISED (AND CENTRALISED) ALTERNATIVES TO SIGNAL: THE CASE OF TELEGRAM

As this chapter has shown, for a number of reasons that range from its centralised architecture and the perceived technical soundness and novelty of its features to its business model and relationship to standardisation bodies and open-source communities – and despite a number of controversies around its development and implementation – Signal has come to assume a central role in the secure messaging field. Yet the 'ecosystem' surrounding it is lively, including other centralised architecture-based applications that – unlike Wire or ChatSecure – are not based on the Signal protocol.

A case in point is Telegram, which was briefly introduced in Chapter 1. Telegram's client-side code is free software, while its **server-side** code is closed-source and proprietary, favouring centralised management; furthermore, Telegram has a centralised architecture, as it runs servers on which correspondence is clearly stored. Telegram's accounts and identity authentication are also tied to telephone numbers. While these features lead both developers and users to situate Telegram unambiguously in the realm of 'centralised' services, it remains the most popular secure messaging app for some user populations – in our research, notably Russian users.

According to our interviews, the usage of Telegram may vary quite substantially according to users' goals and threat models. Several functionalities of the app make it convenient for different user groups: chats, secret chats, group chats, bots and channel broadcasting. Users faced with a low level of threat, not associated with any political activities, tend to adopt Telegram as an alternative to WhatsApp, using it for sending short messages in everyday conversations with their peer groups. Many activists and privacy-concerned users are aware of the absence of 'privacy by default' in Telegram chats (client-to-server encryption); however, they do not always opt for a 'secret chat' option that offers end-to-end encryption. This user group sometimes adopts two-step authentication and self-destruct timer options. Functions such as 'Group chat' are used for group conversations and are popular among activists, journalists or researchers for organisational purposes, as an alternative to Google Groups or mailing lists.

For example, one of our use-cases, a group of researchers working in Eastern Ukraine, use Telegram on a daily basis to coordinate research activities and discuss fieldwork, materials and other organisational information. However, they do not rely on Telegram for very sensitive discussions and prefer face-to-face offline meetings. During Russian anti-Putin protests in spring 2017, Telegram was also very popular, regardless of previously detected security flaws and the absence of end-to-end encryption in group chats. Telegram group chats remain popular among high-risk users despite the fact that the encryption for group chat offered by the app is very basic.

The popularity of Telegram in Russia can be partly explained by the reputation of its founders, Nicolai and Pavel Durov, Russian-born developers and entrepreneurs. Pavel Durov, the founder of Vkontakte, the most famous Russian social network, is colloquially referred to as the 'Russian Zuckerberg' and became *persona non grata* in Russia after his refusal to collaborate with the FSB. Telegram's swift rise on the market of messaging apps reveals a lot about the socioeconomic factors that influence the success of an innovation in the field of secure messaging: indeed, when Facebook bought WhatsApp (resulting in a lengthy black-out for the latter), the Telegram download rate exploded. In contrast to WhatsApp, Telegram can publicly underline its not-for-profit character and lack of ties with any commercial or governmental services.

While the Russian version of Telegram was released in 2012, before the Snowden revelations, Durov claims that the international version of his tool was inspired by the whistleblower:

In 2012 my brother and I built an encrypted messaging app for our personal use—we wanted to be able to securely pass on information to each other, in an environment where WhatsApp and other tools were easily monitored by the authorities. After Edward Snowden's revelations in 2013 we understood the problem was not unique to our situation and existed in other countries. So we released the encrypted messaging app for the general public (Durov, quoted in Healy 2015).

Despite its centralised nature, Telegram servers are located in five different countries around the world, with the aim of improving response times and better responding to national or regional jurisdictions (for example, the data of users who subscribe from inside Europe is stored only in the Netherlands). Due to the geographical distribution of its servers, Telegram's broadcasting function is used by censored media as a way to bypass the blockage, and by bloggers as an alternative to Facebook and traditional blogging platforms (for example, Alexey Navalny's popular bot on Telegram and the Grani.ru channel and bot, among others). However, unlike private communications on Telegram, public channels may be read and blocked by the Telegram technical team (e.g. as of January 2016, 660 channels attributed to ISIS were blocked).

Recent research in usability showed that Telegram was suffering from a number of important problems in this regard (Abu-Salma et al. 2017a); however, our research shows that this application is widely adopted by high-risk users, in Russia, Ukraine, but also in Iran, and reveals a number of 'alternative' practices and room for resistance within a service that has otherwise a number of centralised 'control points' (DeNardis 2014). In Russia, Telegram is widely used by Pirate Party activists (240 users as of 17 June 2017). Users from and living in Iran highlighted several aspects in favour of their choice of Telegram, not all of them directly connected with the privacy or security properties of the app. Users were especially happy with Telegram's functions such as stickers: Telegram makes it possible for users to generate their own stickers, which permits personalised uses of the app. For example, Iranian users explained, in our interviews with them, that adding stickers representing Muslims in their everyday environment, but also specific stickers on the Iranian political situation, was a very important feature that differentiates Telegram from 'first world' apps that only focus on Western lifestyles and emoticons. Furthermore, during our web ethnography focused on usages of Telegram, we observed how Telegram stickers were used to attract attention to a specific cause, as an alternative way of spreading information and setting a trend. Thus, after the arrest of the Tor exit-node operator Dmitry Bogatov in Russia on 10 April 2017, a group of Russian Internet freedom activists (some of them members of Pirate Party Russia), who used Telegram group chat to coordinate the #freeBogatov campaign, generated a sticker pack dedicated to his case. Apart from stickers – that become at the same time tools for community-building and for personalising this messaging app – other elements of customisation are present in Telegram, such as the possibility to set any image as wallpaper/ background for the app, or to use a wide range of colour themes – functions that are absent in Signal.

Finally – as the quotations from the two 'Resistance' group chat participants in Chapter 1 also show – trust in Telegram, according to our interviews, goes beyond the technology to place a special emphasis on Pavel Durov as a 'charismatic leader' (Conger 1989) and on his political positioning. The cryptographic protocol and security and privacy properties lose their importance for users, compared to UI/UX features and the 'aura' surrounding the app's creator.

CONCLUSIONS: CENTRALISED ARCHITECTURES BETWEEN CONTROL AND DEPENDENCY

As we finish writing this chapter, in the summer of 2020, the controversy about phone numbers as means of identification and authentication in secure messaging platforms still unfolds. In late May 2020, Signal released 'Signal PINs', a feature meant to allow users to keep control of their account even if they lose their phone or are forced to switch numbers – a feature which, in the words of a Signal developer, is aimed at 'facilitat(ing) new features like addressing that isn't based exclusively on phone numbers' (randall-signal 2020). Still, the debate about this implying the beginning of the end for phone-number-based identification rages on:

> Signal isn't yet announcing a way to use its product without handing over a phone number at all (…) You still can't use the laptop versions of the app without setting Signal up on your phone first, and you can't set it up on your phone without handing over a real, live phone number right at the start of the installation. PINs aren't a replacement for phone numbers but they do provide a safer way to recover your account in an emergency than a phone number alone (…) It's a start, not least because it means an interfering government or mobile phone company can't lock you out of your account simply by cancelling your SIM card. But you still need a phone to get onto Signal in the first place (Ducklin 2020).

Whether Signal's latest developments indeed herald a post-number-as-ID era for secure messaging tools or not, the fact that this issue – linked with the problem of metadata collection and retention – keeps on being the Apple of Discord for secure messaging systems is revealing of broader controversies around the 'dependencies' of centralised systems upon other entities. Interestingly, these dependencies are discussed in ways that largely overlook the soundness (or lack of) of the cryptographic protocols. On one hand, they are about the ways in which the application's interface, features and particular architectural design choices bind secure messaging tools to other applications and protocols that have, in turn, centralised and/or proprietary structures. On the other hand, they are about the economic and social 'trade-offs' that users must accept in order to use the system – handing over to a server-based service, as identifiers, pieces of information that they consider to be excessively sensitive or revealing, or knowing that a weakness of the system may actually come from the collection and retention of the 'information about information', metadata, that is more concentrated and exposed in centralised applications.

At the same time, centralised architectures make it easier for IM developers to experiment with, for example, particular forms of business models where some form of control or concentration of prerogatives must be retained. The choice of the Signal team to refrain from standardisation so as to maintain the capacity of updating the protocol rapidly enough as a response to the evolutions of the field, and to provide as a service the expertise and specification necessary for a proper deployment of the protocol, is an interesting case in point.

Centralisation may also mean faith in a charismatic developer, for better or worse. Beyond Telegram's Pavel Durov – the centrality of Moxie Marlinspike's figure and interventions in the secure messaging ecosystem is clear in the case of Signal, as well – motivations for the adoption of privacy-enhancing tools are also dependent on the reputation of their creators. In the users' mind, these figures of core developers become a (sometimes very welcome) 'centralisation' point, and their handling of shifting geopolitical alliances that may affect the reach of government agencies and, as a consequence, the users' threat models, is closely monitored and either fiercely supported or blamed.

The (hi)story of the Signal protocol is also interesting from the standpoint of Internet history. Indeed, it is a story of protocols that mutually influence each other, borrow from each other, and even try to revert to their predecessors and renew them in the light of new norms and requirements brought forward by Signal, such as forward secrecy – nowadays accepted as the necessary minimum. The Signal protocol has deeply influenced the crypto protocol field by introducing a combination of properties, such as forward and future secrecy and non-repudiation, combined with a modern interface, that have become a new minimum required for a secure messaging application. As the inventor of the OMEMO protocol (see Chapter 4) explains,

> If you are designing a new protocol for end-to-end encryption now, or even two years ago, for instant messaging having forward secrecy in it is just a good practice. It's just what all the other IM encryption schemes are doing as well. Signal does it, WhatsApp does it.

Boosted by Signal's innovations, older protocols have been refurbished, and new standards are now being discussed that aim at bringing some of these properties to a documented and stabilised form. Signal's impact goes beyond a 'linear' leap from older to modern protocols. The turn to mass encryption has shaken the secure messaging community, instigated protocol renewals and raised new challenges, many of them still unsolved.

The story of Signal is also telling in terms of 'informal' Internet governance. It shows how, as encryption becomes much more of a public concern than it was a few years ago, several end-to-end encrypted messaging developers are becoming sceptical about traditional arenas of exchange and dialogue on potential standards (such as the IETF, XMPP Foundation, W3C or NIST), which they consider less effective (or more 'compromised') than a development-based approach. Does this mean that, as far as widespread adoption of encryption in secure messaging is concerned, we are looking at the 'end' of the standardisation era? Will governance of encrypted messaging happen by infrastructure and by code, by 'something that works'? And if so, is a centralised service more likely to lead the way, due to its 'control points' – technical, financial and organisational – that can make control by design more straightforward for those willing to attempt it? The next two chapters, delving into more distributed arrangements for secure messaging applications – peer-to-peer and federated architectures – will keep on addressing this core question.

NOTES

1 This chapter partially draws upon Ermoshina, K., and F. Musiani, 'Standardising by Running Code': The Signal Protocol and *De Facto* Standardisation in End-to-End Encrypted Messaging', *Internet Histories: Digital Technology, Culture & Society*, 3.3–4 (2019): 343–63.

2 As a reminder (see Chapter 1's 'Instant messaging encryption' for more details), one of the applications built on top of the Signal Protocol is also called Signal and developed by the same team.

3 This independent audit of the OMEMO protocol includes a part dedicated to the Signal protocol and refers to a lack of documentation: https://conversations.im/omemo/audit.pdf.

4 https://signal.org/docs/specifications/xeddsa.

5 https://fdroid.eutopia.cz.

6 https://github.com/mimi89999/LibreSignal.

7 Signal's former and initial name.

8 https://github.com/LibreSignal/LibreSignal/issues/37#issuecomment-217211165.

9 https://github.com/LibreSignal/LibreSignal/issues/37#issuecomment-217231557.

10 https://github.com/LibreSignal/LibreSignal/issues/37#issuecomment-217231557 and follow-ups.

11 The willingness of users to 'stick' with Wire was also the reason why its team implemented a (end-to-end encrypted) chatbot called 'Otto', intended to become users' first contact, a way to get familiar with the app and test it – a way to, in Alan's words, 'show [users] the potential of Wire so that they feel comfortable inviting their friends'.

12 @Snowden on Twitter, 8 June 2017, 8:18 PM: 'Wire seems like a reasonable alternative to Signal, it's just less well-studied. Also lets you register with anon email instead of a phone #'. The tweet is no longer available, although the conversation that followed still is.

13 https://ricochet.im, which stopped development at the end of 2016.

14 In 2017, the Wire team claimed that one-to-one voice calls made via its system no longer collect metadata (Wire, 2017b).

3

PEER-TO-PEER ENCRYPTION AND DECENTRALISED GOVERNANCE: A NOT-SO-OBVIOUS PAIR

IF THERE IS SUCH A THING AS A CONTINUUM IN SECURE MESSAGING APPLI-cations, based on their technical architectures, the services examined in Chapter 2 would most likely situate themselves towards one of its extremes, and those addressed in this chapter would be located towards the other. Indeed, particular populations of users of secure messaging systems, especially those living in high-risk environments or involved in political activism, show an interest towards, and sometimes even a hope in, peer-to-peer architectures, as they see a coherence between their political and economic models, based on horizontal connections, mutual help, self-governance and participation, and the technical architecture of distributed networks. Peer-to-peer, as in previous instances in recent history, also promises less control by both governments and private corporations.

However, as the Introduction to this book has hinted at, this larger apprecia-tion of decentralisation as a principle and a vision may itself become problem-atic; most notably, decentralisation may become an objective in and of itself. Decentralised protocols and applications are too readily assumed, because of their technical qualities, to bring about decentralised political, social and eco-nomic outcomes – 'architecture is politics, but should not be understood as a substitute for politics' (Agre 2003).

Peer-to-peer encrypted messaging faces a number of more specifically tech-nical challenges as well. These include a 'vicious circle' between the adoption barrier and dependency on the number of users; the difficulty of managing users' reputations and identities, as identities are unique but users usually find them hard to memorise due to the form they are presented in; and the mechanisms that lead to trust being invested in the client, which presents a lot of advantages censorship-wise, but may entail risks for users living in authoritarian regimes, where the main threat model remains physical pressure and device seizure.

'Furthermore, while the demand to redecentralise specific components of the Internet has become ubiquitous (Schneider 2019: 266), and despite a long history of tensions which we hinted at in the Introduction, the concept of decentralisation remains uncertainly defined. 'Despite increased research, there remains a great deal of conceptual confusion. Researchers attach a startling diversity of definitions and measures to the decentralisation concept' (Schneider 2003: 32). Practitioners are not on the same page either when it comes to defining what decentralisation means, technically and socially, and which of the many models to opt for when designing a messaging app.

This chapter explores the tensions between the potential and the challenges of decentralised architectures as applied to encrypted messaging, by discussing, in particular, the case of the application Briar. In doing so, it also traces a portrait of the particular populations of users that more frequently adopt these technologies – usually knowledgeable about **mesh networks**, or with a previous history of using decentralised technologies.

THE 'PROMISE' OF PEER-TO-PEER ENCRYPTION

As we have previously discussed in Chapter 1, the discourse linking encryption to peer-to-peer (p2p) is frequently associated with the 'promise' of this decentralised technology for the field of secure messaging. It is cited as such in a number of group chats that we have observed, with a particular focus on Russia[1] and France. These users, whom we have earlier classified as high-knowledge or tech-savvy/tech-enthusiasts,[2] regularly discuss the 're-decentralisation' of the Internet(s) (Rowe 2018). Two main aspects are underlined in these debates: the potential of p2p as a circumvention tool in the context of growing surveillance and censorship, and the particular kinds of metadata protection enabled by the technical features of p2p. Further, the potential of p2p to offer a certain level of technical autonomy useful in case of shutdowns, or in remote areas,[3] as well as the technological 'elegance' of these solutions, are among the key arguments in its favour.

In countries such as Russia, where Internet governance is increasingly state-centred, centralised and authoritarian after a relatively open and decentralised earlier phase (Nocetti 2015), Internet activists suggest not only federation (which will be more extensively addressed in the next chapter), but also p2p as a possibly appropriate technical answer that can potentially help users to 'slip between the cracks' of state filtering and surveillance. In terms of the kind of metadata treatment enabled by p2p, users believe that decentralised solutions will have less impact on privacy compared to Google or Amazon-based solutions, and that metadata can be better protected within distributed or **mixnet**-based systems. Other discussions on re-decentralisation concern infrastructure, at both the physical and protocol levels, for example, how could the Domain Name System (DNS) be re-decentralised. An important place in discussions on re-decentralisation is held by 'alternatives' such as ZeroTier One, a portable client application that provides connectivity to public or private virtual networks, founded by Adam Ierymenko in 2014.[4]

In France, as well, discussions about the need to move away from proprietary and closed-source centralised services are spreading across tech-enthusiast communities. A new trend is developing, which is labelled as a 'relocalisation' of hosting and service providers. With the motto 'host local', a project called CHATONS[5] has been launched by the 'Degooglise Internet' collective, to map local independent hosting, email and XMPP providers. This collective suggests that instead of hosting data in a wide, centralised, remote and anonymous datacentre, it is more privacy-preserving to host it with someone you know personally. Trust relationships, and sometimes even 'IRL' encounters, give an additional layer of protection in addition to TLS and end-to-end encryption.

Mastodon,[6] a federated[7] version of Twitter, is gaining popularity in France (most of its instances are French). Diaspora, a decentralised social network, is also gathering important communities of French privacy enthusiasts, namely through an instance called Framasphere. As one of our interviewees from the French cryptoparty scene commented:

I feel like recently there's a riposte of European services to USA-based ones. I don't really understand why we should give our data to giant datacenters somewhere across the ocean. It's like eating our local food... You like French cheese, French strawberries, why not French hosting? Or even better... you can grow your own strawberries [laughs] or run an instance at your place (A., informational security trainer, France).

In this context of the creation of decentralised and federated projects, p2p solutions become part of a more global trend towards re-localisation, associated with a more responsible and even 'sustainable' attitude vis-à-vis the Internet. De-anonymisation of service providers paradoxically promises better anonymity and online privacy, which goes hand in hand with new protocol designs, often based on IRL contacts and key exchange. Several projects are moving towards a redesign of the backbone and propose a more direct and local, sometimes off-the-grid, device-to-device connection, in order to increase anonymity. Among the promises of p2p, data and infrastructure ownership is one of the most frequently discussed. Unlike centralised applications, which make users delegate part of their data (and therefore, part of their 'freedom') to a server, proponents of p2p submit that such a model guarantees more autonomy and privacy for users.

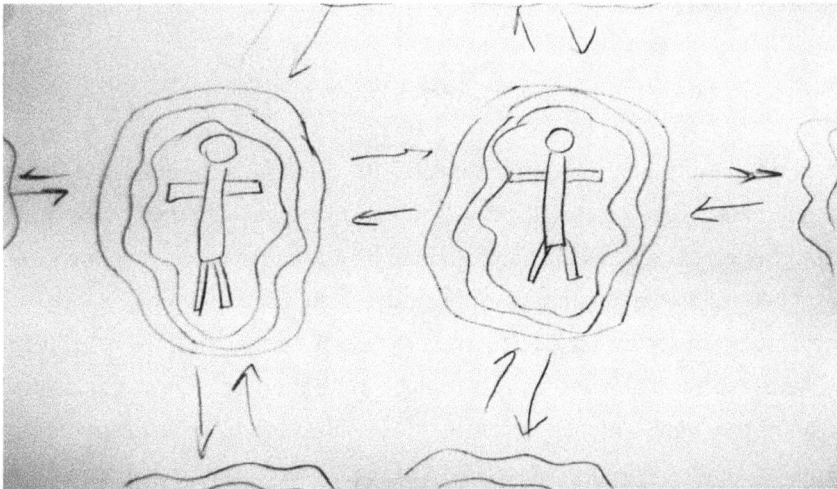

FIG. 3.1 A vision of 'safer Internet'. Drawing made by a feminist activist during a workshop in March 2017 in Saint-Petersburg

The shift towards decentralisation is recursively described as a solution to 'rescue' the Internet, with distributed architectures being considered as possible alternatives to the predominantly centralised, corporate and state-controlled Internet. Interviewees described wishing to 'turn to [the p2p] community to seek digital solutions that defend freedom' and evaluated mesh and peer-to-peer technologies not only as 'more secure' but also as censorship-resistant: 'community-run 'mesh' network ... takes back control from corporations: everyone on the network can agree to keep all content open'.

Drawing on a long-term social and historical perspective on decentralised technologies, these statements can appear too technologically deterministic and blind to the big picture. However, what is most interesting about them from our standpoint, in order to account for the recent history of secure messaging development, is that such arguments are grounded in a perspective on decentralised architectures that sees them as intrinsically charged with a specific political and social vision: as Philip Agre has insightfully summarised, p2p is the epitome of a technical architecture that is seen as a 'substitute for politics' (Agre 2003). This chapter seeks to examine how this vision is entangled with the day-to-day technical challenges and opportunities posed by p2p technologies, and how developers and users attempt to embody the promise of such technologies in artefacts and procedures.

Re-localisation, data ownership, and 'utopias of resilience'

A first facet of the p2p promise concerns the intrinsic technical interest that developers have in decentralised technologies, coupled with their recognition that these technologies are accompanied by a number of challenges unseen in other architectural configurations. Indeed, the overwhelming majority of developers of secure messaging and email applications that we have interviewed express a general interest in decentralisation, and almost all, in the span of the same sentence, underline the technical difficulties related to the implementation of p2p protocols. It is perhaps due to the awareness of these complications that no one calls for the total replacement of centralised architectures in favour of p2p, even though much optimism and sociopolitical promise is invested in distributed architectures. Take the following comment from Sarah, a developer:

> They (centralisation and decentralisation) both have the place in the wild. You'll always have to have collaboration on something centralised, but I think that technology and people are safest when power is distributed, and the way to distributed power is to create decentralised means of communication. My philosophy lies in that. I still see a need for centralisation in few areas, but many of the properties of centralised systems can be created within decentralised systems (Sarah, Ricochet developer).

A second facet of the p2p promise lies in what we call 'utopias of resilience': a number of projects propose solutions for communities in rural areas, or areas at risk (such as war zones), where Internet connections are non-existent, weak or dangerous (for example, if fully controlled by the state). Thus, a Syrian interviewee describes[8] his experience during the first months of the civil war in his country as follows: 'We all became hackers, as we turned to radio waves, walky-talky, mesh and other technologies to coordinate our actions in the absence of network coverage'.

Consequently, countries or areas with frequent Internet shutdowns are also targeted by p2p projects (Vargas-Leon 2016). Among them is Scuttlebutt,[9] invented by a sailor, and a project that proposes an 'off-the-grid' file-sharing, communication and blogging framework. As in Sarah's account above, understandings of power redistribution are once again related to control of data:

> In a database system, all the power is in the database. It's often called a 'single source of truth'. Who can do what is ultimately controlled by whoever administers the database. Here, we have no central database to decide for us what a given action means, instead when you make a post or a 'dig' or change your picture, the other peers (or rather, the software they run) interprets that. A social consensus.[10]

Traffic layer security, or metadata protection, is yet another feature that makes p2p a desirable alternative to models where the metadata collection and retention issue remains unsolved. However, all the developers working on decentralised projects agreed that peer-to-peer presents a number of important challenges usability-wise. They concur that a trade-off exists between the UI/UX features of centralised services that users have got used to, such as stickers, file sharing and calls, and the better level of anonymity offered by p2p-based applications:

> I feel like a whole bunch of people need it [anonymity]. It's really hard to recommend Ricochet over Signal [but w]here Ricochet is gaining it's because it's using Tor hidden services. Part of my goal is to make Ricochet more usable. Compared to Signal, Ricochet is more privacy-preserving because of no phone number. Ricochet is easy but it lacks a lot of features that other IMs have: like sending pictures and files, calls… Ricochet does not have that because this is hard to develop with respect to anonymity (Sarah, Ricochet developer).

Our interviews help shed light on another facet of the p2p promise that may be showing an evolution in the history of decentralised technologies. Traditionally, these architectures have been thought of as best serving the needs of very specific groups of users: on the one hand, activists and strong defenders of civil liberties, members of anti-authoritarian, left-wing movements with a very high-risk profile who seek strong levels of data and metadata protection – so-called 'radical techies' (Milan 2013) – and on the other hand, tech-savvy people interested in 'playing with a new tool', in the more ludic dimension of technology development and testing (Coleman 2011).

However, our interviews with secure messaging users living or working in zones at high risk[11] show that, with the exception of tech workers, these users do not adopt p2p messengers, as they have not been trained to do so. They prefer offline communication on most sensitive issues, or using centralised tools with a deletion timer ('ephemeral messages'). Indeed, digital security trainers who advise Ukrainian or Crimean human rights organisations recommend centralised apps, such as WhatsApp or Signal, as they are worried that p2p will be more difficult to understand and adopt and will present otherwise avoidable technical issues. After a risk assessment (an analysis of real threats and their probabilities in the given context, see Chapter 1), they often conclude that the threat lies on the client side, and the physical seizure or search of devices at borders is more likely to happen than traffic interception. However, digital security trainers or tech professionals like to 'test' new tools, including p2p tools, with their colleagues and friends.[12]

Based on our sample of user interviewees, heavily politicised users, primarily belonging to left-wing movements, are indeed interested in p2p messaging applications, as in their imaginaries of communication technologies a direct connection is established between social and technical decentralisation (Agre 2003); however, actual levels of adoption are very weak, a recurring problem in the history of decentralised technologies (Rowe 2018; see also Musiani 2015b). This aspect of p2p was criticised by a number of our developer interviewees, who share a belief in some of the positive aspects of distributed architectures but underline a number of unsolved challenges:

> People with [...] anti-authoritarian politics bend them [their politics] to a decentralised model and they believe very strongly that all of the technology must follow a decentralised model. And our critique was that... there's a lot of technical problems with decentralised model (Elijah Sparrow, LEAP developer).

BATTERIES AND BUSINESS MODELS: THE CHALLENGES OF P2P ENCRYPTION

Among the problems or challenges of p2p, there is, first of all, a vicious circle of barriers to adoption and a dependency on a critical mass of users (also framed in the past as a 'chicken and egg problem'; see Musiani 2015b and Musiani 2021). Indeed, the more people are using a p2p tool, the better quality of service it can offer; however, it is hard to motivate people to use a relatively unpopular messaging app, due to the poor quality of service in the bootstrapping period. Secondly, projects that offer better levels of anonymity, such as mixnets (for example, POND), have latency issues. These two challenges are very well described by Roger Dingledine, Tor lead developer, in the interview we conducted with him:

> Part of the challenge was that… should we work on this low latency, low security system called Tor or should we work on this high latency, high security system called mixminion? We have a choice – which one is better for the world? And then we did more economic analysis and we realised mixminion will have approximately no users, so while in theory it must be safe, in practice it will not be more safe. So, the answer [to the initial question] was evident (Roger Dingledine, Tor lead developer).

Another problem of p2p tools is the difficulty of managing users' reputation and identity that is often presented as a 'long hash' (as in Ricochet, which uses Tor 'rendez-vous' points). In this context, identities are unique, but users usually find them hard to memorise. The form that identifiers take in a messaging system is most often the result of a trade-off between different properties, as explained by Elijah Sparrow from LEAP:

> (In p2p environments) user IDs are long strings that are hard to remember… There's something that is called Zooko's triangle. For any identity system you get to pick two of the following three choices: you can have something where the names are globally unique, you can have something where the names are globally memorable, and you can have something where the naming system is decentralised. The problem is that everyone wants to get all three, but you have to pick two (Elijah Sparrow, LEAP developer).

These identity management problems result in reputation management issues. This makes it highly problematic for users of p2p environments to be able to authenticate whom they are communicating with – which developers identify as a core issue of today's Internet due to the numerous problematic and potentially damaging practices it hosts (Badouard 2017):

Certain usability properties of identities are very difficult to do in a peer-to-peer decentralised model. And a decentralised model also has issues with Sybil attacks, the question of how you control access, how you establish reputation when there is no barrier to entry. There's essentially no good way for a p2p model to have reputation, which is a very big problem in any online communication setting because there is so much trolling (Elijah Sparrow, LEAP developer).

Another challenge of p2p concerns the trust that is placed on the client side. For example, Beaker Browser[13] promises to turn users' browsing experience 'inside out' by hosting websites on users' clients and using a specific protocol for file sharing. The URLs generated with this process are said to be 'unguessable' and are never sent over the network, the URL itself therefore being a public key helping to decrypt files. While this model presents a lot of advantages for efforts to circumvent censorship, as it makes it almost impossible to block or delete any of the Beaker websites or files, it may present risks for users living in authoritarian regimes where the main threat model remains physical pressure and device seizure (see Chapter 1). Secondly, the p2p architecture requires the user's device, by design, to be constantly online (as every device is also a 'server'), which has significant consequences for battery consumption:

[The] peer to peer promise [says that you] have to trust your device all the time and you have to deal with identities with these long hashes and you have to deal with burning of your battery, memory and mobile device (Elijah Sparrow, LEAP developer).

Improving this aspect is one of the core ongoing tasks for p2p projects, whose developers are being creative in exploring alternatives to this major design constraint, such as whether the client can remain connected to an anonymity network without constantly exchanging data.

A related feature concerns the possibility of planning regular account backups. In distributed applications, it is difficult, by design, to use any kind of cloud platform or other automated or regular backup solution. This feature can be a positive in high-risk situations (deleting an account from a client deletes it 'forever', as no servers are involved). However, it may be a complication for users who prefer to rely on cloud-based solutions or need to keep archives of their communications. Michael Rogers, the lead developer of Briar,[14] which we will be examining extensively later in the chapter, notes in this regard:

> Briar is in a worse situation than some tools, by the moment your own account is stored on your device. If you destroy the device or uninstall Briar, you lose all your contacts and messages (Michael Rogers, Briar lead developer).

To summarise, in the view of the developers we interviewed who are either working on p2p-based tools or considering whether to do so, adoption of p2p systems in the field of secure messaging seems to be limited because of their insufficient usability levels, restricted multimedia sharing capacities, memory and battery concerns. This makes p2p applications harder to adopt in areas where people use older and less powerful phones with lower quality components, smaller memory and shorter battery life. There is therefore the potential for this architecture to contribute to the digital divide (Howard 2007). Developers underline users' 'dependency' on UI/UX features, such as stickers, and agree fact that peer-to-peer solutions cannot compare to centralised applications in terms of usability.

A related question is why p2p solutions are lagging behind centralised applications, when the search for suitable and sustainable business models has been a long-standing issue for decentralised architectures-based applications (see Musiani and Méadel 2015). An immediate answer is that p2p systems have no central intermediary entity that could track – and monetise – social interactions in order to fund the development of applications. Peer-to-peer architectures traditionally attract sizable attention within academia, with a growing number of conceptually complex and promising projects; however, there remains the problem of the 'knowledge gap':

[There is an] enormous conceptual gap between what the designers of an encryption tool think that everybody knows and needs to know in order to make a system work, and on the other hand what a user actually tries to achieve through the use of it (Michael Rogers, Briar lead developer).

In this sense, while usability seems to be less of a burden for centralised systems, users have not yet formed proper 'mental models' to embrace distributed secure communication:

With a certain technical structure that is more centralised, it is definitely achievable [...] But now the question is: can we also bring decentralisation into that picture without breaking all of those mental models that users have and without asking them to learn a lot and make a lot of theoretical effort before they can use that tool. [...] What we're trying to achieve is a balance between asking a user to understand how the system works, which is obviously a burden, or having a system do surprising things because it works differently from what they expect (Michael Rogers, Briar lead developer).

Despite extended critiques by tech and trainer communities, peer-to-peer encrypted messaging apps are developing and some of them are gaining users, funding and media attention. The second part of this chapter turns to analyse the case of Briar, a peer-to-peer, end-to-end encrypted, instant messaging app using Tor hidden services.

BRIAR: RETHINKING ANONYMISATION AND RESILIENCE

Briar is born out of a problem that is activist and academic at once: how to increase anonymity and move communications off the backbone, in the context of Internet shutdowns (Vargas-Leon 2016) and increased governmental control over the network in a number of countries around the world:

I was working on p2p communication networks for my PhD and I reached a point where I realized that being able to observe the Internet backbone gives you the ability to observe all of the endpoints and their interconnections; this shapes the possibilities for having private communications over the Internet [...] if you can see the end points, you cannot get the anonymity (Michael Rogers, Briar lead developer).

In the late 2010s, the lead developer of Briar, Michael Rogers, was contributing to LimeWire, a peer-to-peer file sharing service. In 2009, LimeWire developers were contacted by Iranian journalists from the Green Movement. Activists were wondering if LimeWire would be suitable for use as a communication tool in Iran:

The guy who contacted us worked for BBC Persian service. He had a principal interest [in] getting news from BBC into Iran, but the question was essentially: what can we do to support a movement like this? One part is getting news from the outside world, another part is disseminating news to the outside world, and the third way is internal communication. And those are all things that we kept going as strands within Briar, how do we look at those different use cases (Michael Rogers, Briar lead developer).

At that time, LimeWire was not suitable and secure for high-risk communication; however, Michael suggested building another system with a greater focus on security features. Together with activists, he sketched the rough idea of a network built over social connections, relying as much as possible on local network connections. This technical solution was relevant to the local political context: international connections in Iran were heavily monitored and filtered. In this context, Michael and his team opted for an off-backbone communication: this collective effort took shape, eventually, as Briar. At the time of our fieldwork (late 2017), the team counted four members, with two developers, a UX/UI designer and a security/usability researcher who was also responsible for communications and outreach for the project.

As with most software development projects, its name sheds light on its history and on the *zeitgeist* of its developers. 'Briar' is an organic metaphor: it is a distributed, rhizomatic and ramified structure, which, despite its seemingly hostile appearance, can create a protective environment:

> Briar, as far as I understand, means a thorny plant, and there's a fairy tale about a little rabbit thrown into a briar patch who knows how to avoid it, because for him it's not dangerous, he was born and raised there. So it gives this idea for agility and resilience to escape dangers. And I like the little story behind it (Thorsten, Briar developer).
>
> Indeed, it's an American folk story: it's about a fox that catches a rabbit and says: I am going to tear you into pieces. And the rabbit starts crying: Oh, please, do everything you want to me but please don't throw me into the briar patch! So the fox eventually throws the rabbit into the briar patch, the rabbit runs away in the briar laughing: 'I was born and bred in the briar patch, you know?' [...] In order to communicate privately we have to move away from these centralised services and rely on our social networks, and we have to fall back on these much more difficult structures to communicate (Michael Rogers, Briar lead developer).

The Briar Patch is also a specific region of space featured in Star Trek. According to the plot of the 1998 film Star Trek Insurrection, the Briar Patch emanates a specific 'metaphasic radiation' that is concentrated in the planet's rings, continually rejuvenating their genetic structure – it is a region of space that star-ships usually avoid because of various radiation sources and energy fluctuations that impair communications systems and make it difficult for vessels inside the nebula to make contact with those outside it. This description bears a close resemblance to Briar's architecture and technical features, these being designed for situations where communication with the 'outside' Internet is hard to maintain. Briar focuses on a specific context of state-driven blocking and filtering measures (Bendrath and Mueller 2011; Mueller, Kuehn and Santoso 2012), as well as extreme situations such as a significant Internet blackout or shutdown (Vargas-Leon 2016). Connections in Briar are made over Bluetooth, Wi-Fi and Tor. In this sense, Briar is designed both as a circumvention and an anti-surveillance tool:

What we had in mind specifically was how to get information in and out of the country in times of unrest when it might be blockaded, and it might be particularly difficult to reach Facebook [and other international sites]. One of the problems is how do you tunnel information outside or within the country and then let it spread widely outside the narrow tunnel. And that remains a question that people in Briar think of. People need to use it in conjunction with other tools and especially when they need to reach people who are not part of a movement or whatever social group it is, and who are not using Briar. We need to think about bridges. So we have an import feature to import a blog from a web (Michael Rogers, Briar lead developer).

Briar sees its users as people who are aware of their own need for security and mindful of surveillance-related threats. Briar's threat model sees governments as the main threatening group of actors and attackers, performing filtering and interferences as well as blackouts – not only reading and intercepting communications and metadata. Briar is also intended to be a solution for crisis mapping and disaster response, and as such is aiming to collaborate with humanitarian organisations. Briar's UX/UI and usability concerns are informed by the experience of lead developer Michael Rogers, who previously worked as an informational security trainer for journalists and, in his words, had witnessed in this role the conceptual gap between the expectations of encryption tools' designers in terms of users know and need to know in order to make a system work, and actual user expectations concerning the tool (see also Abu-Salma et al. 2017a and Dechand et al. 2019). In this sense, one of Briar's concerns is to make a usable peer-to-peer tool for secure communication.

From the protocol to the application: A framework for a decentralised alternative

The Briar project consists of two parts: the underlying protocol, called Bramble, and the actual user-facing application, called Briar.

I would say Bramble is a framework, or a library that gives you these peer-to-peer connections with people, without any intermediaries, and it gives you also the notion of groups and of contacts that can interact. And on top of this you can build different applications, and Briar is just one of them, it's a showcase of what the technology can do (Thorsten, Briar developer).

Recently, Briar has been shifting its efforts from the user-facing application to the codebase and infrastructure, and is expecting to guarantee the sustainability of the project without dependency on users – or, to be more precise, in shifting from end-users to 're-users', power-users or lead users (von Hippel 1986) with above-average technical and computing skills who can adapt the protocol to their needs and develop other projects on top of it. The sustainability of Briar is supposed to be guaranteed by separating the protocol from the application, the reason being that, while maintaining pieces of infrastructure is easier in the open-source world as there are several positive precedents (Powell 2012), proper maintenance is more difficult for a user-facing application:

That's partly why we want to make this separation because the user-facing app will probably have to be maintained with crowdfunding from users, or hopefully it can be maintained on a volunteer basis because most of the difficult technical plumbing will be moved into the infrastructure project, where the users don't have to maintain it (Michael Rogers, Briar lead developer).

The Bramble protocol is not yet standardised, and won't be in the near future, because developers see standardisation as the last step in the chain of releases, after the beta-version of Briar application is properly tested, and the final release is published: 'If you standardise it, you need to know that it's the best way to do it', as Thorsten puts it (see Chapter 2). However, the Bramble protocol can follow Signal's route of '*de facto* standardisation', if it is adopted by a sufficient number of other projects. In this way, as with Signal, while the protocol itself is open source, expertise may be needed to implement it. Providing this expertise as a service is now considered a way of providing the project with a certain degree of financial sustainability, which would make the sociotechnical goal of promoting resilient and distributed networks easier to achieve. Indeed, Briar's lead developer sees in this initiative of charging for expertise an embryo of a possible business model for Briar, that echoes Signal's 'non-standardisation as a business model' (see Chapter 2 and Ermoshina and Musiani 2019):

> The idea is that people can build other kinds of resilient networks on top of the same protocol stack and hopefully we can make a sort of consulting business for people who need to communicate with devices out in the field or to communicate within teams that deploy in remote areas, that can be interested to use this kind of networking technology (Michael Rogers, Briar lead developer).

Therefore, the Bramble protocol aims to prepare a framework in order to build distributed alternatives to existing centralised services. In the words of Thorsten, 'I would like as many of the services that people currently use to be transformed to this peer-to-peer model when we don't need anybody in the middle anymore'.

Working at the margins: Threats to metadata and Internet shutdowns

Briar's main 'killer feature', as described by its developers, is intended to be the close attention it pays to metadata protection. As developer Thorsten puts it, Briar 'solves interesting problems that are not solved by other tools on the market, for example, it enables people to chat without needing any servers and without leaking any metadata'. An interesting consequence of this, and of the fact that Briar uses Tor hidden services even for feedback submission and crash reports, is that the Briar team itself does not have any precise data about the number of users, or exact usage statistics:

> All the data only exists on the users' devices. There's no Briar server that can store anything. If two people use Briar in a village in Chad in Africa, we don't know about it, there is no connection made between them and any of the computers we control. The only connection ever made to other people, they add themselves. And we will never know these people even use Briar.

We don't store anything, because it's from person to person (Thorsten, Briar developer).

As mentioned, Briar uses Tor as a 'very well-designed backbone that's designed to know as little as possible on what we do'; however, the team is currently reflecting upon Tor's limitations and security flaws – a concern that mirrors a broader preoccupation in privacy research (Manils et al. 2010). Briar has been conceived to be deployable on any kind of infrastructure; it is not, by design, attached to Tor and could be migrated to a different kind of distributed backbone:

> I think Tor is starting to show its age. Some of the attacks we heard about as theoretical actually went very practical, and we need to think about anonymity infrastructure, privacy infrastructure that is not operated by someone in your house or on your street (Michael Rogers, Briar lead developer).

The Tor vulnerability mentioned by Rogers concerns the exit nodes and is related to the connection point between the onion network and the 'normal' Internet. The traces left by the exit nodes can provoke serious problems for the node administrators – a fact well-known to Dmitry Bogatov, arrested on 10 April 2017 because his exit node was used to post messages judged by a Russian court to be 'extremist' (Hatmaker 2017). The critique of Tor vulnerabilities has led the Briar team to imagine a separate, resilient network, independent from the Internet infrastructure: in the words of Rogers, 'I was looking for something that would work in a sort of partially disconnected environment'.

Briar's particular inspiration comes from the Internet precursor Usenet, when the historical network was running on dial-up connections and supporting early publish-subscribe systems on top of a patchwork of different technologies, before the era of IP addresses (Paloque-Bergès 2017). Some of these ideas had already been developed within the now-dormant Pond project – itself a delay-tolerant, mixnet-inspired messaging system that introduces noise and latency to increase privacy and hide metadata.[15]

One of Briar's central use-cases, which was tested in the field in Brazil with local bottom-up activist communities, is the case of Internet shutdowns. In these scenarios, Briar is meant to still operate using either Bluetooth or any other network that is not connected to the global Internet. Briar received attention from Brazilian activists because of the recent Internet shutdowns and mobile network jamming used by the police during rallies (Internet Without Borders 2018). Briar is also thinking of deploying it in Cuba, where it is common for networks to be disconnected from the global Internet. By not relying on servers, Briar need not be dependent on the Internet as a backbone, and can potentially be run on any kind of autonomous community network:

> When I tried to send you a message on Signal before it did not work because the Internet was down, and the message needed to first go to the Signal servers and then from the Signal server it came back to you. With Briar we make a direct connection in here, in this network. We are all in this network, we have IP addresses and Briar uses these IP addresses to connect to you. It can also use Bluetooth, or other technologies. For example, we have a mechanism when you can use USB sticks, USB hard drives or SD cards. You plug this in your computer, you say for whom it is, who is the contact and it will synchronize or this contact (Thorsten, Briar developer).

For the Briar developers, their interest in not running exclusively on Tor hidden services (which is the case, for example, for Ricochet[16]), is that then Tor becomes one of several possible ways of transporting the data. So, if in some countries Tor is temporarily blocked (as has happened, for example, in China; Winter and Lindskog 2012) users have alternatives, including some that may be developed in the future.

Group chat: A 'social-based paradigm'

Briar's group chat architecture and key discovery processes draw heavily from the observation of social interactions among social movements and grassroots communities. The Briar protocol is, in some way, a 'modelization of social phenomena such as friendship links, affinity-based community formation, attribution of trust' (Musiani 2010: 193), something that has been a longstanding concern of many innovators tackling the development of 'next-generation' P2P applications since the mid-2000s. This 'social-based paradigm' (Pouwelse et al. 2006) works towards achieving trust by relying on both the technical features of the protocol and the social aspects of the 'human' community itself.

Briar's identity management and key discovery are linked to the structures of social movements and to offline communication structures. In this sense, Briar seeks to redistribute the trust relationship between human and non-human agents:

> Social networks are the foundation of all-powerful social movements, so by emphasizing it we bring the attention back to the fact that all the security relies on the people that you can trust, by bringing those trust relationships to the fore… This very difficult constraint can turn into a strength. And I feel again that we are in the position of the rabbit, we're thrown in a supposedly hostile environment that actually is the place where we were born and bred (Michael Rogers, Briar lead developer).

Many interactions are happening offline and face-to-face. The key discovery and contact exchange, for instance, is happening **out of band**. Key discovery in Briar happens in two different ways: directly, by QR-code scanning, and indirectly, on the suggestion or invitation of another user. The first configuration postulates the co-presence of the two users in the same physical space; this use context is considered as the most secure and the 'trust level' shown by the application is 'green'. The second case supposes that two users have one contact in common; the trust level is set to 'yellow'. Yellow can later be transformed into green when the two users meet and verify fingerprints by scanning QR-codes out of band. The 'red' trust level designates participants in a group chat with whom no key exchange has been established. However, Briar also tries to minimise users' interaction with keys and make it as smooth as possible:[17]

> All is end-to-end encrypted by the keys that are automatically created when you add your contacts. You need to be face-to-face to add each other. And when you do, you can be sure that no one is in the middle messing up with

your keys. And you don't see your keys, never. It's encrypted but encryption is invisible to you (Thorsten, Briar developer).

By choosing out-of-band key discovery, Briar tries to solve the **Man-In-The-Middle** problem. However, the QR-code model showed its limits – for very material and physical reasons – in the real-life crash test that we, the authors, performed in August 2017, during a rally on Dvortsovaya square in Saint-Petersburg. A group of 12 activists had installed the Briar application before the rally. We met on the square and had to physically scan QR-codes in order to be able to add each other in the contact list, create a group chat and start the testing. However, the scanning of QR-codes turned out to be hard due to the sunlight. Some users had to hide under their coats in order to scan their codes, and this attracted unnecessary attention from the police and other participants. Other users had their phone screens broken (a very frequent case among left-wing activists), and this has also made the process harder and slower. Moreover, this dependence on offline face-to-face contacts, emphasising the local and the proximity dimensions of the p2p application, made Briar hard to use for coordinating an international movement, or even country-wide one. When we issued a call for Briar user testing in Russia using our contacts in different tech and activist communities across the country, several dozens of people were interested in testing it, but they could not 'add' each other and create a common group chat. Vast distances and decentralised communities with one or two people per city made it harder for the out-of-band system to work.

The latest release of Briar, however, implements a solution to the problem of adding contacts remotely, by making it possible to share a special 'Briar link' (Figure 3.2).

Briar's group chat model is, by far, one of the most interesting across the end-to-end encrypted messengers that we have examined. Briar's group chat structure takes the shape of a star: everyone is connected only via the creator of the group. This offers some degree of metadata protection to the Briar group chat participants. However, once again, the development of this feature was the result of complicated trade-offs:

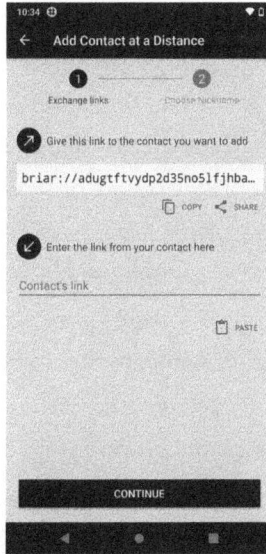

FIG. 3.2 Adding a remote contact on Briar (source: https://briarproject.org/manual).

Doing the group chat was a surprisingly challenging task. We had to make some compromises there. For example, it was a difficult decision – who can add new people to the group? If you allow everybody to pull new people in it, it's a mess and you have a question who can kick them out again. So to simplify things we decided that only the creator of the group is able to add new people. So if you are in a group and you're not a creator and you want your friend to be part of the group, you would ask the creator please invite my friend – it's a social way of doing it (Thorsten, Briar developer).

Human trust is an important aspect that minimises some of the risks related to 'social centralisation' in Briar's group chat architecture:

In a way, there is a certain centralisation aspect again [in the group chat model]. The creator has more control on the group than other people have. But you are not forced in the group, you are invited and you can join when you trust the creator sufficiently to handle this group, not invite bad people into it, and secure their phone properly (Thorsten, Briar developer).

It is the fact that Briar puts metadata protection at the heart of the protocol that led them to develop this unique group chat model. However, a protocol feature has been implemented in Briar that makes it possible to redistribute the power and remove part of the technical and social responsibility from the group creator:

> Because there's no server that distributes messages to everybody, partici-pants need to exchange messages with themselves. So, if there is a creator, she needs to have connections with all the members of the group for the messages to travel, as she distributes the messages. But the implemented mechanism makes it easier because what if the creator loses the phone or is offline? The whole communication stops. So we came up with a solution that allows people to reveal their contact relationships to the group: if we are in the group and Ivan is also in the group and you want to be able to keep the communication running when I, the creator, am not here, you can decide to reveal the fact that you are friends with Ivan to the whole group, and exchange messages with Ivan directly (Thorsten, Briar developer).

However, while this feature continues to be effective in Briar's beta for Android, our observations of user testing in Russia, as well as discussions with testers from around the world, have shown that users do not have a clear understanding of the 'contact reveal' feature. Users tend to think that this involves sharing their social graph and consider this function as insecure and dangerous for them and their community. However, Briar's threat model does not intend that anybody should know who the contacts of a particular user are, and this is why the user needs to opt-in to reveal her contacts so that she can communicate without the creator. The Briar team is using real-life use-cases to explain this feature to their testers:

> Everyone is connected to each other through the creator. But when you reveal the contact it does not mean that you receive a notice saying you are friends with Ivan, it just means that you can exchange group messages also directly with Ivan without the creator being connected. It can happen

that people need to make more connections to each other so that they can exchange messages more fluidly: if you are in a bigger group at a protest and you send 'the police is coming, you need to run away', this message will not arrive to all the members if only the creator is distributing messages (Thorsten, Briar developer).

Enrolling users: Community-building on top of research

A number of theoretical problems have been revealed during the work on the beta version of Briar's group chat, for example '**gossiping**', i.e. making sure that data are disseminated to all members of a group after a user has left it (the nature of peer-to-peer makes it hard to let all users know about it at once, and this may confuse users). The Briar team is looking at both academic work and other projects for solutions but has concluded that existing efforts do not solve these problems. A possible solution may lie in the collaboration between Briar and other anonymity-centred projects, such as Panoramix, Loopix or Pond. At present, Briar does not collaborate closely with any project, but it is following the overall 'galaxy' of encrypted messaging applications, even centralised ones, to keep track of the UI/UX features that users want to have. Briar wants to learn from these popular messaging apps and propose a smoother way for users to 'migrate' from centralised messengers to Briar:

> We usually look at Signal, WhatsApp and Telegram, simply because in this space these are the biggest three apps that fit... With Signal, since the source code is open, we look at it and use some of it, for emojis for example. If we want to solve some UI problem, we do look at how other projects do it. Because if we have our own way, it may be confusing for people because they are already used to other ways. [We want] for the users to have it easier switching from other apps to our app (Thorsten, Briar developer).

However, Briar has a very different approach to the protocol governance and centralisation/decentralisation debate. Briar is actively distributing its Android

Package, which allows the distribution and installation of their application, via F-Droid; however, they cannot at this stage give users absolute freedom to modify the protocol, for interoperability reasons. Thorsten explicitly states that Briar has a different philosophy to Signal, inasmuch as Briar does not attempt to centralise the protocol and distributions of its apps: 'They [Signal] are very strict in having control over it [the protocol and distributions] while we encourage other implementations'. (Thorsten, Briar developer)

The Briar project is now experiencing a transition phase as the team is choosing which path to take in the near future; during this transition phase, primary concerns include the aforementioned separation of the Bramble protocol from the Briar app, and the search for alternatives to Tor as a backbone.

An important issue to underline is that Briar has become available to users only very recently; until spring 2018, test builds were available for Android devices on request, and the Briar team was organising usability workshops to test different features of the tool.[18] Thus, the 'chicken and egg' problem of getting a critical mass of users interested and motivated has not yet had to be fully confronted. However, the decentralised tool project, though unused by the general public thus far, has been tested in 'field' conditions in remote rural areas, where participants could communicate successfully in the Briar mesh at a limited distance. Furthermore, even though Briar does not yet have an actual user base, it is an interesting example of a project that is driven at the same time by research interests (usable p2p encrypted instant messaging in the context of resilient communications and blackouts) and by activist- and community-based motivations (the team members are frequent participants of Circumvention Tech, now Internet Freedom Festival, and are collaborating with the Guardian project, GNUNet, Unlike Us and Open Internet Tools). This community-building dimension with relevant actors is understood by the Briar developers as a dynamic that will structure developments in the near future, as an important motivation for developers:

> The sense of community is really important to have everybody motivated to work on these projects that are very open-ended, and somehow against the flow that society in general is taking… where there is less and less privacy

and more and more social control. It's nice to be reminded to know that other people are going in the same direction (Michael Rogers, Briar lead developer).

Ultimately, Briar is a sociotechnical experiment (alongside other projects from the galaxy of p2p encryption tools, such as the MIT-based Vuvuzela) and as such, illustrates important questions about the limitations and problems of p2p-based secure messaging, while at the same time showing its potential.

CONCLUSIONS: THE DIFFICULT DAY-TO-DAY PRACTICE OF THE 'PROMISE OF INTERNET EQUALITY'

In the galaxy of end-to-end encrypted messaging tools, decentralised ones appear to be subject to the highest degree of experimentation. If we consider this in a historical perspective, we see that the nexus between p2p and secure messaging today is an important manifestation of a longstanding and complex tension related to decentralised technologies – between their alluring promise of interoperability, horizontality, mutual help, self-governance, participation, reduced control by governments and the private sector, and, on the other hand, the multiple technical and economic challenges standing in the way of its widespread implementation, including the 'chicken and egg' problem of user motivation vs technical dependency on the number of users, and the difficulty of how to manage users' reputation and identity.

As the 'promise of Internet equality' (Agre 2003) of p2p technologies remains strong, particularly in specific activist and academic settings, seeking solutions to the different challenges posed by decentralised architectures to encrypted messaging is at the heart of a substantial portion of current privacy and anonymity research. However, there seems to be a gap between academic research fields and activist needs and questions:

It's one of the greatest unsolved mysteries [...] The computer science problems that activists care about are not necessarily close to the computer science problems that are prestigious to work on in computer science. For me, as an activist working on usable communication this is a great unsolved problem (Elijah Sparrow, LEAP).

Some projects, such as LEAP, Delta Chat (see Chapter 4) and Briar are trying to work in between the two; the NEXTLEAP project, via the work of the authors and other members of the consortium, has operated in the same direction, with our focus on activist use-cases (both high- and low-risk) and collaboration with open-source developer communities (Autocrypt).

We have selected the Briar case among decentralised secure messaging projects as we believe it demonstrates well the new potential of peer-to-peer encrypted messaging applications, as well as the challenges presented by p2p. However, in a broader context where net neutrality is put under increasing strain, and Internet censorship around the world is growing and becoming more pervasive, it is important to acknowledge that some of Briar's technical and social solutions can be reused, and possibly improved upon, by other projects. Alongside Briar, several projects sharing its foundational interest in decentralised architectures show a trend towards reinventing the Internet backbone itself, and migrating to other networks – seeking a freer, more decentralised Internet that would be less controlled by both governments and private corporations. New projects develop and define themselves as real 'ecosystems' suitable for any kind of data exchange, such as Matrix.org (see Chapter 4), CJDNS,[19] i2p[20] and Yggrasil,[21] decentralised and encrypted network protocols that have a growing user base in countries like Russia, as a response to the country's current trend towards more centralised control over the Internet.

As the secure messaging field grapples with the issue of delegating too much trust to the creators of centralised IMs (an illustration of this has been the Pavel Durov vs Moxie Marlinspike case, described in Chapter 2) or to the infrastructures they manage, p2p messaging applications seek to somehow *re-distribute* the trust between humans and protocols. However, our research on this type of secure messaging systems has shown that many users are still very much bound to centralised architectures, except for specific technical communities or openly anti-authoritarian activists.

NOTES

1 E.g., Telegram chats of Pirate Party Russia, Cybersecurity chat, internal Rublacklist chat

2 And questioned/challenged this label in Chapter 1.

3 See projects such as Secure Scuttlebutt: https://scuttlebutt.nz.

4 https://zerotier.com.

5 https://chatons.org.

6 https://joinmastodon.org.

7 See Chapter 4.

8 Discussion at the Citizen Lab Summer Institute, session on armed conflicts and information control, July 2017.

9 See above: https://www.scuttlebutt.nz, a 'decentr(alised) secure gossip platform'.

10 https://github.com/ssbc/handbook.scuttlebutt.nz/blob/master/principles/legacy.md.

11 E.g., in the frame of a 'corollary' project of NEXTLEAP, in January 2018 we interviewed 28 Ukrainian and Crimean journalists, tech workers and activists.

12 See, e.g., the 2017 wave of interest in Tox messenger among the tech community in Kyiv, Ukraine.

13 https://beakerbrowser.com.

14 https://briarproject.org.

15 https://youbroketheinternet.org/secure-email#pond.

16 https://ricochet.im.

17 We will discuss in the final chapter how this and other similar strategies fall into a tendency which we define as the 'opportunistic turn' in encryption.

18 The authors participated in a usability workshop for Briar at University College London in February 2017. Eleven people took part in the workshop, all of them being UCL PhD or postdoctoral students in computer science or usability. We tested several functionalities, such as **key exchange**, invitations for a one-to-one chat, group chat creation, blacklisting and changing the 'trust level' of contacts.

19 https://github.com/cjdelisle/cjdns.

20 https://geti2p.net/en.

21 https://yggdrasil-network.github.io.

4

FEDERATION: TREADING THE LINE BETWEEN TECHNICAL COMPROMISE AND IDEOLOGICAL CHOICE

WITH THE GROWING POPULARITY OF THE SO-CALLED 'FEDIVERSE', MAINLY known by its main projects, Mastodon[1] and Pleroma,[2] the introduction of OTRv4 and the vibrant scene of 'chat-over-email' projects, federated architectures are currently experiencing a phase of increased development and use. They are presented as alternatives, on the one hand, to centralised applications that introduce a 'single point of failure' in the network and lack interoperability, and on the other hand, to the p2p apps that necessitate higher levels of engagement, expertise and responsibility from the user (and her device). Federation is sometimes described as an ambitious technopolitical project; federated architectures open up the 'core-set' of protocol designers and involve a new kind of actor, the system administrator, responsible for maintaining the cluster of servers necessary for federated networks. Federation is believed to help alleviate the very high degree of personal responsibility held by a centralised service provider, while at the same time distributing this responsibility and the 'means of computing'[3] – the material and logistical resources needed by the system – with different possible degrees of engagement, favouring the freedom of users to choose between different solutions and servers.

As the previous chapter has also shown, the community of developers involved in the field of secure messaging is conducting lively debates about the limits and potentials of decentralised protocols – debates which we have retraced online. The discussions of the tensions between centralisation and more distributed architectural forms, such as federation, go hand-in-hand with debates over standards. Supporters of federated solutions claim that reusing existing standardised protocols or developing new open standards can enhance interoperability and solve the problem of 'messaging silos' (Kent 2019). Indeed, federated architectures appear to be well-suited to promoting localism and community-oriented smaller solutions, whose business model does not depend on the sheer numbers of users and the availability of their data for harvesting and aggregation. On the other hand, according to advocates of centralised solutions, federation can present problems in terms of security, as it is harder to audit all the different implementations of a federated protocol and ensure that all servers are well configured.[4] Indeed, federated messaging solutions add a layer of complexity to the governance of the sociotechnical networks they structure, as they introduce the need for the decentralised administration of servers (or 'instances').

This chapter retraces debates about federation in encrypted messaging and analyses the shaping of federation as both an infrastructural and a social experiment, one that seeks a compromise between the distribution of responsibilities onto a larger number of actors, high levels of security, and better usability. We discuss federation as a political as well as a technical project that recognises the dangers inherent to centralised solutions but suggests a middle ground between centralisation and full-fledged distribution as in the case of peer-to-peer tools, the latter considered as requiring a steeper learning curve. In the chapter, we will analyse two approaches to federation. Firstly, we examine projects that develop new protocols, such as OMEMO and Matrix. org. Then, we analyse the 'ecological' approach to protocol development, which consists of **upcycling** older protocols and existing open standards, with the example of 'Chat-over-email' projects such as Delta Chat. The chapter shows how community-managed infrastructures and practices of 'social encryption' are used to enhance security beyond encryption protocols. We also analyse federation as a way to make messaging apps resilient to censorship, a factor that plays a more and more important role for users living in repressive contexts.

DECENTRALISING TO WHAT EXTENT?
THE 'DEPENDENCIES' CONTROVERSY REVISITED

When it comes to the community of developers debating online, the tensions between centralisation and federation are paralleled by debates over standards; the discussions have as a *fil rouge* the controversy about 'dependencies' which we introduced in the case of Signal, and the impact of different aspects of dependency for users' Internet freedoms.

A well-known argument in favour of centralisation – and against standards – was made by Moxie Marlinspike, Signal's lead developer, in a previously introduced (Chapter 2) blogpost (Marlinspike 2016), which attracted considerable attention and was widely quoted by developers, trainers and advanced users as a reason to opt for centralisation. According to this point of view, centralisation offers a better control 'by infrastructure' or 'by design', while federation can be 'dangerous' in terms of security, as it is hard to audit all the different implementations of the protocol and ensure correct updates. This first argument therefore frames the debate in terms of governance of a given project and its implementations. According to Marlinspike, it is the evolution of the market of end-to-end encrypted messengers that demands centralisation:

> One of the controversial things we did with Signal early on was to build it as
> an unfederated service [...] it's entirely possible to build a federated Signal
> Protocol based messenger, but I no longer believe that it is possible to build
> a competitive federated messenger at all (Marlinspike 2016).

Marlinspike argues that only centralised solutions can satisfy constantly changing consumer demand and the overall instant messaging 'ecosystem'. Interestingly, he explains the success of current popular online communication systems as a result of the progressive evolution of federated protocols into centralised services (he uses, more precisely, the word 'cannibalisation'):

> It's what Slack did with IRC, what Facebook did with email, and what
> WhatsApp has done with XMPP. In each case, the federated service is stuck

in time, while the centralised service is able to iterate into the modern world and beyond (Marlinspike 2016).

According to Marlinspike, decentralisation seems to bring about more problems in keeping older and newer versions of an application interoperable. Michael Rogers, Briar's lead developer (see Chapter 3), tends to agree when he explains why the Briar app public release took longer than expected:

> We have an app that runs, it's fairly stable, it looks like a fairly complete finished application. The reason that we do not release it now is because we need to change the data format and protocol details, and keeping interoperability with older versions in the decentralised network when you're changing data format and protocol details is really difficult. So we want to postpone having to deal with that problem as late as possible by just doing limited test until those things stabilize before doing public releases (Michael Rogers, Briar lead developer – January 2017).

Thus, the Briar team implements 'expiry dates' into its releases in order to make it technically impossible to communicate between users of newer and older versions. This problem was also present in the case of a federated messaging ecosystem, Matrix.org, during its transition towards end-to-end encryption, when a multitude of older clients became incompatible with e2e. Therefore, decentralisation supposes a certain amount of coordination and community-oriented effort.

With respect to federation, another argument in favour of centralisation concerns the security that comes with greater control over changes in protocols and server administration. Marlinspike claims that social centralisation is needed to successfully respond to unsolved challenges, such as metadata protection:

> If anything, protecting metadata is going to require innovation in new protocols and software. Those changes are only likely to be possible in centralised environments with more control, rather than less. Just as making the

changes to consistently deploy end to end encryption in federated protocols like email has proved difficult, we're more likely to see the emergence of enhanced metadata protection in centralised environments with greater control (Marlinspike 2016).

Peter Sunde, co-founder of The Pirate Bay and developer of the Heml.is messaging app, whom we have already met in Chapter 2, agrees – despite his preference for federated architectures, which were the initial model envisaged for Heml. is – that centralised control over servers may help enhance users' privacy (social graphs, metadata):

> The idea to begin with [when developing Heml.is messaging app] was to do federated servers, but then we realized that it was not possible because we also wanted to protect social graphs of how people communicate and in order to do that we needed to make sure that we have control over the servers ... All these ideas and technological solutions are always a trade-off (Peter Sunde, Heml.is).

The previously discussed trade-off between security and usability (Norman 2009; Cranor and Garfinkel 2005; Yee 2004) also reappears when it comes to older federated protocols, such as XMPP. Despite the fact that this protocol is defined by its promoters as a 'living standard', in Marlinspike's words, due to its capacity for protocol extensions, it is often criticised for its weak support of rich media and for the difficulty of developing it for mobile uses. Due to the relative freedom developers have to deploy a variety of XMPP-based clients, XMPP suffers – according to Marlinspike – from fractured client support, and the difference between various XMPP clients results in lack of consistency regarding feature support in various clients. This may create confusion for users:

> Someone's choice to use an XMPP client or server that doesn't support video or some other arbitrary feature doesn't only affect them, it affects everyone who tries to communicate with them. It creates a climate of uncertainty,

never knowing whether things will work or not. In the consumer space, fractured client support is often worse than no client support at all, because consistency is incredibly important for creating a compelling user experience (Marlinspike 2016).

However, developers from the PGP and the XMPP/OTR community, and the growing galaxy of 'Chat-over-Email' projects, strongly oppose this critique from Signal in their own blog posts and on a number of mailing lists where developer discussions take place. For example, a developer involved in the Conversations and OMEMO projects argues that the 'extensibility of XMPP is not a danger in itself. A good extension will spread naturally. Moreover, there's a permanent incentive to innovate in XMPP'. This has led developers in certain communities to try to standardise versions of the Signal protocol applied to federated projects; for example, the OMEMO protocol has been submitted to the XMPP Foundation in order to be standardised.

Signal developers believe that older protocols like PGP and XMPP actually harm user security and should be abandoned; and as Chapter 2 shows, the Signal protocol has been crucial in boosting updates to these older protocols and setting up a 'required minimum' of features for instant messaging applications. Signal has deeply affected the market of instant messaging, not only by 'informally standardising' a number of technical features, but also by attracting financial investments towards centralised projects as opposed to decentralised or distributed ones:

I believe that the problems with decentralisation we have right now are more a problem of the lack of funding than a conceptual problem that decentralisation does not work. Most XMPP clients are developed by volunteers in their spare time. And it's kinda obvious that one single developer that donates two hours a week of his spare time to develop an IM client is unable to compete with five full time developers like Open Whisper Systems for example (ChatSecure developer).

GIVING (OR RECLAIMING) CHOICE, DISTRIBUTING
RESPONSIBILITY

Opposed to Signal's strong discourse on 'consumer space', which has modified the scene of secure messaging by inviting to the discussion table a more
varied set of actors than the techno-idealists and crypto-enthusiasts of the
early days, are discourses such as that of the LEAP team, which strongly
defends open federated protocols (as opposed to self-made, closed or partly
closed protocols):

> Moxie came out recently and 'arrowed' himself as a centralist in his blogpost
> about this topic. I disagree with him. His argument is that... open feder-
> ated protocols are simply too slow to adapt and they are too difficult to
> implement because there's too many different players, you make a change
> and you break everything [...] I think just because there are examples
> in the past of being difficult to change protocols does not mean that the
> idea of open protocols is dead. I think there's definitely ways in which we
> can recognize the problems with open protocols so that we still can have
> interoperability but not be locked in an unchanging [ecosystem] (Elijah
> Sparrow, LEAP developer).

The arguments put forward by our respondents in favour of federated architectures concern several aspects: first of all, the danger of trusting one person
or entity behind the service ('putting all your eggs in one basket', as Elijah puts
it) and potentially enabling easier metadata leaks. From this standpoint, the
personal responsibility of a centralised service provider is very high and puts
the provider itself and all its users at risk. A federated solution would help to
distribute this responsibility:

> Signal is trusted because it's Moxie, but if I was the government I could
> force Moxie to hand over the keys and tell him like... you can't say anything
> anymore. But he would at least shoot the system down, like the case with
> Lavabit, the email service that Snowden used. That guy closed the service

down instead of working for the government. But most people will not do that... The way to solve it is to have a federated system like you have your own data at your own location (Peter Sunde, Heml.is).

Even though developers agree on the fact that decentralised systems are harder to design, their motivation to work on federated systems seems to be grounded in both the political and technical aspects of federation, first and foremost the 'empowerment' it can offer to the user by providing the means to control their own data and enable better metadata protection:

> I know there are journalist organizations that run their own XMPP server, primarily using desktop clients. I'd like to allow people to run their own infrastructure around their own data as much as possible. There are other great tools that do encryption, at that point you can use WhatsApp or Facebook, they are using the same Signal protocol. But you're still not owning your data, all the metadata is controlled by a centralised system, they know all your contacts, who you're messaging at what time. [...] Other people feel differently. Like Moxie really wanted to do a vertically integrated centralised solution because it's a lot more usable if you control all the technology pieces (ChatSecure developer).

Another argument in favour of federated architectures – this time, as opposed to both centralised and purely p2p ones – emphasises the freedom for users to choose between various services, as Matrix's lead developer explains:

> I had a long running dispute with Moxie Marlinspike about [decentralisation versus centralisation] basically because Matrix obviously is an interoperable decentralised network and he considers that a privacy risk because you can't control the whole network, there may be implementations that may not be secure, there may be bugs that you cannot control, that leak sensitive information and that is a thing for privacy. I would argue however that decentralisation is also important for freedom, and the user's ability to pick which service to use (Matrix lead developer).

In this sense, federated protocols are often compared to political systems, where users can 'vote with their feet' by leaving a server in favour of a better one. Federated protocols are said to provide better accountability and better control over the service providers. Moreover, the ease of migration offered by interoperable environments makes it possible for users to choose a better option without losing their social graphs.

> There's no way to establish any kind of accountability for centralised services that lock people in. It is very easy if people have federated services, they can just pick up and leave if their provider does something they may not like. So tomorrow Signal started to do that people were critical of, it would be very difficult to get people out of Signal to use something else (Elijah Sparrow, LEAP developer).

Indeed, our user interviews revealed among frequent XMPP users a peculiar attitude of 'proximity' with XMPP service providers, as well as a specific set of feedback practices between users and providers. The possibility of developing a client on top of an open federated protocol, with features needed by a specific user community, was also underlined as a positive aspect of federation, albeit that it limits the usage of these solutions to a more tech-savvy audience, or else requires localisation efforts.

Unlike developers, many high-risk users did not bring up the need for federation explicitly, but they raised it implicitly in how they formed trust relationships. Federation provides a suitable infrastructure for specific communities to organise without having to rely on intermediaries. In this sense, developers, high-risk users and trainers tend to build associations between specific configurations of political organisation and of technical infrastructure. For example, some developers and trainers justified federation as mirroring the organisation of anti-authoritarian social movements, which echoes w the conceptual analysis of the sociotechnical meanings of decentralisation proposed by Nathan Schneider (2019). Thus, there was a preference for systems that were considered politically trustworthy p by high-risk users; federation was generally viewed as positive in this regard by a minority of high-risk users. These users expressed concerns about centralised systems collecting their metadata, although few realised this would also be possible in most federated systems, albeit in a distributed form – which attests to the important ideological component included in the notion of federation.

Some developers believed the choice of federation to be inherently connected to not collecting metadata, and felt that models existed which were both usable and decentralised:

> With Signal, it's impossible to create a decentralised system because phone numbers aren't decentralised. With XMPP it's like an email address. Even users who aren't technologically savvy can understand this is my user ID, and this is my server (OMEMO lead developer).

The 'chat-over-email' paradigm is also based on understanding the risks associated with synchronising contact books and depending on mobile operators. Moreover, federated projects promote interoperability as a solution to the walled gardens of secure messaging applications. Building a potentially open system, pluggable and modifiable according to the needs of a community, also means removing parts of the work from the developer team.[5]

The remainder of this chapter explores three federated protocols and the applications based on them: Conversations (and OMEMO protocol), Matrix. org, and the 'chat-over-email' effort, with projects such as Autocrypt/Delta Chat, LEAP and Pixelated. Through the case studies, we aim to explore the tensions between the elements of technical innovation and the politico-ideological choices that shape particular definitions of 'freedom', both for users and developers, in federated arrangements.

Conversations and OMEMO: Bringing future secrecy to XMPP

The federated end-to-end encrypted messaging app Conversations is based on XMPP and OTR/OMEMO.[6] This project could be defined as a 'one-man app', its core developer working alone, driven by his own technical curiosity and relying on his own previous experience as user of XMPP and OTR:[7]

> I am an XMPP user. When I got my first Android phone there were no good examples available for the platform. I actually decided to write my own app. I did maybe 95% of the code by myself. I do have occasional contributors on github but was pretty much alone (Daniel, Conversations/OMEMO lead developer).

Conversations is an end-to-end encrypted instant messaging application that offers users a choice of three encryption algorithms and an unencrypted (TLS-only) mode. This design solution is unique in the field and makes Conversations an interesting case-study. The choice between three different algorithms was, as one of the Conversations developers explained to us, his version of an answer to the interoperability problem; when he started working on Conversations, end-to-end encryption methods were available for different clients, and Conversations tried to be compatible with them all, so it had to implement OpenPGP as well as OTR.

As a third choice for encryption, the OMEMO protocol (recursive acronym for OMEMO – Multi-End Message and Object Encryption) was created with the idea of providing future and forward secrecy and deniability and gives the possibility of message synchronisation and offline delivery, which are both important features for a federated protocol. According to its creator, OMEMO was developed to solve specific limitations and problems that existed both in OpenPGP and in OTR:

> One of the main limitations of OTR was that it didn't work with multiple clients. If you are logged on your mobile client as well as your desktop client, OTR does not work. Open PGP had downsides as well: there wasn't any verification built in, it did not have any forward secrecy or any other nice crypto traits that you wanted to have (Daniel, Conversations/OMEMO lead developer).

OMEMO was developed during the Google Summer of Code in 2015, using the LibSignal library.[8] Daniel, Conversations and OMEMO's lead developer, acknowledges the lack of standardisation and lack of specification of the Signal

Protocol, which we noted in Chapter 2 ('The underlying cryptography was not very well documented, and we were just basically making through the library'). However, Daniel was able to work with the library well enough to implement the Double Ratchet, the up-and-coming 'golden standard' of instant messaging promoted by the widespread acceptance of the Signal Protocol:

> I personally don't have a very strong cryptography background, I try to rely on what's already there, what's already popular right now. Like Signal protocol with double ratchet is quite widespread these days and seems to be well received by various cryptographers. So it makes sense to base OMEMO on something that's similar (Daniel, Conversations/OMEMO lead developer).

OMEMO, being, in Daniel's words, an 'XMPP wrap around LibSignal', brings Signal's innovative features, such as future secrecy, to XMPP. In this sense, protocol design choices for Conversations and OMEMO are determined by the overall development and state of the art of modern cryptography (see Chapter 2: 'Signal does it, WhatsApp does it.'). Instant messaging, over the development of OMEMO, is understood as a set of tools for the exchange of information that is intrinsically 'temporary', and users are likely to favour a feature such as future secrecy over the possibility of permanently accessing their archives. However, Conversations does not support the function that leads to the disappearing of messages, even though users, according to our interviews, have been asking for it. Instead, Conversations opts to entrust users with more choice, but also with the increased responsibility that comes with it:

> If you are looking into data hygiene, not keeping around the history is something that you should do for yourself on your own device according to your own rules and Conversations has a setting that allows you to delete all messages both sent and received on your device and regulate intervals, for example a month or a week. It is a more honest solution. Because you can control when these messages are deleted. It is up to each individual user to decide what to do with the data (Daniel, Conversations/OMEMO lead developer).

Interestingly, this approach of entrusting users with both choice and responsibility differs from the automatic, or 'opportunistic' turn in encryption embraced by applications aimed at the general public (e.g. Signal), whose creators actively work on concealing a lot of options from users to make the application more immediate and comfortable to use. Conversations seems to be targeted more towards those users for whom freedom equates to having more control over the application and, in the words of one of our respondents, 'see[ing] encryption happening'.[9]

The kind of 'freedom' that Conversations aims at giving users extends not only to the server, but also to the encryption scheme that they prefer or are more used to. The intention is to help attract more users, regardless of the encryption algorithms that their peers support, as Conversations can talk to OTR- and to OpenPGP-only clients. The language elements of 'user choice' return here: 'They can choose Open PGP and will not have forward secrecy but will have some other features in return'. [Daniel, Conversations lead developer]

This freedom of choice is, as we have demonstrated in the section above, is mentioned as one of the advantages of federation. It also gives users the possibility to gain certain security, privacy or usability features that exist in some protocols but not in others. For example, OpenPGP offers archiving, which, for low-risk users, may sometimes be more important than future- and forward secrecy:

> There are a couple of users who don't want to move away from OpenPGP because all these modern encryption schemes that provide forward secrecy do not have the ability to retrieve your messages, so when you're setting up a new client you can't access the archive with all your messages. And OpenPGP allows you to do that. That's arguably a very niche use case, less secure in some ways because it doesn't have forward secrecy and stuff like that, but some users really prefer to have the ability to access the archive if they are not under high risk (Daniel, Conversations/OMEMO lead developer).

As the app's developer explains it, Conversations is aimed at a specific user-group, that – if we were to go back to categories we questioned but found useful earlier in the book – could be defined as high-knowledge, low-risk and privacy-aware users, who strongly support XMPP, federation and open source, and opt for Google-free and privacy-preserving solutions such as the minimisation of data storage, with both technical and ideological components subtending their choices. While applications such as Signal, Telegram and Wire are arguably starting to be considered as mainstream, and are often covered in the media, in the case of Conversations, user enrolment happens via specific digital security training sessions, advice from tech-savvy friends, personal technical knowledge and interest in XMPP and federation. These users are, in turn, introducing their close network and peer groups to the app via word-of-mouth dynamics.

OMEMO is not yet a standardised protocol, though it has already been adopted by a number of XMPP clients (listed on a dedicated website).[10] At the time of writing (16 September 2019), the website lists 18 XMPP clients fully supporting OMEMO and 33 clients that are currently working on being compatible with OMEMO. OMEMO has been submitted to the XMPP Foundation for standardisation and is currently at the first stage of the standardisation process.

However, our interviews with the developer teams of both Conversations and ChatSecure have revealed that these projects, though well known within the XMPP scene (developers mention that they regularly attend XMPP-related events), are almost invisible within more hybrid events aimed at privacy advocates and high-risk users and other stakeholders (Internet governance organisations, lawyers, researchers), such as, for instance, the Internet Freedom Festival or RightsCon. These applications could have had a wider adoption, especially given the strong modern-state cryptography implemented in both tools; however, their authors remain disconnected from the 'high-risk, low-tech' communities. Media coverage is also partly responsible for that disconnect: both applications are much less visible in non-tech-savvy oriented media, and cannot draw on the support of well-known public figures such as Edward Snowden, or organisations such as EFF, AccessNow or Tactical Tech. The latter are more eager to cover centralised applications (except for the Tor browser) and are *de facto* not involved in advocacy for technical decentralisation or federation.

Matrix.org: Facing the interoperability problem

Lyon, France, 25 May 2017: Ksenia attends the European Lab session on privacy-enhancing technologies and decentralised identity management systems. At some point, an interesting discussion takes place, which illustrates the state of the art in the field of encrypted messaging quite well. The panel moderator, himself a user of multiple encrypted messaging tools and protocols including PGP, Signal, Wire and Jabber, asks the audience: 'How many messaging applications do you use on your mobile phone?' After a brief round of answers from the public, he counts that among the forty people present, the average number of messaging applications is five per person, while several people say that they regularly use more than seven messaging applications. This question allows him to bring to the table the important problem of digital 'silos' (Kent 2019): how do people communicate in this 'mess of messengers', being separated by the walled gardens (Musiani 2016) of their favourite messaging clients, but also, more deeply, by various encryption protocols that are incompatible with each other.

While Conversations suggests a solution for interoperability between encryption protocols (OpenPGP/OTR/OMEMO), it still runs over XMPP and requires users to have an account on an XMPP server (or 'even better, run [their] own XMPP server for [them] and [their] friends', as OMEMO's inventor puts it). However, interoperability remains a problem for users of centralised messaging applications (Kent 2019). Individual projects have attempted to solve the interoperability problem, such as by bridging Jabber – a free IM service based on XMPP – to centralised applications. For example, the Russian Pirate Party has developed a 'Jabber bot' for Telegram, that helps Pirate Party members who do not trust Telegram to continue communicating within their community using Jabber.[11]

Another project that addresses the interoperability problem is Matrix.org, which works on giving users the possibility to bridge various messaging applications and let users connect without laying on them the 'burden' of having to migrate from their favourite tools. The underlying idea of Matrix.org is meant to go beyond an instant messaging application; it is framed by its developers as an ecosystem that could be used for any kind of data sharing:

> The model is very much inspired by the phone network, in terms of the phone network being a global way to exchange communication data. But in the end it's closed, it's not open, it's quite centralised to the telcos. So we wanted to create a complementary network which has the openness and the decentralisation baked in (Matthew Hodgson, Matrix lead engineer).

The main goal of the project, as underlined in several articles, is to 'create an architecture that tackles the interoperability problems that were not addressed by previous approaches'. This interoperability is meant to become a substantial comparative advantage and enrolment factor for users: 'where IRC has a high barrier to entry, requiring you to know exactly what server you're connecting to and configure accordingly, Matrix would let you associate with as many public identities as you're willing to share (phone number, email address, Facebook, Google, and so on), as long as they support the Matrix standard. Otherwise, it requires no setup – it's just like if you were using any consumer messaging service' (Weinberger 2014).

Matrix is an open-source, non-profit project under Apache license, and was financed by Amdocs until 2017. Since then, the Matrix team has created its own foundation, called 'New Vector', that offers consulting services to those who want to use hosting services within Matrix or use Matrix for commercial purposes:

> We offer help to build bridges between various messaging platforms. If I have an enterprise where everyone is using Slack, I can pay huge amounts of money to Slack to buy their corporate solutions, or I can pay a couple of bucks per month to Matrix to maintain bridges (Matthew Hodgson, Matrix lead engineer).

Recently, New Vector obtained funding from an Ethereum startup, and Matrix attracted interest from the French government that asked for support in deploying an internal messenger for civil servants, built on Matrix/Riot.[12] As of 16 September 2019, the team counted sixteen members, eleven of them based in London and five in France. They support Android, iOS and Desktop versions. Currently there are 5000+ chat rooms registered on Matrix, focused mostly on 'the techno-privacy aware community, computer scientists and normal developers', in the words of Matrix's lead developer.

Unlike LEAP (which will be addressed in the last part of this chapter) and Signal, the Matrix team does not take an explicitly political or ideological stand and does not aim at providing software for specific audiences with a political agenda or engaged in political arenas, such as activists. The creator of Matrix positions his team as 'sort of moderate, really centrist', and adds:

> I am very sympathetic to the human rights issue and privacy but we haven't
> set up with Matrix to build something like Tor or Signal or Ricochet or any
> of those tools which are optimized very specifically for privacy at all costs.
> Instead we're trying to do the best we can and be very mindful of it, whilst
> also building an ecosystem that works and is practical (Matthew Hodgson,
> Matrix lead engineer).

Matrix's creator identifies his position as a kind of 'liberal pluralism', which is reflected in the very architecture as well as the users of his system. From the point of view of the architecture, it is a federated system that bridges a great variety of different messaging tools, thus leaving a certain amount of freedom to users, allowing them to retain their usual interface, while making it possible for them to connect with others. As Matrix's lead developer points it, Matrix is trying to respond to the problems of walled gardens, produced by the quick and somewhat 'chaotic' development of the messaging ecosystem, especially on mobile. As an illustration of his objective, during our interview, he showed us his mobile phone with around 10 different instant messaging applications (from Wire, Threema, WhatsApp and iMessage to Signal).

In terms of user pluralism, Matrix has a variety of rooms addressing a wide variety of subjects, from cryptography and open source, cryptocurrency and decentralisation to psychological help, furries, subcultures and fan communities, left-wing groups and alt-right Donald Trump supporter rooms. Two of the main lingering problems for Matrix are managing spam and maintaining a decentralised reputation system – issues that, according to Hodgson, are still open for research, and need to be supported by a 'morally neutral' positioning.

Within the ecosystem of mail and messaging applications, Matrix identifies itself as a compromise, in a positive sense, between centralised and completely decentralised systems, that seeks to provide satisfactory security solutions while running a partially decentralised system:

> Signal is pretty much saying: we'll run it [Signal] as a centralised service therefore we can guarantee its security. Email in the current state has no privacy and security but it's being 100% decentralised. So we're basically a middle-ground approach (Matthew Hodgson, Matrix lead engineer).

For the main developer of Matrix, the relation between decentralisation and security is a thorny issue: according to him, 'the two things definitely pull against each other'. He sees email as an insecure system, because of the independence of email service providers. In this sense, an attempt to introduce a standardised, automatic mail encryption, that could be implemented by various **Mail User Agents** with relatively low resources, could be a possible step against many passive attacks. Due to the convergence of interests in this regard, Matrix was invited to present its current work at the Autocrypt hackathon in December 2016; this event gathered different projects that discussed not only email encryption but also decentralised reputation and identity systems, such as Scuttlebutt. Introducing encryption through headers also becomes a form of 'governance' via federation, between the multitude of mail service providers: this kind of governance, unlike Signal, is based on a very detailed specification, which could be approved by the galaxy of email service providers who take part in the Autocrypt effort.

For Matrix as a decentralised system, the frequency of passive attacks made the implementation of end-to-end encryption a crucial step; it was also a specific way to establish trust within federated infrastructures, where trust is spread across a large number of server administrators:

> In decentralised systems, you end up with a large attack surface. If you were running a server and I am running a server, and I send a message, the message is on both of our servers that means that we have to trust a sysadmin of both

of the servers. In a big room with 5000 people, and, say, 1000 servers, you have an even bigger problem. If you're sending something sensitive or private, it will be shared across all of the servers. Getting end-to-end encryption is critical so that the servers get an encrypted copy of the message rather than the real message so that you don't need to worry about system administrators spying on messages (Matthew Hodgson, Matrix lead engineer).

As a federated project, Matrix is deployed on a multitude of servers (according to its lead developer, more than 15,000 as of 21 December 2018) that are not under the control of the Matrix team. Moreover, as Hodgson explained in the interview, each server can have its own privacy settings and policies for collaborating (or not) with lawful interception. Thus, self-hosting is promoted by Matrix as a way to increase security, in addition to enabling encryption. In the case of Matrix, end-to-end encryption was adopted two years after the beginning of the project – while, as our research has shown, when a system has not been designed with end-to-end encryption from the very beginning, the transition is rather slow and difficult. In the case of Wire, originally built with no end-to-end encryption, the team had to remove part of the server-side code that still contained the possibility of a plain text message being sent before going fully open source. In the case of a decentralised system, the problem of implementation is even harder, as some of the older clients run with no encryption and additional steps must be taken in order not to block users who use older clients:

So by now it's an opt-in on a room basis. But once we're out of beta we'll be turning e2e on by default by every private room, and we'll have a proxy migration path for other clients so that simple clients that know nothing about cryptography can easily join and participate (Matthew Hodgson, Matrix lead engineer).

The protocol implemented for end-to-end encryption in Matrix is called Olm and is a version of the Signal Double Ratchet. Interestingly, while Wire had difficulties in implementing the Signal Protocol (see Chapter 2), Matrix did not encounter hostility or tensions from the Signal team,[13] except for an explicit condition to avoid using names or references to Signal (or its predecessor, Axolotl). Hodgson attributes the cause of this relatively successful collaboration with Signal to the political economy of open source and to the very architecture and nature of Matrix, which opens the possibility of bridging a large number of other projects:

> The difference between us and Wire is that Matrix.org initiative is non-profit and entirely open source. The Apache license that we use is aggressively permissive [...] And I spoke to Moxie and explained what we were doing. And he said: you're crazy, and if it works then go for it, it will be great, but you guys have fun doing that and I will keep doing Signal. He does not want to persecute us. [...] Whereas other companies, which are doing proprietary commercial messaging solutions even if some parts of it are open source, he [Moxie] will see them as competition. We are more like idealistic altruistic hippies who should probably fail while building this white elephant of Matrix, and if we don't it will be a good thing for everybody including him [Moxie]. So why not support us? (Matthew Hodgson, Matrix lead engineer).

Currently, Matrix.org[14] is working on minimising the spread of disinformation and spam. Indeed, while centralised platforms such as Twitter or Facebook are increasingly subject to critique for enabling the spread of disinformation and hate speech, federated alternatives, such as Mastodon or Pleroma seem to offer some ways to counter or minimise the spread of disinformation, by a mix of social and technical moderation by server or instance administrators. The Matrix team hopes to address this problem by deploying a reputational system and seeks a way for users to filter content by developing a system of open and modulable filters. Furthermore, as a response to the increased risk of Internet shutdowns in politically unstable regions, such as Belarus, Iran, Kirghizstan and others, in June 2020 Matrix released an alpha peer-to-peer version of its software, which is not dependent on an Internet connection provided by telecom operators.

Autocrypt: Email encryption as a community-building effort

Email remains stubbornly unencrypted, due chiefly to problems with key management. Proprietary closed-source projects offering 'encrypted email solutions' exist; however, they are not managing to solve the interoperability and fragmentation problem. End-to-end encryption in Protonmail, for instance, works only if both users have Protonmail installed; this is reminiscent of how centralised instant messaging clients work: binding users to specific applications. Furthermore, users' awareness of this constraint is unclear; our early-stage research showed that users do not always know about this particularity of Protonmail and think that all Protonmail emails are encrypted by default.

However, email 'remains the largest open federated identity and messaging eco-system, anchors the web, mobiles and continues to relay sensitive information between people and organisations'.[15] In the context of centralisation in the field of IM apps, with telephone numbers being massively used as unique identifiers, several initiatives have recently been launched to revive encrypted email, such as Autocrypt, pEp, the Google End-to-End project and LEAP/Pixelated. These efforts have not yet been finalised or have not reached widespread adoption; this process 'in-the-making' should be analysed, from an STS perspective, as a technosocial, community-building effort that may have important consequences for the whole encrypted messaging/mail ecosystem as it suggests a '(re)turn to federation' and proposes alternative approaches to identity and key management.

Because of its decentralised architecture, automatic email encryption implementation demands a strong community effort and the enrolment of a multitude of actors (namely, Mail User Agents-MUAs, and email service providers). These actors need to agree on the protocol, its documentation and modalities of implementation, but also its UI/UX features, logo, funding sources and so on.

Unlike centralised mobile applications for instant messaging, that can impose their own protocols (often unstandardised) and try to 'own' or capture users who interact within the IM app, the federated email ecosystem remains largely open. It blurs the borders between users and service providers, as the barrier of running a privately-owned email service has become lower, involving more people in the ecosystem. Migration costs from one email server to another are also relatively low, and users can shift identities or have several ones. Thus, there is fundamentally no way (nor will) to control all of the MUAs and service providers at both the technical and ideological levels. However, there are several ongoing attempts to create a tool that can connect different actors without centralising the whole ecosystem – an artefact that Michel Callon would probably consider a 'translation' tool.

One of the most recent innovations in this field is Autocrypt, a project run by an international group of email program developers and crypto enthusiasts from the open-source privacy-aware community. An Autocrypt plugin was added to the Mozilla Thunderbird email client in August 2019, marking an important step for this young project towards greater user adoption. Autocrypt provides a possible answer to the problem of key discovery, exchange and key management, thus addressing two important challenges: usability and 're-decentralisation'. Instead of keeping public keys on a centralised public key server (which may create vulnerability), and proposing that users retrieve, exchange and verify keys by themselves (which may create confusion) Autocrypt puts key material in the header of the email.

Usability-wise, this automatic key discovery process helps to solve important problems related to key exchange, verification and management. The part of our research focused on users showed that they rarely verify keys or can even define what a key is. High-risk users tend to verify the authenticity of their contacts when they receive notifications on an IM app about the changes in the key material, using 'real-life' non-cryptographic solutions such as voice calls or contacts over social networks. However, this behaviour is rare. And when it comes to email, advanced key verification rarely happens. Moreover, as our interviews with trainers show, the general tendency in the trainer community is to avoid explaining keys during informational security seminars, as 'the old metaphors of padlocks are not really clarifying what's going on there, and we waste a lot of time on it', as a French trainer from the hackerspace Le ReSet explains. The general turn to 'automatic' or opportunistic encryption makes the key discovery process invisible to the user, and this is seen by several trainers as a positive step towards the mass adoption of encryption; McLemon, a cryptotrainer from

Austria, points out that 'having encryption as a default mode means a user does not have to learn about all the math beyond the crypto [. This] is the key part in making encryption popular'.

The Autocrypt solution addresses the problem of centralised public key storage and proposes a new form of coordination or federation of the email app developer community, which has been for a long time rather dispersed and has not really had a place to 'meet each other', in the words of Autocrypt's promoters. In this sense, email headers become instruments of 'self-governance', communication and coordination of MUAs, leaving a lot of freedom to MUAs while providing a standard that helps to keep encryption working across different agents. The usability and federation of MUAs are interconnected, as scalability is necessary in order for automatic encryption to work, which implies collaboration between the multitude of third-party projects.

In order to work and to be spread widely, Autocrypt relies on the joint efforts of professional communities – service providers in one case; mail client developers in the other. In short, it relies on the widespread enrolment of email app developers. This community-based approach is very different from the one offered by Signal-like centralised applications, where the authors of the protocol seem to have greater control over the implementations, and various implementations do not offer interoperability.

Until recently, Autocrypt was focused on passive attacks only, primarily targeting a low-risk audience. However, this has served as only the first step towards providing more sophisticated solutions against active attacks and targeted surveillance: indeed, the most recent development of Autocrypt includes a solution against the active attacks of a network adversary.[16] Even though Autocrypt initially focused on low-risk users, the Autocrypt motto 'email encryption for everyone' implies in the longer term a benefit for high-risk users: mass adoption of email encryption makes both mass surveillance and targeted surveillance more expensive and harder. By now, Autocrypt has been supported by an important number of email app developers, and starting in June 2017, the Autocrypt specification has been adopted by a new project, Delta Chat, that brings the Autocrypt encryption scheme into the field of instant messaging, offering interoperability between email and the new instant messenger.

Delta Chat: Secure messaging over email as an Autocrypt offspring

The Delta Chat secure messaging application is the pioneer of what is now called the 'messaging-over-email' effort. Similar to Matrix, this project is driven by a push for social decentralisation aiming to unbind users from 'messenger silos', relying on the pre-existing email infrastructure to favour scalability to billions of email users. The general effort to reuse the interfaces of existing popular messaging apps (inspired by the Telegram and Signal UI) draws from the same core principle: avoid creating yet another silo and offer users something they already know and are familiar with, in order to minimise migration and to focus on protocol upcycling. In the words of Delta Chat's lead developer, 'Delta Chat's take is not so much in designing protocols but using existing federation. But of course, this in turn, is based on protocols, SMTP/IMAP, OpenPGP and others'.

Delta Chat's approach to social decentralisation includes specific approaches to teamwork and collaboration with other projects – from crypto libraries to decentralised file sharing solutions. While it originally started as the 'lone wolf' project of German developer Bjoern Petersen, Delta Chat soon joined other projects and has gradually become a collaborative effort drawing upon a galaxy of communities. Delta Chat claims a strong focus on usability and to that end interacts with user groups in various at-risk regions, from Ukraine to Cuba, Hong Kong, Taiwan and the MENA region.

Some of the sets of protocols used by Delta Chat are long-term standards (SMTP, IMAP, OpenPGP for instance), while others are in active development. In terms of protocol governance, one of the fundamental elements of Delta Chat that makes it 'pluggable' and interoperable with other applications is the Autocrypt specification, first released in December 2016 – a set of guidelines that 'describe how e-mail programs negotiate encryption capabilities using regular emails' (Holger Krekel, Delta Chat lead developer).

Several key contributors to Delta Chat have also been active in the Autocrypt community and both share a set of practices. Both have been quite 'loosely coordinated' with around a dozen active contributors, from developers and crypto library designers to UX/usability experts. These contributors, many of whom work on a voluntary basis, are mostly decentralisation or crypto enthusiasts, who have known each other from various offline hacker gatherings or online discussions and collaborations around email and IM encryption, decentralisation and certain politically engaged hacker circles, including 'activist tech collectives'. Moreover, many contributors to both efforts use Internet-Relay-Chat (IRC) on freenode, a major gathering point for open-source developments. The #autocrypt and #deltachat rooms each have 60–70 participants, and in September 2018 Delta Chat had around 5500 posted chat lines. Both efforts also use the github.com site and the 'git' versioning tool to collaborate, and to discuss and review each other's changes.

Even if the recent funding for Delta Chat provided by the Open Technology Fund since July 2018 has stabilised the core team working with Delta Chat, many regular and active contributors continue working without any official affiliation. Delta Chat seems to share a tacit agreement about certain modes of collaboration that avoid reproducing what is understood as the 'startup way', which attributes fixed roles to team members and establishes hierarchies within teams. Instead, the work is organised around a set of main components of Delta Chat, such as Core, Desktop, Android and iOS versions, legal and licensing efforts, as well as usability and need finding. Currently, Delta Chat operates more as a decentralised 'ecosystem' than as a messaging app: instead of offering a specific solution, it works towards bridging various solutions with the aforementioned components of Delta Chat. The priorities for development and collaboration are partly informed by fieldwork and constant informal communication with targeted user communities, mainly high-risk journalists and human rights activists and NGOs. Interestingly, while some of Delta Chat's development and collaboration decisions are pushed forward by various Delta Chat team members out of their personal technical or political preferences, others are also driven by the design of the current funding proposal, supported by the Open Technology Fund.

Delta Chat is also working with email service provider communities, pushing for certain changes, namely, to identify Autocrypt-friendly providers who currently support Delta Chat. Indeed, one of the drawbacks of the Autocrypt solution is the spam problem, with headers often being read as junk by email providers. Currently, Delta Chat is deepening its collaboration with activist-oriented email providers to work on new features such as automatic account creation, tailored for specific use-cases, for example those involving field missions for journalists and activists with self-destroying temporary accounts.

While being essentially a non-for-profit and activist-inspired project, Delta Chat aims to be usable by larger user communities. Recently the team has gained a Mozilla Public Licence in order to open up collaborations with for-profit actors: 'The move to MPL is meant to be more inviting for commercial collaborators as it is now easier to incorporate Delta Chat's core chat/contact and IMAP/SMTP/Autocrypt implementations in all kinds of offerings' (Holger Krekel, Delta Chat lead developer).

LEAP/Pixelated: An 'encryption as a human right' infrastructure for providers

As its website sums up, the LEAP project 'fights for the right to whisper'.[17] Indeed, in a less subdued way than several other projects analysed in this and previous chapters, the LEAP project is structured by a political vision, most of its members having previously been involved in so-called 'radical tech *collectifs*' (see Milan 2013). However, if LEAP's initial target was high-risk users, the scope of the project gradually has come to include a wider audience of Internet users, as LEAP frames encryption as a human right:

> Like free speech, the right to whisper is a necessary precondition for a free
> society. Without it, civil society and political freedom become impossible.
> As the importance of digital communication for civic participation increases,
> so does the importance of the ability to digitally whisper. LEAP is devoted
> to making the ability to whisper available to all Internet users.[18]

While Autocrypt engages email app developers and opts for an in-band approach, LEAP primarily addresses email service providers. The server-side part of LEAP, the LEAP Platform, is also called 'provider in a box' and is a 'set of complementary packages and server recipes automated to lower the barriers of entry for aspiring secure service providers'. The client-side part is called Bitmask, a cross-platform application including a local proxy that a standard email client can connect to, and an easy one-click Virtual Private Network (VPN) service. Bitmask offers full end-to-end encryption, while public keys are automatically discovered and validated. The LEAP project was developed in response to both the crisis of email encryption infrastructure, and usability issues that make it difficult for users to use encryption without compromising their confidentiality and the confidentiality of the people they communicate with.

LEAP's architecture and protocol design solutions have been forged through discussions with other tech collectives, questioning the 'coherence' between certain types of politics and architectural solutions, namely, anti-authoritarian leftist politics and peer-to-peer models. LEAP develops its own philosophy of decentralisation, that is far from being an apology for radical decentralisation or p2p, and quite clearly suggests that a third way is necessary:

> There are three architectural models: centralised, federated and peer-to-peer. And LEAP came out of a shared understanding [...] about the way in which people with certain type of politics, with anti-authoritarian politics, they bind their politics to a decentralised model and they believe very strongly that all of the technology must follow a decentralised model. And our critique of that was that there are a lot of technical problems with the decentralised model, and that you can't actually... the politics and the tech architecture... there is some correlation but trying to [correlate them directly] does not work at all. So for all these reasons and many more we were upset with how people from anti-authoritarian politics were mapping this directly to a decentralised architecture which we felt had potential but there are a lot of hard research problems that are unsolved (Elijah Sparrow, LEAP founder).

In response to problems found in both p2p and centralised models, LEAP proposes to initiate a transition of the whole modern encryption ecosystem towards open federated protocols – these can also become an important turn in Internet governance, as they can become an instrument to redistribute power relations and re-decentralise infrastructures, nowadays owned by a minority of big actors:

> We felt that we needed a revival of the 1990s. [The] 1990s were like before the craziness of the dotcoms, everything if you wanted to communicate you had to use an open protocol that was federated, that was the way everything worked. [...] We felt that ... the time was right to take some of the new innovations in the last 20 years and start to turn those into open protocols that can be federated and do not lock people... do not chain them to the monopoly powers of the Internet, Google, Amazon, Microsoft and Apple... (Elijah Sparrow, LEAP founder).

In this sense, LEAP refers to a specific vision of the history of the Internet(s), that postulates the existence of a 'golden age' of decentralised open protocols (Oram 2001) – a vision that is controversial within other communities, such as the one gathered around Signal. The same kind of 'nostalgic' turn to federation has been observed among Russian tech and privacy-aware user communities, from the growing interest in Matrix.org, to the revival of such formats as XMPP-based 'microblogging' as alternatives to Twitter. However, the early-stage federated protocols were accessible only to specific communities of tech-savvy users. Nowadays, as ChatSecure's lead developer noted in a previously cited quote, setting up and maintaining federated infrastructures for larger segments of the online population is far from easy due to a number of infrastructural, financial and human constraints. In this context, one of the main goals of LEAP is to spread federation by deploying 'kits' of interlaced protocols, sets of packages necessary for a quick deployment of a secure infrastructure:

> One reason that holds back the federated model is that properly hosting secure services on the web now is very difficult, beyond the reach of people who do not specialize in keeping their servers secure. So we want to be able to encapsulate all the skills and best practices for maintaining an infrastructure into an automated suite that allows people with moderate skill to be able to do it properly (Elijah Sparrow, LEAP founder).

LEAP is mostly built on existing open federated protocols;[19] the contribution of the project is understood by its members as the combination of these protocols and their 'translation', in Callon's sense, for easier deployment. LEAP is also interacting with other solutions, such as mixnets, in order to solve important 'hard' research problems, including how to keep keys up to date and reduce metadata leaks – problems that are, in fact, linked:

> Initial key discovery is only half of the problem. The harder half is your keys up to date. You have to be constantly refreshing them and that potentially leaking a lot of information. That's particularly where the metadata leaking becomes important. LEAP also works on it [to] build a mixnet infrastructure for different purposes – e-voting and email (Elijah Sparrow, LEAP founder).

As Conversations, LEAP aims at being 'backwards compatible', supporting older protocols and older clients without radical transition towards post-PGP protocols; it also aims at supporting different encryption protocols; however, currently, the only supported protocols are OpenPGP and S/MIME. As a consequence, LEAP-based solutions also lack important security properties, such as forward secrecy. However, this is not inherent to LEAP per se but is, more broadly, a problem of the actual state of the email encryption ecosystem; as Sparrow points out, it is 'baked in the OpenPGP as a protocol itself'. LEAP proposes an alternative solution to the lack of forward secrecy in OpenPGP, which consists in discarding the encryption and signature information once the message is obtained and re-encrypting it in a new format. Forward secrecy is inherent to the specifics of mobile and instant communication, but the LEAP team argues that email usage is very different, including having a different attitude to time and archiving: users do need archives in email, whereas disappearing messages are suitable and needed for IM communication.

On the client side, LEAP contributes to the development of solutions such as Pixelated, an automated mail encryption client which aims at bridging the gap in user experience between existing mainstream proprietary solutions and open-source tools based on a federated infrastructure with a strong encryption dimension ('that's the goal. Same user experience', says Sparrow). Indeed,

Pixelated is aimed at a specific audience of users with low technical expertise. As our interviews showed, this tool has been tested *inter alia* with a community of Brazilian farmers, a radical collective fighting to keep their land.[20] As Pixelated's UI/UX designer notices, the client has been developed for conditions of low-quality Internet connection, and for a user group that has few interactions with email and online services in general.

In Pixelated, key verification is invisible for users and happens automatically. When we assisted at the Pixelated usability workshop at the Chaos Communication Congress in December 2017 (33c3), it was interesting to observe the reaction of its audience (tech-savvy people, frequent GPG users) to Pixelated UI/UX. A number of participants remarked that they did not feel their emails had been encrypted because they had 'nothing to do'. To them, feeling secure meant the ability to 'see encryption happening', possibly with additional effort and user involvement; however, being a hosted/cloud solution, Pixelated is specifically built to place less trust on the client side. This solution turns out to be interesting for specific use-cases, such as journalism and situations of physical device threat/seizure:

> Let's say you're a journalist [...] If you are travelling and doing reporting and crossing borders, your situation changes dramatically. You probably don't have a device that's always in your presence that you may trust, and maybe you don't want to have one. So suddenly it makes sense to have a hosted version and to be able to say may be only on a temporary basis or on a permanent basis, I am gonna move my trust, my most sensitive things like my private keys that unlock my universe of communication archive, I'd like to move that to the web. And the unique thing about what we're doing with Pixelated and LEAP is that by moving that trust from your personal device to a server, you don't have to change your trust relationship with your email provider (Elijah Sparrow, LEAP founder).

CONCLUSIONS: COMMUNITY, COMPATIBILITY, CUSTOMISATION AND CARE — THE FOUR CS OF FEDERATION

Retracing recent debates on federation in encrypted messaging, this chapter has sought to analyse the shaping of federation as both an infrastructural and a social experiment. We have seen how, in the different examined projects, developers seek to achieve a compromise between high levels of security and better usability, in a constant dialogue with 'ideological' motivations such as distributing responsibilities onto a larger number of actors and offer particular versions of online freedom, such as giving users the choice of the level of autonomy they wish to achieve.

We suggest that a tentative systematisation and conceptualisation of what has been seen in this chapter can be attempted with what we will call the 'four Cs of federation': community, compatibility, customisation and care. We offer some conclusions about these four aspects below.

In terms of community, (self)-governance and advancement of federated projects implies an important community-driven effort and depends on engaging a variety of service providers and clients into accepting new open protocols or new libraries. Communication and consensus among various projects are needed in order to be able to advance in a federated environment. The transition towards next-generation encryption protocols within federated ecosystems is likely to be slow and difficult; however, our research quite clearly demonstrates the rise of a powerful and diverse community of interested actors involved in a co-production of elements (protocols, packages, libraries and others) necessary to prepare the ecosystem for adopting automatic encryption in federated environments. Autocrypt is one of the core examples of such community-based efforts, now collaborating with K9, Enigmail, Mailpile and other important MUAs and service providers. Conversations (with its underlying OMEMO protocol) is another federated project that undertakes important community-oriented efforts to move the secure messaging ecosystem forward. These efforts are recognised across projects: Elijah Sparrow, the leader of LEAP, remarked in our interview with him that 'the guy who wrote Conversations... he has done a lot to adapt XMPP, wrote a good demonstration client, and encouraged the servers to support this set. It's a good example of other "can-be-changed" protocols'.

Federation comes with challenges of 'compatibility', which we identify as its 'second C'. One of the practical examples of compatibility is the so-called 'backwards compatibility' that makes a harmonious transition from older to more recent protocols possible, without blocking or boycotting 'by design' some of the clients. As seen previously, the field of end-to-end encrypted instant messaging applications is highly competitive, with important tensions happening among protocol and application developers, implementers and open-source community activists. Due to the very nature of centralised and non-interoperable encrypted IMs that 'lock users' (as Sparrow puts it) within a tool with specific interfaces and sets of features, IMs compete for users. Email being an open federated ecosystem, it is structured by a number of collaboration and coordination efforts. However, these are not exempt from tensions and points of controversy; besides the difference in the technical approaches of different projects, such debates also involve the necessity to enrol an important number of email app developers in order to implement and spread their solution and being able to secure users.

Federated messaging solutions are currently taking shape as attempts to solve several important challenges experienced by contemporary communication infrastructures: on the one hand, fragmentation of the web and lack of interoperability, concentration of power and aggregation of data by centralised applications and platforms, and on the other hand, the high sociotechnical entry barrier into p2p networks, which necessitates greater expertise and responsibility from users and better performance of their devices.

This is where the 'third C', customisation, comes in. Federation offers users the option of choosing among multiple service providers and migrating from one server to another without losing their social graphs. The 'bigger/better' paradigm is thus questioned by federated messengers, whose business models do not depend on the number of users or on collecting and aggregating their data. In federated projects, users move beyond the role of 'data workers', in the words of Spanish artist and media philosopher Manuel Beltran;[21] smaller user groups appear to be easier to manage, and federated architectures make it simpler to customise and localise implementations, adapting them to the needs of a specific user community without losing the ability to interact with broader networks (by developing bridges, bots or other means to 'plug' systems to each other). Federation offers space for creativity; small projects proliferate, challenging researchers who fail to document all the various implementations of a given protocol.

At the same time, implementations of a federated protocol are harder to control, and this may create compatibility problems and security vulnerabilities across different instances or clients. A successful development of federated communication tools therefore necessitates new forms of organisation and decision-making, which is especially challenging for loose, decentralised networks. Federated forms of project governance take shape through the variety of ways in which protocol documentation is laid out and improved; constant negotiations across involved actors; physical, often informal, gatherings and new efforts at standardisation. Working standardised or quasi-standardised protocols function as instruments of self-governance, communication and coordination among actors of federated networks – what Yochai Benkler (2006) has called 'coordination without hierarchy'.

However, federation adds a layer of complexity in the governance of IMs as sociotechnical networks by introducing new key players, notably the system administrators, responsible for the maintenance and growth – the 'care' (Denis and Pontille 2015) – of federated infrastructures, our fourth and final 'C' of federation. The stability of federated ecosystems depends, as well, on the successful enrolment of maintainers, which requires the development of good documentation and guides with 'best practices', and the dissemination of technical expertise through offline educational events for future sysadmins.

In federated systems, 'caring about the plumbing' (Musiani 2012) is especially important and acquires an architecture-specific meaning, as no single entity can be counted on to maintain the system as a functioning one, but the necessity of care is distributed across the multiple sysadmins and other actors that manage the different instances in the federation. The growth of federated platforms marks a turn towards community-managed 'safe spaces', with more power delegated to human moderators (administrators of email or XMPP servers in the case of Delta Chat or Jabber, or instances in the case of Matrix or Mastodon). This introduces new risks of the re-centralisation of power within federated networks (Raman et al. 2019), requiring more research on the role of infrastructure maintainers, administrators and moderators, besides the core-set of protocol designers.

Among the main challenges of federated messengers are spam and reputation systems, as well as the discoverability of contacts and content that becomes harder without a centralised registry. On federated social networks like Mastodon or Matrix, the absence of data aggregation and filtering algorithms is viewed as beneficial for users' privacy. However, it is considered by some researchers as a challenge for wider user adoption, because it makes it harder for users to discover relevant topics or find other users (Trienes et al. 2018). At the same time, federated social networks are seen as a beacon of hope by those categories of users whom we call 'disinformation refugees' – users who abandon centralised social networks, such as Twitter, because they are tired of disinformation or hate speech.

At the end of this journey through architectural models in secure messaging and their impact on the configuration – social and economic as well as technical – of encrypted messaging tools, we now turn to examine the ways in which actors in the field have attempted to make sense of the 'mess of messengers' through initiatives of categorisation and classification. In a field at this level of maturity, these initiatives contribute to shaping and defining what constitutes 'good' privacy and security, and what constitutes a well-performing 'concealing for freedom' tool.

NOTES

1 https://joinmastodon.org.
2 https://pleroma.social.
3 https://www.chapsterhood.com/2019/03/09/decentralize-or-perish.
4 See, for example, the recent important hack of Matrix.org's default server (https://matrix.org/blog/2019/04/11/we-have-discovered-and-addressed-a-security-breach-updated-2019-04-12).

5 In the federated messaging space, we distinguish two main approaches, that we can call 'protocol innovation' and 'protocol upcycling'. Even if innovative protocols are built on existing libraries and standards, they tend to narrow interoperability, while 'upcycling' means developing systems that can be reachable via older protocols.

6 See the protocol history section in the Introduction.

7 ChatSecure, and its core developer, have a similar profile and history.

8 https://github.com/signalapp/libsignal-protocol-c.

9 For example, during our observations of Autocrypt usability tests at 33c3 in December 2016.

10 https://omemo.top.

11 The actual bot is called Jabbergram; similar bots now exist that bridge Telegram to IRC and Matrix.

12 https://matrix.org/blog/2018/04/26/matrix-and-riot-confirmed-as-the-basis-for-frances-secure-instant-messenger-app.

13 The harshest critique of Matrix.org actually comes from within the XMPP community, downplaying Matrix.org's innovative aspect and considering that they *'reinvent the wheel'*.

14 https://matrix.org/blog/2020/06/02/introducing-p-2-p-matrix.

15 Autocrypt project background: https://autocrypt.org/background.html.

16 Countermitm: https://buildmedia.readthedocs.org/media/pdf/countermitm/latest/countermitm.pdf.

17 https://leap.se/en/about-us/vision.

18 Ibid.

19 However, the project also works on new protocols, such as SOLEDAD and BONIFIED.

20 The name of the collective was never explicitly mentioned, for security reasons.

21 https://www.youtube.com/watch?v=TtvYipmFoBg.

5

WHAT IS 'GOOD' SECURITY? CATEGORISING AND EVALUATING ENCRYPTED MESSAGING TOOLS

CLASSIFICATIONS AND CATEGORISATIONS ARE, TO PUT IT IN BOWKER and Star's (1999) words, 'powerful technologies', whose architecture is simultaneously informatic and moral and can become relatively invisible as they progressively stabilise, while at the same time not losing their power. Thus, categorisation systems should be acknowledged as a significant site of political, ethical and cultural work. Building upon the variety of different architectural and interface formats that we examined in the previous chapters, this chapter examines how this 'work' by actions of categorisation and classification happens in the field of encrypted messaging tools.[1] We examine, as a case study, one of the most prominent and emblematic initiatives in this regard: the Electronic Frontier Foundation's 2014 release of the Secure Messaging Scorecard. A particular focus is on the debates it sparked, and its subsequent re-evaluation and evolutions. We show how the different versions of the SMS, as they move from an approach centred on the tools and their technical features to one that gives priority to users and their contexts of use, actively participate in the co-shaping of specific definitions of privacy, security and encryption that put users at the core of the categorisation system and entrust them with new responsibilities, while at the same time, ultimately warning users that 'we can't give you a recommendation' (Cardozo, Gebhart and Portnoy 2018). We also show how this shift corresponds to an evolving political economy of the secure messaging field: instead of a model of 'one app to rule them all', new approaches emerge, such as those mentioned in Chapter 4, that embrace the freedom of users to choose from or use simultaneously a multitude of apps, according to their social graphs and contexts.

THE EFF SECURE MESSAGING SCORECARD: THE SHAPING OF A 'COMMUNITY OF PRACTICE' THROUGH CATEGORISATION

For the Electronic Frontier Foundation (EFF), a digital rights group based in San Francisco, the question of what the most secure and usable tools are, in today's diverse and crowded landscape of messaging systems, has been at the core of their advocacy work for several years. Their most prominent initiative in this regard has been the 2014 release of the Secure Messaging Scorecard (SMS),[2] a seven-criteria evaluation of 'usable security' in messaging systems.

While the 2014 version of the SMS (1.0) displayed a number of apparently straightforward criteria – including, but not limited to, encryption of data in transit, ability to verify contacts' identities, available documentation for security design assessment, and whether a code audit has happened in the recent past – our research shows that the selection and formulation of these criteria has been anything but linear.[3] This was made particularly evident by the EFF's 2016 move to update the SMS. Acknowledging that 'Though all of those criteria are necessary for a tool to be secure, they can't guarantee it; security is hard, and some aspects of it are hard to measure', the foundation proceeded to announce that this was why it was working on 'a new, updated, more nuanced format for the Secure Messaging Guide'.[4]

Indeed, in a digital world where, as Chapter 2 has shown, the words security and privacy are constantly mobilised with several different meanings – even within the same debates and by *a priori* alike actors, and even more so when profiles of needs and adversaries vary – it seems relevant, so as to shed light on yet another facet of the making of encryption, to take SMS's first release as a case study. We can see its subsequent discussions and renegotiations as processes that destabilise, negotiate and possibly restabilise particular definitions of security, of defence against surveillance and of privacy protection. This chapter intends to show that initiatives such as the SMS and the negotiations around the categories that are meaningful to qualify and define encryption are in fact contributing to shape what makes a 'good' secure messaging application and what constitutes a 'good' measurement system for assessing (usable) security, able to take into account all the relevant aspects – not only technical but also social and economic. In addition to the fieldwork and interviews that are the basis for previous chapters of this book, the present chapter particularly relies on three in-depth interviews with current or past EFF personnel, conducted in November and December 2016. These are the person in charge of the first SMS (R1), the coordinator of the second SMS (R2) and the trainer and coordinator of the EFF Surveillance Self-Defense Guide (R3).

As Geoffrey Bowker and Susan Leigh Star remind us in their seminal work *Sorting Things Out* (1999), issues such as the origin of categorisation and classification systems, and the ways in which they shape the boundaries of the communities that use them, have been an important preoccupation for the social sciences in the last century. STS scholars in particular have explored these systems as tools that co-shape the environments or the infrastructures they seek to categorise and have addressed their particular status as both a 'thing and an action', having simultaneous material and symbolic dimensions (Bowker and Star 1999: 285–286). As this chapter will show, the EFF's attempt to define an appropriate categorisation system for assessing the quality of secure messaging tools is indeed simultaneously a thing and an action, co-shaping the world it seeks to organise.

From an STS perspective, classification and categorisation processes are strictly linked to the shared perception different actors are able to have of themselves as belonging to a community. In many cases, these processes highlight the boundaries that exist between communities and constitute the terrain where they might either move closer or drift further apart:

> Information technologies used to communicate across the boundaries of disparate communities [...] These systems are always heterogeneous. Their ecology encompasses the formal and the informal, and the arrangements

that are made to meet the needs of heterogeneous communities—some cooperative and some coercive (Bowker and Star 1999: 286).

Categorisation processes, as Goodwin (1996: 65) reminds us, are meant to 'establish […] an orientation towards the world', to construct shared meanings within larger organisational systems.

Borrowing from Cole (1996: 117), Bowker and Star point out that the categories produced by such processes are both conceptual (as they are resources for organising abstractions, returning patterns of action and change) and material (because they are inscribed, affixed to material artifacts). The act of using any kind of representation, from schematisation through to simplification, is a complex achievement, an 'everyday, [yet] impossible action' (Bowker and Star 1999: 294) that is, nevertheless, necessary to become part of a 'community of practice' (Lave and Wenger 1991), or in Becker's words, a set of relations among people doing things together (Becker 1986). The community structure is constituted by 'routines' and 'exceptions' as identified by the categorisation system – the more the shared meaning of this system is stabilised among the members of the community, the more the community itself is stabilised as such:

> Membership in a community of practice has as its sine qua non an increasing familiarity with the categories that apply to all of these. As the familiarity deepens, so does one's perception of the object as strange or of the category itself as something new and different (Bowker and Star 1999: 294).

We will see how, in the highly unstable environment of the EFF's initial attempt to categorise secure messaging tools with a view to providing guidance on their quality, the embryo of a community of practice started to emerge. At the same time, it went beyond – and revealed the manifold points of friction between – the relatively homogeneous group of cryptography developers, to include users of different expertise, trainers, civil liberties and 'Internet freedom' activists.

Classifications and categorisations, despite their embeddedness in working infrastructures and consequent relative invisibility, should be investigated as a significant site of political, ethical and cultural work (Bowker and Star ibid.: 319) – three aspects that our analysis of the SMS negotiations will unfold. In these three respects, categories are performative (Callon 2009): the reality of the everyday practices they subtend reveals that, far from being 'enshrined [...] in procedures and stabilized conventional principles that one merely needs to follow in order to succeed' (Denis 2006: 12, our translation), they actively participate in the construction of the relation between the different actors that have a stake, or a role, in the categorised environment; categories, from this perspective, are one of the components of a complex network of actors and technologies.

THE SECURE MESSAGING SCORECARD 1.0 AND THE UNVEILING OF 'ACTUAL SECURITY'

In November 2014, the EFF released its Secure Messaging Scorecard. The SMS was announced as the first step of an awareness campaign aimed at both companies and users – a tool that, while abstaining from formal endorsement of particular products, aimed to provide guidance and reliable indications that 'projects (we)re on the right track', in an increasingly complex landscape of self-labelled 'secure messaging products', in providing 'actual [...] security'.[5] According to R1, 'We tried to hit both audiences, we wanted to provide information for users and we also wanted to encourage tools to adopt more encryption to do things like release source code or undergo an audit'.

Overcoming the security vs usability trade-off

The EFF closely linked the SMS initiative to the Snowden revelations, mentioning that while privacy and security experts had repeatedly called on the public to adopt widespread encryption in recent years, Snowden's whistleblowing on governments' 'grabbing up [of] communications transmitted in the clear' has made widespread routine adoption of encrypting tools a matter of pressing urgency. R1 suggests that the need for such a tool came out of a need expressed by the general public:

It kind of came out of conversations at EFF [… we] got a lot of queries with people asking which messaging tools they should use. So there have been a couple of projects in the past, like the guide 'Who has your back', a project that is a sort of scorecard of Terms of Service and how companies handle data, that's where the idea came from … try to use the same approach to put information out there that we thought was useful about different messaging tools. (R1)

In the EFF's view, adoption of encryption to such a wide extent 'boils down to two things: **security and usability**'. It is necessary that both things go hand in hand, while in most instances, the EFF observes a trade-off between the two:

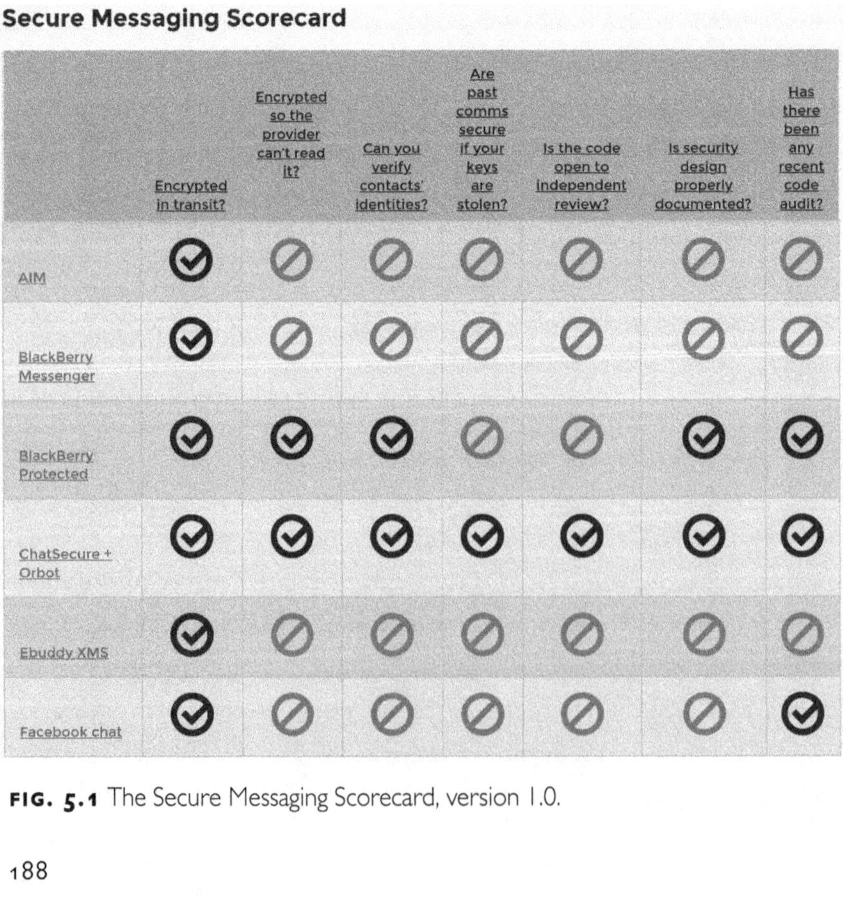

Secure Messaging Scorecard

	Encrypted in transit?	Encrypted so the provider can't read it?	Can you verify contacts' identities?	Are past comms secure if your keys are stolen?	Is the code open to independent review?	Is security design properly documented?	Has there been any recent code audit?
AIM	✓	✗	✗	✗	✗	✗	✗
BlackBerry Messenger	✓	✗	✗	✗	✗	✗	✗
BlackBerry Protected	✓	✓	✓	✗	✗	✓	✓
ChatSecure + Orbot	✓	✓	✓	✓	✓	✓	✓
Ebuddy XMS	✓	✗	✗	✗	✗	✗	✗
Facebook chat	✓	✗	✗	✗	✗	✗	✓

FIG. 5.1 The Secure Messaging Scorecard, version 1.0.

Most of the tools that are easy for the general public to use don't rely on security best practices – including end-to-end encryption and open source code. Messaging tools that are really secure often aren't easy to use; everyday users may have trouble installing the technology, verifying its authenticity, setting up an account, or may accidentally use it in ways that expose their communications (R1).

Citing collaborations with notable civil liberties organisations such as ProPublica and the Princeton University research Center on Information and Technology Policy, the EFF presents the SMS 1.0 as an examination of dozens of messaging technologies 'with a large user base – and thus a great deal of sensitive user communication – in addition to smaller companies that are pioneering advanced security practices', implicitly involving both established and emerging actors, with arguably very different levels of security and usability, in the effort. The visual appearance of the SMS is presented in Figure 5.1: a simple table listing specific tools vertically and the seven classification criteria horizontally. These are the following:[6]

1. Is your communication encrypted in transit?
2. Is your communication encrypted with a key the provider doesn't have access to?
3. Can you independently verify your correspondent's identity?
4. Are past communications secure if your keys are stolen?
5. Is the code open to independent review?
6. Is the crypto design well-documented?
7. Has there been an independent security audit?

The table includes intuitive symbology and colours to account for the presence or the lack of a requirement, and a filter giving the possibility of displaying only specific tools or getting a bird's-eye-alphabetised-view of all the examined tools.

Thus, as we can see, the political and 'quasi-philosophical' rationale behind the SMS was clearly presented. It is interesting to acknowledge, in this context, that the 'Methodology' section in the presentation page was very matter of fact.

It presented the final result of the categorisation and criteria selection process, but EFF provides very little information on the thought processes and negotiations that led to the selection. The page states, 'Here are the criteria we looked at in assessing the security of various communication tools', and proceeds to list them and the definitions used for the purpose of the exercise.

Yet, as researchers exploring the social and communicational dimensions of encryption from an STS perspective, we hypothesised that selecting and singling out these categories had been anything but linear, and that the backstage of these choices was important to explore – not merely to assess the effectiveness of the SMS, but also as a way of exploring the particular definition of encryption and security the EFF was inherently promoting at it was pushing the project forward. Indeed, it seemed to us that by fostering the SMS project, and due to its central role as an actor in the preservation of civil liberties on the Internet, the EFF was not merely acknowledging and trying to accumulate information about a 'state of things' in the field of encryption and security; rather, it was contributing to shaping the field, with the categories chosen to define 'actual' or 'usable' security being a very important part of *co-producing* it.

An ongoing reflection on the 'making of' the criteria

While the SMS's main presentation page focused on the criteria in their final form, there were some indications of the EFF's ongoing reflections on the 'making of' such criteria, and of their online presence. A post in early November 2014 by chief computer scientist Peter Eckersley, 'What Makes a Good Security Audit?', acknowledged that the foundation had 'gotten a lot of questions about the auditing column in the Scorecard' (Eckersley, 2014). Eckersley proceeded to explain that obtaining knowledge about how security software had been reviewed for 'structural design problems and is being continuously audited for bugs and vulnerabilities in the code' was deemed as an essential requirement, but it was also recognised that the quality and effectiveness of audits themselves could vary greatly and have significant security implications. This in turn, he suggested, opened up discussions that eventually led to the inclusion of three separate categories accounting for the process of code review (regular and external audits, publication of detailed design document and publication of source code) (Eckersley, 2014). Despite the fact that methodologies for code audit vary, Eckersley gave examples of fundamental vulnerabilities that a 'good code audit' may decrease. The code audit criteria thus refer to other systems of classifications, such as the CVE (Common Vulnerabilities and Exposures), an international standard for Informational Security Vulnerability names.[7] Other 'Notes' attached to some of the criteria are indicative of backstage negotiations, as they mention 'compromises' both on forward secrecy (encryption with ephemeral keys, routinely and permanently deleted after the communication, a 'hybrid' version of which is accepted 'for this phase of the campaign') and on the source code's openness to independent review ('only require[d] for the tool and not for the entire OS').[8]

In parallel, musings on the SMS came from several actors in the encryption/ security community at large. Some criticised the lack of hierarchy among the criteria, the phrasing of some of them and even the messaging tools' alphabetical ranking.[9] Others conducted alternative reviews of tools included in the SMS and questioned their quality, despite the fact that they had been scored positively on the EFF grid (Hodson and Jones 2016). Yet others concluded that the EFF was being 'pushed to rethink' the SMS (Zorz 2016). Indeed, relying on these documentary sources, it seems that reflections within the EFF on the quality of the SMS categories and their possible alternatives and evolutions, and, on the other, more or less constructive external criticisms of these same aspects, took place in parallel and paved the way for a subsequent version of the tool – all the while shaping 'good' security and 'good' encryption, as well as how users and developers could grasp what this meant.

In early August 2016, these reflections seemed to have reached a turning point as the EFF 'archived' its SMS main page, labelling it a 'Version 1.0', and announced it would be back in the near future with a new, improved and 'more nuanced' guide to encryption tools, explicitly referencing the ongoing revisions that had characterised and were still characterising their categorisation work: 'Though all of those criteria are necessary for a tool to be secure, they can't guarantee it; security is hard, and some aspects of it are hard to measure' (Figure 5.2).[10] It also anticipated that the term 'scorecard' would be dropped in favour of 'guide'.

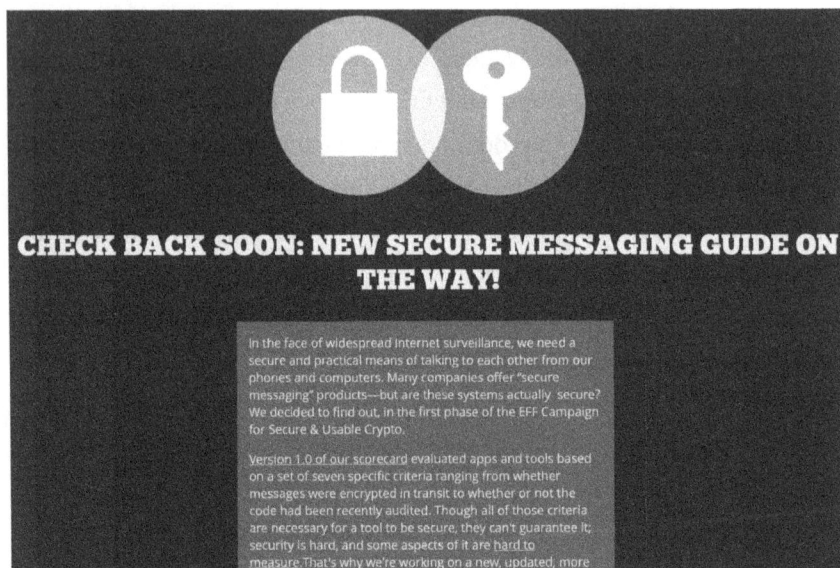

CHECK BACK SOON: NEW SECURE MESSAGING GUIDE ON THE WAY!

In the face of widespread Internet surveillance, we need a secure and practical means of talking to each other from our phones and computers. Many companies offer "secure messaging" products—but are these systems actually secure? We decided to find out, in the first phase of the EFF Campaign for Secure & Usable Crypto.

Version 1.0 of our scorecard evaluated apps and tools based on a set of seven specific criteria ranging from whether messages were encrypted in transit to whether or not the code had been recently audited. Though all of those criteria are necessary for a tool to be secure, they can't guarantee it; security is hard, and some aspects of it are hard to measure. That's why we're working on a new, updated, more

FIG. 5.2 Secure Messaging Scorecard main page between August 2016 and its withdrawal in 2018 (https://www.eff.org/secure-messaging-scorecard).

What did the first SMS do? Performativity and performance of a categorisation tool

And thus, Version 1.0 of the SMS was no more, except in the form of an archive preserved 'for purely historical reasons' of which the EFF itself discourages further use.[11] Nonetheless, our interviews with EFF members and with security trainers in several European countries – as well as the fact that the EFF decided to leave the SMS visible to the public while putting it in context – demonstrate that the first SMS *did* a lot of things to and for the encryption and security community, and contributed to shaping the field itself.

Indeed, the first SMS appears to have had a performative effect on the community: the EFF has a central role as a protector of online civil liberties and setting up a scorecard in this field was a pioneering effort in its own right. In an otherwise mostly critical discussion thread among tech-savvy users,[12] it was recognised as such ('The EFF scoreboard carries the embryo idea of a global crypto discussion, review, comparison and knowledge site that could also serve as a great resource for non-crypto people and students to learn a lot about that field'), and most interestingly, it led the encryption technical community to be reflexive about itself and its own practices.

There were a number of reasons for this reflexivity. The first was because a 'hybrid' organisation – EFF includes some technical people but also individuals with a number of other profiles – spearheaded this effort ('Isn't it a bit strange that a small organisation of non-computer scientists produce something that was painfully missing for at least 50 years?'). The second was because it prompted reflection on parallel categorisation efforts that may better respond to what the technical community sees as 'good security'. As one contributor put it:

> The highly valued information you and other experts are dropping [...]
> should be visible in a place that collects all that stuff and allows for open
> discussion of these things in the public, so people can learn to decide what
> security means for them. If such a thing exists, please show me. If not, please
> build it.

Indeed, by its very creation, the SMS caused a reaction in the developer community, making them wonder whether a categorisation effort of this kind was worthwhile, including the EFF's particular efforts. Despite the flaws they saw in the scorecard, developers seemed to perceive EFF as a sort of standardising or trend-setting body; they knew that many users would rely on the SMS if they perceived it to be the advice of EFF, in part thanks to some of the other initiatives aimed at bridging technical soundness and user-friendliness, such as the 'crypto usability' prize.[13]

Interestingly, and despite the EFF's announced intentions, we can retrace some early ambiguity and perhaps confusion about the SMS's intended target audience. The simplicity and linearity of the grid, the symbols used, the way categories were presented – each of these aspects could indeed lead the encryption technical community to think that it was aimed at both developers and users (confirmed earlier by R1, as well), and perhaps primarily at users. However, there are other indications that it might have been the other way around – in which the primary target would be fostering good security practices among a wide number of developer teams, with usability being a subsequent target. According to R2,

> what motivated us to make the scorecard, is to survey the landscape of secure messaging and to show developers: 'look that's what we think is important. So you should use all these things to make a truly secure tool', and then we can get to the usability part.

And later, even more clearly:

> Originally the target of the SMS was not users, telling users 'you should use Signal or you should use something else'. […] It was … we were trying to make a grid so that developers could see 'ok I need to get this and this to check all the boxes'. But it backfired….

So, it appears that one of the core things the SMS did was to prompt practices by end users that to some extent escaped the EFF team's intentions and control: intended as an indicative checklist for developers, the SMS actually assumed the shape of an instruction tool for users and cryptography trainers – a 'stabilised' and defining artefact, when in fact it was anything but.

Ultimately, and despite the EFF's warnings,[14] developers appeared worried that the SMS and its set of criteria would appear to guidance-seeking users as a performance standard that tools should achieve in order to qualify as 'good encryption'. Take, for instance, this comment by 'tptacek' on Hacker News:

> Software security is a new field, cryptographic software security is an even newer field, and mainstream cryptographic messaging software is newer still. The problem with this flawed list is that it in effect makes endorsements. It's better to have no criteria at all than a set that makes dangerously broken endorsements.[15]

This concern is echoed by EFF, with R2 pointing out during our interview how the organisation became worried about the SMS's use as an endorsement, or a standard, especially by those users whose physical safety actually depends on the security of their communications – those user profiles we defined as 'high risk' in Chapter 1. Indeed, the effect of SMS 1.0 on 'real life', relating both to how it was engineered and presented, appears as one of the primary motivations to move towards a second version, as we will explore further in the following section of this chapter.

'SECURITY IS HARD TO MEASURE': REVISITING THE SMS, (RE-) DEFINING SECURITY

In the interviews we conducted with them, EFF members describe how, since the early days of the SMS's first version, there had been an ongoing process of thinking back to the different categories. Taking into consideration what actors in the encryption community considered 'errors' (shortcomings, misleading presentations, approximations, problematic inferences), and revisiting their own doubts and the selection processes used during the making of 1.0, the EFF team started to analyse how the choice of these categories contributed towards building specific understandings of encryption and security. With this in mind, they started to consider how the categories could evolve – and with them, the definitions of 'good encryption' and 'good security' they presented/suggested to the world.

Questioning the grid: Incommensurability of criteria and the 'empty tier'

A first, fundamental level at which the reflection took place concerned the choice of the format itself. The feedback on the first version of the SMS revealed that in the attempt to be of use to both developers and users, the scorecard might have ended up as problematic for both:

> We got a lot of feedback from security researchers who thought that it was far too simplified and that it was making some tools look good because they have hit all the checkmarks even though they were not actually good tools. So we ended up in a little bit in between zone, where it was not really simple

enough for end users to really understand it correctly, but it was also too simple from an engineering standpoint (R1).

But in the making of the second version, according to R2, they wanted 'to make sure [...] that we can put out something that we're confident about, that is correct and is not going to confuse potential users'. Especially in light of the meanings that users bestowed upon SMS 1.0, a key question arose: was a grid the most useful and effective way to go? Perhaps the very idea of providing criteria or categories was not suitable in this regard; perhaps the updated project should not take the form of a grid, to avoid the impression of prescription or instruction to users that may previously have been given by 'cutting up' such a complex question into neat categories. As R2 explained, while discussing the possibility of creating a second version of the scorecard,

> we are definitely abandoning the sort of grid of specific check boxes [...]
> A table seems to present cold hard facts in this very specific way. It is very
> easy to be convinced and it's very official [...] we are definitely going
> towards something more organic in that way, something that can capture
> a lot more nuance. [...] there's a lot more that makes a good tool besides
> six checkmarks.

As both R1 and R2 suggest, we see how this intended additional 'nuance' was at some point being created not by eliminating categories, but by revisiting them. A suitable second version of the SMS may have divided the messaging tools in a set of different groups – R2 calls them 'tiers': the first group would include tools recommended unconditionally, whereas the last group would convey an 'avoid at all costs' message (e.g. for those tools that have no end-to-end encryption and present clear text on the wire). Within each group the tools would again be presented alphabetically, and not internally ranked; however, instead of visual checkmarks, each of them could be accompanied by a paragraph describing the tool in more detail, specifically aimed at users. As R2 comments, 'this is essentially so that we can differentiate [between tools] ... because we realize now that users are using this guide...'. And R1 suggests that it is also for the benefit of diverse user groups, with different levels of technical awareness: 'the goal is for people who are looking on the scheme on a very high level [to] say these tools are the best, these are bad, and there will be a slightly more nuanced explanation for people who really want to read the whole thing'.

Interestingly, the EFF team declared to us in early 2017 that, if the tiered model was going to be used, there were plans to keep the first tier... empty. This had strong implications for the definition of good encryption and security, basically implying that an optimal state has not yet been achieved in the current reality of the secure messaging landscape, and as of yet, a mix of usability and strong security is still an ideal to struggle for. One of our interviewees, for instance, commented that there is currently no tool that provides sufficient levels of insurance against a state-level adversary. Interestingly, the feeling that a 'perfect tool' is lacking has found its graphical representation in drawings collected as part of our fieldwork (see Chapter 1, Figures 1.2, 1.3, 1.4). The new SMS would convey the message that nothing is actually 100% secure and make users aware of the fact that there is no 'perfect tool', yet it can still be recommended without reservation. R2 gave us practical examples of why the team came to this conclusion, citing WhatsApp's practices of data sharing with Facebook (its parent company) or Signal's reliability problems for customers outside the United States.

In passing, the EFF team was defining what, according to them, would ideally be a 'perfect' secure messaging tool: end-to-end encrypted, but also providing a satisfactory level of protection from the risks of metadata exploitation, which, as we saw in Chapter 1, is still the core theoretical and practical issue for the developers of secure messaging tools. The emptiness of the tier represented a strong message to begin with, but was of course bound to evolve:

> If a tool got pretty close, and did not provide perfect protection against metadata analysis, we still might put it up in that tier and say look, these people have made a really strong effort [...] But so far, it is going to be empty. Just to emphasize that there's still plenty of distance for tools to go, even the best ones.

Thus, the EFF was not planning to skip its 'recommender' function which was at the core of the first version of the SMS; however, as we will see later in more detail, the focus was going to be placed on contexts of use and on the different 'threat models' of various user groups. Thus, weaknesses 'may not be shown in a check-box'.

The graphic and spatial organisation of the second version of SMS was planned to radically differ from 1.0's table. First of all, moving from a table to a list implies a different way of working with the information and undermines the idea of a direct, linear and quantified comparison offered by the table. A list of tiers with nuanced descriptions of different apps and their properties offers room for detailed and qualitative explanations, while tables tend to put different tools on the same surface, thus creating an illusion of commensurability and immediate quantified comparison. As R2 says: 'It's [...] definitely not gonna be a table [...] it will be more like a list: here is the first group, here's the next group, here's the next group, here's the group you should never use'.

The idea of 'filters' adds a certain degree of user agency to the classification of tools: the lists become modulable as users may set up a criterion that could graphically reorganise data, providing cross-tier comparisons. This offers a different way of classifying the data and 'making sense of it', compared to a table. The latter is, as Jack Goody puts it, a graphically organised dataset with a structure that leaves little room for ambiguity, and as such becomes an instrument of governance (Goody 1979).

Another problem posed by the grid format, that the new version of the SMS sought to address, was the projected equivalence of the different criteria, from the open-source release of the code to its audit and the type of encryption. The 'checklist' and 'points' system created the impression of an artificial equality between these criteria, and therefore led to the idea that one can 'quantify' the security of a given tool by counting points. In fact, the presence of some criteria rather than others, or the degree to which they are implemented, may result in different impacts on security and privacy, in particular for users in high-risk contexts:

> [If you were] someone who does not know anything about crypto or security, you would look at this scorecard and would say, any two tools that have, say, five out of seven checkmarks are probably about the same [while] if...

one of those tools actually had end 2 end encryption and the other did not, even though they both had code audit or the code was available, or things like that, their security obviously isn't the same. [The SMS 1.0] artificially made the apps that were definitely not secure in the same way look secure. And we were worried it was putting particular users whose safety depends on… you know users in Iraq or in Syria, in Egypt, where their security of their messages actually affects their safety.

The EFF team also realised that some developers and firms proposing secure messaging tools had, while presenting their tools, 'bent' the 1.0 grid to their own advantage – more precisely, they had presented a high conformity to the SMS as a label of legitimacy. Again, R2 emphasises that this was a problem particularly in those cases when users lack the technical background or expertise to build their own hierarchy of the criteria's relative importance, according to their needs or 'threat model' (see Chapter 1).

In 2017, a piece of research on user understanding of the SMS, authored by Ruba Abu-Salma, Joe Bonneau and other researchers with the collaboration of University College London, showed that indeed, users seem to have misunderstood the 1.0 scorecard in several respects. Four out of seven criteria raised issues: 'participants did not appreciate the difference between point-to-point and e2e encryption and did not comprehend forward secrecy or fingerprint verification' (Abu-Salma et al. 2017b), while the other three properties (documentation, open-source code and security audits) 'were considered to be negative security properties, with users believing security requires obscurity'. Thus, the assessment concluded, 'there is a gap not only between users' understanding of secure communication tools and the technical reality, but also a gap between real users and how the security research community imagines them' (ibid.).

'Not everyone needs a bunker'! From a tool- to a context-centred approach

The additional expertise needed by the user to understand the difference between various criteria and their importance emerged as a crucial flaw of the first version of the grid. One of the keys for a 'new and improved' SMS, thus seemed to be the fact of taking user knowledge seriously, as a cornerstone of the categorisation: for it to be meaningful, users needed to identify and analyse their respective threat model, i.e. identify, enumerate and prioritise potential threats in their digital environment. R3 remarked that this is one of the core objectives of EFF in several of its projects beyond the revision of the SMS, and noted that there are no direct tools to indicate what threat model one has, but users need to uncover the right indicators in their specific contexts of action:

> We're not answering what someone's threat model is, we just help guide them in their direction of what to read. We can say like journalists might have good secure communication tools that they might wanna protect their data, but we can't say how much of a threat any journalists are under because different journalists have different threats.

Furthermore, R2 pointed out that the same wording used to identify a particular threat might have very different meanings or implications depending on the profile of the user who utters it and on the geopolitical context she operates in: 'there's still a difference between "I am worried of a state-level actor in Syria" versus "I am worried of a state-level actor in Iran" versus China versus US'. In this regard, the more 'qualitative', descriptive nature of the new SMS should be useful to trigger the right reflexes.

In the absence of a universally appropriate application, the new SMS should take the diversity of the users – and the corresponding diversity of their threat models – as a starting point. R2 again resorted to specific case-examples to illustrate this point, citing Ukrainian war correspondents and 'hipster San-Francisco wealthy middle-class people' as opposites in terms of needing to worry about the relationship between their safety and the security of their messages. Helping individuals to trace their profile as Internet users, and the different components of their online communication practices, would be a first step towards identifying the threat model that best corresponds to them:

> Not everyone has to put on a tin foil hat and create an emergency bunker. Lots of people do, but not everybody. I think that would be great to have an

[ideally secure] app but since it's not there I think it's useful to tailor things, tailor the threat model.

If for the user the choice of a strong secure messaging tool is in this vision strictly linked to the understanding of his or her threat model, for its part the EFF acknowledges that just as there is no universally appropriate application, the same applies to the definition of what constitutes 'good' encryption – 'good' security and privacy. Beyond the strength of specific technical components, the quality of being 'secure' and 'private' extends to the appreciation of the geographical and political situation, of the user's knowledge and expertise... of whether privacy and security are or not a matter of physical and emotional integrity, which can only be contextually defined and linked to a particular threat model. A high-quality secure messaging tool may not necessarily always be the one that provides the greatest privacy, but the one that empowers users to achieve precisely the level of privacy they need.

Comparing with other categorisation systems

The efforts to revise the SMS could not, for the EFF team, do without a comparison with other categorisation systems. On one hand, the new version of the SMS would interact with the Surveillance Self-Defense Guide, developed by the EFF itself and destined for the purpose of ' defending yourself and your friends from surveillance by using secure technology and developing careful practices'.[16] Indeed, the contextual approach to users' needs and threat models appears to be dominant in this project: in stark contrast to the technical properties-based criteria of the first SMS, on the guide's home page, a number of 'buttons' introduce the reader to different paths of privacy and security protection depending on... user profiles and 'ideal-types' (Figure 5.3). The revised SMS should have partaken in this shift.

According to R3, this approach based on facilitation, induction and personalisation is informing more broadly the recent EFF efforts, and goes back to identifying the right level of relative security for the right context:

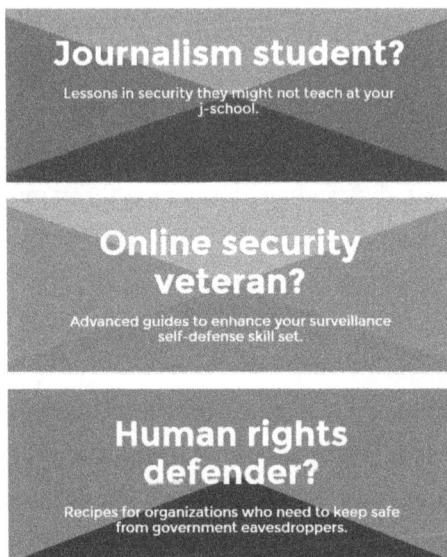

FIG. 5.3 Sample of 'user paths' on the SSD home page as of early 2017. These 'user profiles' have as of 2019 been turned into a 'Security Scenarios' menu (https://ssd. eff.org/en)

> We don't distinguish threat models; we give tools to help users figure out what are their threat models. [...] I still would not say we were putting an answer to the question out there. The key to the guide that we've created is that we want people to start with understanding their own personal situation.

The EFF was also looking at categorisation systems in the same field produced by other actors – acknowledging that SMS 1.0 has been, in turn, an inspiration for some of them and that there seems to be a need, generally identified in the field, for tools to provide guidance in the increasingly complex landscape of secure messaging.[17] R1 engaged in dialogue with several organisations which had the same kind of categorisation projects ongoing or were considering establishing one. A few of these organisations explicitly acknowledged that they were drawing ideas and concepts from the first version of the SMS, but re-elaborating it, which EFF considered a positive thing. Both R1 and R2 refer in particular to the similar effort by Amnesty International in 2016,[18] and while R1 acknowledges that they were really trying to produce something very simple and consumer-based and I think they did that, their report was much easier to digest for the general public', R2 mentions how 'I feel they suffer a lot from the same problem that Scorecard had, which is they [...] rely on a single number, they gave this score, like 90.5 points out of a 100 [and] you can't reduce security down to a single number.

The alternative, user-centred approach arose not only as a result of internal reflections on the first version of SMS, but also in relation to how parallel categorisation attempts were performed by other actors promoting online civil liberties. This includes informational security trainers and their recent pedagogical shift from tools to threat model evaluation, as described in Chapter 1.

Conformity to criteria: Evidence-seeking, evidence-giving

A final set of evolutions was meant to move beyond the building of the categorisation system itself. It aimed to question how EFF would request proof of the different secure messaging tools' conformity to their guidance, and how this evidence would subsequently be provided by the developers of the tools, as well as the encryption/security community at large. Indeed, one of the early criticisms of the first SMS did not have to do with the format of the grid, but concerned the opacity of the ways in which its 'binary' recommendations were evidence-supported.

In SMS 1.0, 'green lights' had sometimes been awarded for specific criteria as a result of the private correspondence between R1 and the developers, says R2: 'He would just email [...] sometimes he knew who was the developer but most cases it was just like contact @ ...'. The subsequent version of the SMS would thus adopt a more transparent approach and encourage display of public evidence from the developers, the lack of which may be a deal-breaker:

> This time around we are not going to accept as proof of any criteria any private correspondence. If an app wants to get credit for something, it has to publicly post it somewhere. I mean, we may be contacting developers to

encourage them to publicly post it. [... but] we don't want to have to say, 'well, we talked to them'. We want to say they are publicly committed to it. (R2)

In particular, one of the criteria that had raised more objections in terms the evidence provided was the review of the code – a developer, contributing to the previously-mentioned SMS-focused Hacker News discussion thread, asked: 'What does "security design properly documented" even mean?'. The EFF did not have sufficient resources to review the code line by line, and for several of the tools the code was not available, which is why the 'external audit' criterion was added. The lack of resources to dedicate to this task continued to be a problem, one more reason why, in the second phase, the EFF meant to concentrate on what app developers made public via their official communication channels. In parallel, the criterion calling for an independent audit – which, as we recall, had elicited a lot of internal methodological reflection since the beginning – was no longer meant to have a place in the second version of the SMS, once again because of evidence-seeking requirements and their material and human costs. As R1 pointed out, 'the cost of really doing a crypto audit of a tool is really high. The audit of 40 tools would have taken an entire year for me. So we just did not have the resources'. Interestingly – and while he agrees that the criterion needs to be dropped as such – R2 points out that several companies do their own audits, and the fact that they keep the results private does not necessarily affect their quality:

> There are companies like Apple or Facebook [...] it's almost certain they're doing an audit with an internal team so they will not release it publicly. It does not necessarily mean that the internal team did not do a good job. [...] For that reason we feel like the whole audit category does not do a lot. But we are going to still include if the code is open for an independent review because we think that's important [for some threat models].

Finally, to support the arguments provided in the new SMS, the EFF team expressed the wish to build on the competencies of the encryption communities of practice – cryptographers, professors, people in industry and digital security trainers – in order to get feedback about whether they possessed enough information about a particular tool, and whether the available information was correct. The EFF team anticipates that the search for feedback will be ongoing, to avoid falling into the same trap that had led commentators to wonder why the making of the first SMS had seemingly been a mostly 'internal' matter for EFF[19] and also to be able to react promptly to important changes in the tools: 'We try to make it clear that we're keeping the door open to feedback after we publish it, for anyone we did not get a chance to talk to before we published it. We can't get feedback from everybody before it goes live'. As tools evolve, what constitutes 'good' security evolves, or may evolve, as well.

CONCLUSIONS: SOMETIMES NARRATIVES ARE THE BEST CATEGORIES

Using the Electronic Frontier Foundation's prominent attempts at building a grid or guide to assess secure messaging tools, this chapter has sought to examine the role of categorisation and classification in defining 'good' encryption, privacy, security and secure messaging. In doing so, it has analysed how, by challenging, re-examining and re-shaping the categories that are meaningful to define the quality of secure messaging tools, the EFF has sparked a 'global crypto discussion'[20] that currently contributes to shape what constitutes 'good' security and privacy in the field of encrypted messaging.

Indeed, on one hand, the EFF's activities, epitomised by the SMS and its revisions, seem to contribute to the 'opportunistic turn' in encryption (IETF 2014) that gained momentum in 2014 after the Snowden revelations, and consists in a progressive move of the crypto community towards making encryption 'seamless', with almost no efforts required on the part of users. In terms of design choices, this entails a 'blackboxing' of quite a few operations that used to be visible to users and that needed to be actively controlled by them (e.g. key exchange and verification, or the choice of encrypted/unencrypted status etc.). The opportunistic turn calls for 'encryption by design', and constructs a new user profile, one who 'does not have to' have any specific knowledge about cryptographic concepts and does not have to undertake any additional operations to guarantee a secure communication. That shift may also be explained by the growing popularity of 'usable crypto' that undermines experts' monopoly on encryption and makes easy end-to-end encryption accessible outside of the tech-savvy user groups, where users used to be at the same time designers, developers and cryptographers.

However, while calling upon developers for improved usability – demanding that the technical crypto community make some properties, such as key verification, easy for users and independent from user agency – the EFF also puts users at the core of its attempt to develop a better 'guiding system', and in doing so, entrusts them with an important decision-making responsibility. To put it in R2's words, '[The aim] is still to push the developers to improve but we realise that people are using it to make choices, so now the idea is [to do this,] instead of just showing the developers here's what you have to do'. As it is often the case with categorisation and classification systems, the SMS was re-appropriated by the different actors in the community of practice, beyond the intentions of its creators – and several users in particular have relied on it heavily. Attempts at an evolved SMS intended to take this into account to a greater extent; but within the new paradigm that guided attempts to move beyond the SMS 1.0, there is an understanding that users have to question their threat models, increase their awareness of them, and have to know how to make technological choices according to their particular situation – a tool, from this perspective, is 'good' if pertinent to the context of use. This paradigm shift is also experienced and reflected upon by the trainers, organisers of cryptoparties and informational security seminars whom we have interviewed in different countries.

The reader may wonder at this point whether there is an (ongoing) epilogue to this story, given the fieldwork for this particular strand of our research ended in 2017. The answer is both that there is continuity with our conclusions above, and at the same time, things have moved in a slightly surprising direction. In March 2018, Nate Cardozo, Gennie Gebhart and Erica Portnoy of EFF published a piece with a provocative title: 'Secure Messaging? More Like a Secure Mess' and an equally provocative first sentence: 'There is no such thing as a perfect or one-size-fits-all messaging app' (Cardozo et al. 2018). As we kept on reading the article, we realised that we were in fact looking at the latest, and likely the final, iteration of the SMS – one that in describing the intention to create a 'series', reads like a selection of articles, all attempts at schematisations and categorisations gone, including the 'tiers' organisation that our interviews had unveiled as the EFF's intended next step:

> For users, a messenger that is reasonable for one person could be dangerous for another. And for developers, there is no single correct way to balance security features, usability, and the countless other variables (...) we realized that the 'scorecard' format dangerously oversimplified the complex question of how various messengers stack up from a security perspective. With this in mind, we archived the original scorecard, warned people to not rely on it, and went back to the drawing board. (...) we concluded it wasn't possible for us to clearly describe the security features of many popular messaging apps, in a consistent and complete way, while considering the varied situations and security concerns of our audience (...) So we have decided to take a step back and share what we have learned from this process: (this series will) dive into all the ways we see this playing out, from the complexity of making and interpreting personal recommendations to the lack of consensus on technical and policy standards.
>
> For users, we hope this series will help in developing an understanding of secure messaging that is deeper than a simple recommendation. This can be more frustrating and takes more time than giving a one-and-done list of tools to use or avoid, but we think it is worth it. For developers, product managers, academics, and other professionals working on secure messaging, we hope this series will clarify EFF's current thinking on secure messaging and invite further conversation (Cardozo et al. 2018).[21]

Ultimately, the EFF's conclusion – after, as Cardozo and his colleagues themselves point out, 'several years of feedback and a lengthy user study' – can be understood as the celebration of the 'relational' concept of risk we introduced in Chapter 1, and as a consequence, of the impossibility, when it comes to secure messaging, of a classical categorisation system including lists, schemas, regroupings, bullet points, tables, columns and rows. The soundness and 'goodness' of privacy and security protection in the field of secure messaging cannot be accounted for in a system intended to provide a set of possible answers for *all* possible readers – even if categories were expressed as open-ended questions aimed at personalising feedback, instead of red crosses versus green dots. A similar approach has been taken by the Citizen Lab's Security Planner[22] project, an interactive online digital security guide that gives a personalised and detailed 'action plan' including recommendations on security measures and tools based on users' responses to a set of questions.

The epilogue of the EFF's experimentation first with a scorecard, then with a guide, brings us to the conclusion that our fieldwork on the transition from the first to the second version had already unveiled: if a tool is good when it is pertinent for the user(s) and their social, geographical and political context of use, the best categories cannot possibly be anything else than narratives – narratives that do not prescribe, but inspire reflection on who a person is and what they want to do, who their adversary is, and what they want their communicative act to be. For some things and some times, suggests the EFF, open questions and narratives may be the best categories – and a field such as encrypted messaging today, which 'is hard to get right – and […] even harder to tell if someone else has gotten it right' (Cardozo et al. 2018), is very likely to be one of those things and times.

NOTES

1   A previous version of this chapter was published as Musiani, F. and K. Ermoshina, 'What is a Good Secure Messaging Tool? The EFF Secure Messaging Scorecard and the Shaping of Digital (Usable) Security', *Westminster Papers in Communication and Culture*, 12.3 (2017), 51–71 <http://doi.org/10.16997/wpcc.265>. Sections are reproduced and adapted here under a CC-BY 4.0 license. The paper was also presented and discussed at the annual conference of the International Association for Media and Communication Research (IAMCR) in Cartagena de las Indias, Colombia, on 19 July 2017.

2   https://www.eff.org/node/82654.

3   See e.g. the discussion of the code audit criterion at Peter Eckersley, 'What makes a good security audit?', EFF Deeplinks, 8 November 2014, https://www.eff.org/deeplinks/2014/11/what-makes-good-security-audit, which will be addressed in more detail later in the chapter.

4 https://www.eff.org/secure-messaging-scorecard.

5 https://www.eff.org/node/82654. This webpage, introducing SMS v1, is now preserved 'for purely historical reasons' on the EFF website. Citations in this section are from a version of this page that was online at the time of our fieldwork (2016–2017) unless otherwise noted.

6 We will return to them in more detail below.

7 http://cve.mitre.org/cve.

8 https://www.eff.org/node/82654.

9 Discussion thread on Hacker News, https://news.ycombinator.com/item?id=10526242.

10 Formerly at https://www.eff.org/secure-messaging-scorecard, which was taken offline during 2018.

11 https://www.eff.org/node/82654: 'you should not use this scorecard to evaluate the security of any of the listed tools'.

12 https://news.ycombinator.com/item?id=10526242. Citations in this paragraph are from this thread unless otherwise noted.

13 https://www.eff.org/deeplinks/2014/08/recap-first-eff-cup-workshop.

14 See also https://www.eff.org/node/82654: 'the results in the scorecard below should not be read as endorsements of individual tools or guarantees of their security; they are merely indications that the projects are on the right track'

15 https://news.ycombinator.com/item?id=10526242.

16 https://ssd.eff.org/en.

17 This issue had also been brought up in the Hacker News SMS-related thread: 'Isn't it a bit strange, that there is no such thing as that scoreboard produced by an international group of universities and industry experts, with a transparent documentation of the review process and plenty of room for discussion of different paradigms? (see https://news.ycombinator.com/item?id=10526242).

18 https://www.amnesty.org/en/latest/campaigns/2016/10/which-messaging-apps-best-protect-your-privacy.

19 See https://news.ycombinator.com/item?id=10526242: 'Why didn't they consult any named outside experts? They could have gotten the help if they needed it; instead, they developed this program in secret and launched it all at once'.

20 Ibid.

21 We license this text from the EFF website under a CC-BY license: https://www.eff.org/copyright.

22 https://securityplanner.org.

6

CONCLUSIONS: ENCRYPTED COMMUNICATIONS AS A SITE OF SOCIAL, POLITICAL AND TECHNICAL CONTROVERSY

WE NOW CONCLUDE THIS JOURNEY AMONG EXPERIMENTS IN 'CONCEALING for freedom'. During this journey, we have explored the choices made in technology and governance that lead to both a variety of configurations of encrypted tools and to a diversity of intended publics and action repertoires (Tilly 1985) for these tools. We have also witnessed the attempts to categorise and make sense of the 'mess of messengers' that seek to respond to the challenges associated with the increasing variety and complexity of the field.

In the final pages of this book, we seek to draw some conclusions about encrypted communications as a site of social, political and technical controversy today. Encrypted messaging tools remain at the centre of a powerful double narrative, with on the one hand a strong positive discourse around empowerment and better protection of fundamental civil liberties and, on the other, an equally strong critical discourse shaped by allegations concerning the technology's links to (and fostering of) terrorism. Furthermore, we can see how there are two 'turns' in the ecosystem of online communication: the cryptographic turn, that has seen Internet companies implement a number of cryptography-based organisational and technical responses aimed at restoring user trust in their cloud-based services, and the 'opportunistic turn', a progressive move by the crypto community towards making encryption seamless and requiring almost no effort from users to actively control most of the messaging tool's operations.

Issues related to encryption and its adoption in messaging systems inextricably entangle with issues of standardisation (both formal and informal), the political economy of software development and adoption, and the consequences of choices about technical architectures. This concluding chapter will offer some reflections on these different aspects as informed by our fieldwork and will then tie the different ways in which political effects can be achieved through technological choices to broader contemporary political concerns related to privacy, in particular, how they can interact with recent supra-national legal instruments such as the General Data Protection Regulation (GDPR). Finally, we will comment on the implications of our study and of cognate research for the development of social studies of encryption and for its interactions with Internet governance research, in particular work inspired by STS.

INTERNET RIGHTS AND FREEDOMS 'BY ARCHITECTURE'

Throughout its chapters and its various stories about the development and use of encrypted messaging systems, this book has addressed the question of the relationship between different kinds of technological architecture – most notably those that support the concealing of metadata, data or communications – and Internet freedoms and fundamental rights.

The relationship between human rights and Internet protocols is starting to become an issue in a few arenas, both political and technical; for example, the IRTF and its Human Rights Protocol Considerations research group (which will be further discussed below). As Stéphane Bortzmeyer (2019) aptly contends, the idea progressively taking hold in such arenas is that

> the Internet is not just an object of consumption, that the customer would only want to be fast, cheap, reliable, as it would a car or the electrical grid. We do business, politics, we talk, we work, we get distracted, we date: The Internet is not a tool that we use, it is a space where our activities unfold.

It is, to paraphrase Carl Schmitt (2003), the *nomos* of the twenty-first century, a normative universe where fundamental rights, as constrained or enabled by the platforms and protocols of the Internet, are in many cases just as important for people as the guarantees provided by governments.

The Internet as a multifaceted public space intersects with a pre-existing human rights framework. Human rights are formalised in texts such as the 1948 Universal Declaration of Human Rights (UDHR), where they are claimed to be universal, indivisible and inalienable. Despite such claims, it is clear that human rights are not absolute, as they may be in conflict with one another – in fact, they usually are. For example, the right to freedom of expression may conflict with the right not to be insulted or harassed, and freedom of expression may conflict with the right to privacy, if we want to prevent the publication of personal data. Historically, it has been the task of the legal system to determine the balance between such rights. In the networked age, the question is whether the technical space of the Internet, including its rules, limits and capabilities, has an influence on human rights, or whether it transforms human rights; and, if the latter, what concrete policy measures are needed as a consequence?

In 2012, the co-inventor of the Internet and Google evangelist Vint Cerf put forward the proposition that 'Internet access is not a human right', arguing that 'technology is an enabler of rights, not a right itself', as a human right 'must be among the things we as humans need in order to lead healthy, meaningful lives, like freedom from torture or freedom of conscience' and so 'it is a mistake to place any particular technology in this exalted category, since over time we will end up valuing the wrong things' (Cerf 2012). Nonetheless, some countries have made Internet access a basic right – Finland, for example – and this sentiment has been echoed by other entities, such as, for example, the Constitutional Council in France. Relatedly, it has also been argued that, while Internet access per se may not be a human right, the empowerment such access can provide probably is. As Tim Berners-Lee and Harry Halpin point out, considering the ability to access a particular technical infrastructure as a human right may be less important than defining as a new kind of right the ensemble of social capabilities that the Internet engenders (Berners-Lee and Halpin 2012).

Thus, Internet rights and freedoms may be promoted or enforced 'by architecture', including by 'technology-embedded' proposals around network neutrality and encryption. Data protection as an Internet right extends the notion of privacy to the digital age, fundamentally reshapes it and puts it into tension with new, similarly transformed networked forms of the right to free expression. This book has unveiled different ways in which technical developments of encrypted secure messaging systems, and of the associated governance models, construct Internet rights and freedoms, and are then in return shaped by them. The makers of 'concealing for freedom' technologies, their users and their regulators, operate within arenas of social, political and technical controversy ranging from standardisation and political economy of software development to choices of technical architecture and business models. The following pages draw conclusions about each of these aspects.

On (de-)centralisation: Choices of architecture as (a substitute for) politics

This book has provided thorough empirical evidence that, in the field of secure messaging as in other fields of protocol and software development, the choice of more or less centralised technical architectures is a context-based compromise, and not the result of choices between abstract models that might have intrinsically better or worse qualities. Decentralised architectures are a suitable solution in particular situations; but just as centralised architectures can, in some cases, have useful and rights-preserving qualities and, in others, be highly problematic, decentralised architectures are not always the ideal solution. The case studies we have examined in Chapters 2 to 4 illustrate, via concrete cases, the extent to which technical decisions contribute to enacting particular configurations of governance and repertoires of action.

Many Internet protocols have a client/server architecture. This means that the machines that communicate are not equivalent. On one side is a server, permanently on and waiting for connections, and on the other is a client, who connects when it has something to ask. This is a logical mode of operation when the two communicating parties are distinct, which is the case on the Web: when visiting a website, a user is a reader, and the entity which manages the website produces the content to be read. Yet not all uses of the Internet fit into this model. Sometimes one wants to exchange messages with an acquaintance. The communication, in this case, is not reader-to-writer, one-way, but peer-to-peer.

In this case, the machines of two humans communicate directly, something the Internet allows via peer-to-peer architecture.

So why go through an intermediary when it is not always strictly necessary? Usually, as Chapters 2 and 3 in particular have shown, it is because the intermediary serves a variety of purposes, that range from technical functioning and optimisation to business model, and to organisational/governance forms providing different extents of control. An example is the storage of messages in the case where the correspondent is absent, and their machine off. The Simple Mail Transfer Protocol (SMTP), which is the basis of the sending and relaying functions in email services, does not provide for messages to be sent directly from Alice's machine to Bob's. Alice's software sends the message to an SMTP server, which then transmits it to the SMTP server that Bob uses, which will then retrieve it via yet another protocol, probably the Internet Message Access Protocol (IMAP). The consequence of this architecture is that now, Alice and Bob depend on third parties, the managers of their respective SMTP servers. These managers can stop the service, limit it, block some messages (the fight against spam always causes collateral damage), and, if Alice and Bob do not use encrypted email protocols, read what passes through their servers. In practice, this may not happen, but the possibility exists, and it is technically very simple to archive all the messages being transmitted.

Since passing through an intermediate server has consequences, the question inevitably arises: which server to use? A personal machine that we install and manage ourselves, which is the closest a user can get to complete decentralisation? A personal machine run by a friend who knows and takes care of everything? A server or a cluster of servers run by a local collective, as in federated networks? Servers run by actors that mostly operate on centralised architectures, such as a public body, or a Silicon Valley platform like Gmail that is now able to extract information from a sizable portion of the world's email? The choice is far from obvious, both for developers when they are faced with technical choices, and for users who have to pick one or two communication tools out of many, based on often obscure criteria.

From the point of view of privacy and freedom of expression, centralised architectures are frequently criticised for posing the greatest threats. However, as Chapter 1 has shown, it is not always possible to individualise these problems: even if one does not use Gmail, others using Gmail may leak the contacts being made to your non-Gmail email to Google.

Still, in principle any third party that controls a server has the ability to abuse its power, and machines that are managed by a particular individual, local company or even public administration in federated networks may not, ultimately, be safer than the giant centralised actors of Silicon Valley, as they will simply have fewer resources to solve security and privacy-related issues. A machine run by a well-intentioned but overworked and not necessarily competent amateur can present high risks, not because the amateur is untrustworthy, but because it can be relatively easy to successfully attack the system. At the same time, it should be pointed out that professional servers are not necessarily safer: a number of recent hacks of very large companies have shown that they ultimately present perhaps larger targets. Servers managed by public bodies are an option, but even an administration that is well-meaning at a particular point in time may eventually evolve into one that violates rights and liberties. In this regard, federated systems, which allow servers to be easily interchanged, have some benefits in terms of sustainability. For example, Mastodon, the decentralised microblogging service (à la Twitter), is made up of hundreds of independently managed servers, some of which are administered by an individual (thus, their future is uncertain if this individual abandons this role), some by associations and yet others by companies of different sizes.

What are the implications of decentralised and peer-to-peer architectures for Internet rights and freedoms? First, as we have seen in Chapter 4, we should recall that these terms do not designate a particular protocol, but a family of highly diverse protocols. The most well-known peer-to-peer application in recent Internet history has been for the exchange of media files (e.g. music, video), but peer-to-peer is a very general architecture. And despite being accompanied by a rhetoric of openness and freedom, decentralised architectures also have their problems from the standpoint of Internet rights and freedoms. In the era of Google and Facebook as dominant, centralised, totalising platforms that seek to exert control over all user interactions, it has been easy to often present peer-to-peer as the ideal solution to all problems, including censorship. But as this book has shown in its analysis of the field of secure messaging, the situation is far more complicated than that.

First, peer-to-peer networks have no central certification authority for content; thus, they are vulnerable to various forms of attacks, ranging from 'fake data' to 'fake users'. It should be remembered that at one time, rights-holders circulated fake MP3s on peer-to-peer networks, with promising names and disappointing content, that lured users and eventually led them to be identified by their act of downloading. An attacker can also relatively easily otherwise corrupt the data being shared, or at the very least the routing that leads to it. Furthermore, in terms of net neutrality, because the peer-to-peer protocols that account for a good deal of Internet traffic are often identifiable within a particular network, an ISP may be tempted to limit their traffic. Many peer-to-peer protocols do not hide the IP address of users; for example, in the popular peer-to-peer file sharing client BitTorrent, if you find a peer who has the file you are interested in, and you contact them, this peer will learn your IP address (unless you disguise your IP address by using a VPN). This can be used by rights-holding individuals or organisations as a basis for issuing threatening letters or for initiating legal proceedings, as it has been the case with the HADOPI[1] in France (Arnold et al. 2014). There are peer-to-peer networks that deploy protection against this leak of personal information, such as Freenet, but they remain rarely used by the public at large.

Another danger specific to peer-to-peer networks is 'fake users', also called Sybil attacks: i.e. if verifying an identity can be done without needing something expensive or difficult to obtain, nothing prevents an attacker from creating millions of identities and thus subverting systems. It is in order to combat this type of attack that different systems and platforms have resorted to other ways of verifying identity. Bitcoin uses 'proof of work', a form of cryptographic proof in which one party to a transaction proves to the other parties that a particular amount of computational resources has been dedicated to a specific objective. Organisations like the CAcert certification authority (Tänzer 2014), or informal groups like users of the Pretty Good Privacy (PGP) encryption program, use certifications created during physical meetings, which include verifying a user's national identity documents. There is currently no general solution to the problems of Sybil attacks, especially if any solution is required to be both ecologically sustainable – which is not the case of the proof of work mechanism – and fully peer-to-peer – which is not the case for conventional enrolment systems, as they require a privileged actor to approve a participant's entry. Solutions based on social connections, such as the one proposed by PGP, pose problems to privacy, since they expose the social graph of the participants – the list of their correspondents. In this field of alternative methods for identity verification, experiments aimed at allowing gossip in social networks to help verify identity,[2] while remaining privacy-preserving, are on the way;[3] but the road is far from linear.

As the most recent generation of secure messaging tools develops, and more broadly, the blockchain takes hold as an often more politically acceptable decentralised technology – even as we are learning more and more about its governance and technical flaws – the relationship between different architectural models for networking and communication technologies, the choices made and the roads not taken, are likely to remain a controversial issue. Attempts to deploy decentralised technologies and communities within particular territories are currently being piloted.[4] More traditionally political arenas are involved in the decentralisation debate: in early 2019, declarations of intention by political officials in several European countries indicated an intention to actively favour decentralised technologies, blockchain in particular, via legislation. French President Emmanuel Macron, for example, referred to blockchain as a possible way to bring transparency and traceability into the agricultural industry to ensure better quality, and argued that Europe should adopt a 'homogeneous policy' in this regard. Within Europe at least, it is therefore likely that further proposals to use blockchain or decentralised technologies for such purposes will see the light in the coming months and years.

The success of the blockchain is perhaps still greater in research projects and imaginaries of intermediary-less futures than in fully working applications, and we can recognise, as in previous 'expectation cycles' related to distributed architectures and a number of other technologies (see e.g. Borup et al. 2006; Brown and Michael 2003), interactions between both potential and hype. Yet, the blockchain and its myriad variants have some specific features that will be very interesting to observe in the coming years. In particular, it seems to be the first decentralised networking technology to be widely accepted — 'celebrated' would be more accurate — by national and supra-national institutions, despite its first widespread application, Bitcoin, being born with the explicitly stated goal of making each and every institution obsolete, and despite its birth, development and functionality being subject to several controversies (Musiani and Méadel 2016).

Thanks to the role that local and distributed technologies have played, relying on networks such as TOR, in rallying and organising social movements and grassroots resistance tactics, decentralised architectures are increasingly seen as technologies of empowerment and liberation. Yet they do not escape a powerful double narrative, fuelled by previous narratives depicting peer-to-peer as an allegedly 'empowering-yet-illegal' technology. On the one hand, the discourse around empowerment and better protection of fundamental civil liberties is very strong; on the other hand, several projects that have sought to merge decentralisation and encryption to improve protection against surveillance have needed to defend themselves from allegations of use by terrorists and other unsavoury publics (a defence some projects are technically unable to mount).

This dialectic is taking place in the broader context of discussions about civil liberties and governance by infrastructure (Musiani et al. 2016), some of them particularly related to encryption (or the breaking of it), such as the Apple vs FBI case or WhatsApp proposing, since April 2016, encryption by default (Schulze 2017). Indeed, both the (re-)distribution and the (re-)decentralisation of networks are strictly linked – much more so than a few years ago, and in particular after the Snowden revelations – to discussions of surveillance and privacy, and find themselves frequently associated with discussions about encryption, and its practical implementations. The next section will discuss this relationship and its challenges.

ON ENCRYPTION: STRATEGIES OF CONCEALMENT AS INTEGRITY (AND POWER) TOOLS

As we have seen throughout the book, encryption is a controversial issue. As the case studies unfolded, we could see how the different developer teams – and, often, the users of the systems they develop – cope with the fact that debates over encryption policy are framed as pitting security at the cost of civil liberties against new technological freedoms that may pose security risks. While technologists, including several developers and security trainers interviewed for this book, hold that without encryption the right to privacy remains purely theoretical given the ease of spying on digital communications, encryption is frequently framed in political debates as a mechanism that allows criminals to conceal the content of their communications from the judicial system and police.

Our research allows us to point out several ways in which this debate should be nuanced, as we have examined the 'making of' encryption and its interplay with Internet rights and freedoms. We have observed how cryptography is not only used to conceal information, i.e. to make data confidential, but also to provide checks on the integrity and authentication of data, even data that is public. For example, in order to check that data has not been modified either by accident or with ill-intent, we have seen hash functions – functions that shrink data to a small code that can be checked independently – being used to check the integrity of the data. We have also seen cryptographic techniques being put to use with both private secrets, called private keys, that can work with public information, and public keys, to both authenticate as well as encrypt data. With public keys and hash functions, digital signatures can be created to make sure that we know the identity of the entity that originates particular data. This approach, widely used in secure messaging, is useful in a variety of scenarios, including e-Signature schemes that can help reduce bureaucracy or to prevent the spread of false information. Thus comes the dilemma that, in the field of secure messaging, has been exemplified by the FBI vs Apple case (Schulze 2017): if a government implements a policy to reduce the scope of encryption so that its police or intelligence services can 'read' digital messages, there is a clear danger that the government would accidentally prevent other uses of encryption that would damage the ability of users to place any trust in data circulation and processing by third parties, with wide-ranging negative economic consequences.

For this reason, and acknowledging that developer teams' respective strategies in terms of architectural choice or standardisation greatly vary, we can recognise a common trend in the different stories of development we have examined: strong resistance to making the encryption of data illegal, for any reason. Actors in the secure messaging field share the belief that cryptography needs to be legal as digital technologies not only increase the possibilities of surveillance, but they do so in a fundamentally asymmetric manner that is incompatible with democracy (see also Bortzmeyer 2019); platforms gather a lot of information about us, but these platforms are opaque to citizens, and the same issue holds true of various state intelligence agencies; furthermore, this data processing happens *en masse*.

Our observation of the development processes of secure messaging tools as 'situated practices' reveals the limits of presenting encryption primarily as a mechanism that will prevent states and police forces from conducting their investigations properly. As we followed developers in their endeavours, we could see that for them, end-to-end encryption – where the endpoints are the users, and no entity in the middle has the ability to decrypt the message – actually, and partially, restores the social norms around communication that were expected prior to the advent of digital communication, so that messages are clearly given to be from a particular sender and can only be read by a particular recipient, with interference to the message being detectable.

With a revival post-Snowden (e.g. Barr 2016), but having its roots in a long-standing academic and political debates (Rivest 1998; Soghoian 2010), one heavily debated, controversial policy option concerning encryption has been and is its 'selective weakening' by allowing both the use of encryption and its possible breaking in specific cases – for example, in case of investigation of a case of terrorism, the idea of a 'backdoor' to allow decryption of encrypted messages. From the standpoint of technologists, this arrangement is highly problematic as, regardless of the choice of technical architecture, the mathematical algorithms that form the core of encryption cannot work only in some cases, but not in others: either they make it possible for data to be accessed by anyone who has the key, or they have a flaw, which is exploitable by anyone who is aware of it – an argument made, most prominently, by the *Keys Under Doormats* report (Abelson et al. 2015). In proposals for 'backdoors', one decryption key would be the legitimate receiver's key, but another key would exist, controlling a 'middlebox' that decrypts the message and re-encrypts it to the intended recipient. This key is considered to be under 'key escrow', which means stored by a third party such as the government, and perhaps only available in special circumstances. However, such a solution would, for clear enough reasons, not work in open-source and free software projects (including those examined in Chapters 3 and 4), where the review of any code would show the backdoor. It would be more realistic in contexts such as those described in Chapter 2, where the user does not have control over the software she is using, and the software she is given may include the backdoor from the start.

As one of the developers we interviewed pointed out, though, 'Obviously, any real threat to the state will not use the latter tools, but [will instead] search for software without backdoors. But this method can work with the honest citizen who, unlike the terrorist, trusts proprietary software, and who communicate with each other through Silicon Valley platforms'. Thus, from the standpoint of this developer and others among our interviewees, the purpose of anti-encryption campaigns for 'backdoors' is not, or not primarily, about finding solutions allowing authorities to decrypt for anti-terrorism purposes, but a way to pressure Silicon Valley and other technical actors to include backdoors in their communication software, in order to enable and/or sustain systems of mass surveillance.[5] In response to this scenario, the European Commission has recognised in its recent cybersecurity strategy (European Commission 2017) that encryption allows fundamental freedoms to be exercised, and digital freedoms organisations such as European Digital Rights (EDRi) have argued that as such, encryption should be recognised as a tool for countering the arbitrariness of state governments and dominant private actors (EDRi 2017).

Developers of the variety of secure messaging systems examined in this book are coping with several levels of complexity. Their use of modern cryptography and, most often, formally verified protocols, has the aim of reducing security problems (e.g. those linked to backdoors) and mistakes. They also predominantly work on the assumption that the cryptography they develop should be understood by decision-makers in order to be deployed; as one of our interviewees put it, 'no policy-maker should have to know the difference between the Decisional Diffie-Hellman and Computational Diffie-Hellman property'. They also mostly share an understanding that privacy is 'hard to get right', due to the varieties of social contexts involved, which we examined in Chapter 1. They are aware that in order for notions of privacy to be meaningful and applicable to development processes, it is necessary to carefully define the threat model and run simulations to see various empirical ways to measure phenomena such as proximity or unlinkability. Finally, several developers are aware that in order to rule out the possibility of backdoors in their or others' software, the algorithms and protocols using cryptography need to be formally verified or audited by external parties – an aspect that, as the reader will recall from Chapter 5, was also included by the EFF in earlier versions of its evaluation grids. However, for the reasons mentioned above, privacy is harder to actually *verify*, and does not fit within formal verification frameworks; thus, it is complicated to determine exactly what kinds of privacy are being discussed and whether a given system can support it.

While developers do not expect policymakers to have cryptographic knowledge, they operate within national and supra-national contexts where encryption, and the ability to compromise it, is an intensely political issue if not an outright proxy for power – and, post-Snowden, increasingly so. In 2013, a few months after Snowden's revelations, the NSA was revealed to have discreetly lobbied for the US National Institute of Standards and Technology (NIST) to include a weakened, possibly deliberately flawed algorithm in a 2006 cryptography standard (Greenemeier 2013). And in 2016, a financial industry group proposed a protocol called eTLS, omitting from it the forward secrecy feature which had been incorporated into the latest version of the Transport Layer Security (TLS) protocol. The European Telecommunications Standards Institute (ETSI) released eTLS, rebaptised ETS to minimise ambiguity, as a standard in the autumn of 2018, to great controversy (Leyden 2019) and steadfast opposition from the Internet Engineering Task Force (IETF).

Standardising bodies such as the IETF and its parallel organisation, the Internet Research Task Force (IRTF), have shown, in the above controversy as well as others, that they are well-positioned, via entities such as the IRTF-chartered CryptoForum Research Group,[6] to issue authoritative advice about the safety of cryptographic algorithms. However, there are other important sources of authoritative advice. In Europe, the promotion of best practices in the use of public cryptographic algorithms, their verification and the generation of cryptographic standards was until recently undertaken by the European Union Agency for Cybersecurity (ENISA, which still uses this abbreviation, in reference to its original name: European Network and Information Security Agency); however now this function is being devolved down to the nation-states, which may entail risks (as discussed, pressures to introduce backdoors, or uneven levels of cryptographic knowledge within different national contexts).

Furthermore, several debates are taking place at the national level in European countries on end-to-end encryption and on how to strike a balance between the protection of digital rights and law enforcement. In 2017, the French Digital Council (CNNum) issued advice on encryption, reaffirming the usefulness and necessity of encryption technologies in light of the repeated attempts by the Ministry of Interior to challenge their use due to their potential exploitation by terrorists and criminals (CNNum 2017). In 2019, new and worrying signals came from Germany, where, after more than twenty years of unequivocal support for strong encryption (Herpig and Heumann 2019), a law is being examined that would force chat app providers to hand over, on demand, end-to-end encrypted conversations in plain text; this inclusion of Internet services providing encryption software would expand German law, which currently 'merely' allows communications to be gathered from a suspect's device itself (Chapman 2019). In the United Kingdom, within the debates concerning the Investigatory Powers Act,[7] the government issued a revised version of the bill that 'clarifies the government's position on encryption, making it clear that companies can only be asked to remove encryption that they themselves have applied, and only where it is practicable for them to do so' (Carey 2016).

In response to the controversy around encryption in Germany, Roman Flepp, from a Swiss-based end-to-end encrypted instant messenger platform called Threema, that is popular among German-speaking users, asserted that: 'Under no circumstances are we willing to make any compromises in this regard' (quoted in Chapman 2019). However, as this book has shown, the road to 'no compromises' is in practice, for developers of secure messaging tools, paved with compromises – some of which relate to technical choices, others to the user publics they target and still others to the broader geopolitical scenarios and debates they operate within. Such debates will no doubt continue as encryption remains a matter of intense public concern, which technologists are actively involved in it, in both actions and words.

ON STANDARDISATION: SETTING (OPEN) NORMS AS SOLIDARITY AND TRANSPARENCY

The stories of secure messaging tools development told by this book are also revealing about how the field is currently approaching issues of standardisation, a process that is simultaneously technical and political; there is an 'intimate connection between standards and power', a power that 'lies in [standards'] very subtlety' (Busch 2011). Standards describe the specifications for code, and this code may then be independently implemented in conformity with the specification of various licensing options, ranging from open source to proprietary. Geoffrey Bowker and Susan Leigh Star have long since noted that standards play an important role in the making of public policy and, more broadly, of social order: 'standards and classifications, however imbricated in our lives, are ordinarily invisible [...yet] what are these categories? Who makes them, and who may change them? When and why do they become visible? How do they spread?' (Bowker and Star 1999: 94). A number of case study analyses of competing standards in information technology have contributed to shed light on these processes, including the birth of the QWERTY keyboard (David 1985) and the VHS vs Betamax controversy (Besen and Farrell 1994), and, more recently, debates about the respective merits of two different Internet protocols – IPv4 vs IPv6 (DeNardis 2009).

Technical standards take shape at once in material forms, in social and economic interactions, and in their intended or inferred use. Several standards are developed (and recognised as such) intentionally and result from regulatory actions or from being voluntarily adopted. Such formally endowed standards are developed by dedicated organisations, such as the International Standardization Organization (ISO) or, for the Web, the World Wide Web Consortium (W3C), with the standards taking the form of documents that describe objects, their properties and the extent to which they can be put under strain or stress without breaking or being compromised. One example is the IETF's Request for Comments, or RfC, whose very evolutions over time contribute to making visible the transformations of the IETF, including changes in both its organisational forms and practices (see Braman 2016).

For 'ordinary' users, the meaning and pervasiveness of standards in their everyday lives, as operative in a myriad of different situations, often escapes understanding (Star and Lampland 2009). The publication of a standard is only the beginning of the norm-making process – and indeed, as the Signal case examined in Chapter 2 has shown, sometimes it is not even a necessary step. The adoption of something close to a 'standard' may occur either de facto or accidentally, with seemingly minor decisions and actions becoming crucial for the development of a field in a particular direction. In some instances, what determines the adoption of an object, process or protocol as a standard is its ability to circulate and gain recognition: factors such as popular demand, perceived quality and the credibility of its developers become crucial for the standard's success. The spread of standards through social, technical and institutional media is a multifaceted process; mechanisms of standardisation are economic, social and technical – with different degrees of intentionality – alongside the 'official' institutional practices of certification and harmonisation (Loconto and Busch 2010).

The issue of open standards seems particularly salient for encrypted messaging and their potential for 'concealing for freedom'. Open standards are produced by standardising bodies that allow anyone to participate in the process. This openness is seen as maximising both transparency and the collective intelligence gained through the 'wisdom of the crowds' – this is argued to be particularly useful in standards around security and cryptography (Simcoe 2006). Open standard bodies have produced most of the technical standards that form the core of the Internet, like TCP/IP, HTML and TLS. As we started seeing at the end of the previous section, however, standard-setting bodies can be subject to lobbying and wider agenda-setting strategies that can, in some instances, even be characterised as manipulation. As we saw in Chapter 2, the perception of standard bodies as possibly fragile in the face of lobbying is the reason why secure messaging developers increasingly emphasise the institutionalisation of standardising bodies and their progressive distancing from coding communities, which often creates an environment that is less suitable for experimental and unfinished projects (as is the case for several 'young' systems in the secure messaging field).

However, our developer interviewees also emphasise that they perceive differences between standardisation bodies, with several national and closed standards organisations being seen as more prone to manipulation, whereas open standards bodies are seen as having more rigorous processes. One of our respondents referred to the contentious standardisation of Office Open XML file formats in the late 2000s, which was ultimately designated as an 'open' standard by the International Standardization Organization – ISO, a standards body composed solely of representatives from nation-states – following pressure from Microsoft (see also Ryan 2008).

Unlike standards bodies comprising only commercial organisations (e.g. ECMA, the European Computer Manufacturers Association), open standards bodies usually employ a multi-stakeholder model, including public institutions, private companies, universities and individuals. Open standards bodies for the Internet include the IETF and, for the Web, W3C. A key aspect addressed by such bodies is **patent disclosures**. Open standards, particularly those with a royalty-free licensing policy like those produced by the W3C, are perceived by our interviewees to be highly important due to their prohibition of patent licensing fees. Bodies like the IETF force patent disclosures, and have been protagonists in several controversies (e.g. the ETS controversy mentioned above) in their efforts to prevent patented elements from becoming part of open standards.

When it comes to the code underlying the systems we analyse in this book, we can see a consensus among several developers – predominantly those involved in federated and decentralised secure messaging solutions, but also including some involved with centralised components, as we will see later with Signal. Open source, our interviewees argue, should be supported both as a technological principle and as a matter of policy, with some interviewees also suggesting that policies should go even further to foster the adoption of free software (as 'a matter of liberty, not price'[8]), as a political programme. This would include guaranteeing four fundamental 'user freedoms', in which the user should be able to: run the program in question as they wish, for any purpose; study how the program works, and potentially change it; redistribute copies; and distribute copies of their modified versions to others. This political programme is meant to go a step further than ensuring code is 'open source' and 'open access', although it assumes open access to code is a necessary precondition for freedom.

The free software movement originally came out of Richard Stallman's acknowledgment that the practice of sharing software, with its hacker culture heritage (Coleman 2013) was being increasingly 'enclosed' by commercial ventures. In order to create a legally binding form of resistance to these new enclosures, Stallman created the GPL (General Public License[9]), which postulated that the copyright on a given piece of software is allocated by default to the developer and that the developer can license their software to an unlimited number of people. The GPL license requires that all derivative works also use the GPL, thus preserving for posterity the aforementioned four fundamental user freedoms and enabling the software commons to grow virally. The GPL has proved to be a successful license and software methodology: GNU/Linux, which depends entirely on the GPL, subtends most of the Internet's architecture today and even Google's Android is based on a free software kernel, although Google outsources vital components to its proprietary cloud.

However, the 'virality' of the GPL can pose problems when there is the need to integrate with commercial software, as is often the case in public administration, a point that our interviewees are well aware of. Less strong open-source licenses, which retain the possibility of private actors copying a piece of software and making a proprietary version of it, again carry the risk of enclosure – as has been explored in recent work, this kind of 'weak' open licensing is an important motivation for many companies to fund open-source projects, as it opens the way to eventually fork parts of them into proprietary versions (O'Neil et al. 2020; Birkinbine 2020).

An interesting path for software designed in the public interest – which has, in the field of secure messaging, a notable precedent in Signal, one of its most widespread protocols and applications – seems to be a 'dual license' policy, with server-side software being published using the Affero GPL (AGPL[10]), while client-side software uses the GPL v3.0. The AGPL software prevents free software from being made available as a service over a network, such as a web service, without the code being released. If someone wants to use this software in combination with commercial software, then the creators of the AGPL-licensed software retain the right to grant a non-exclusive and non-transferable 'dual license' on its use. This license can be granted for free to public administrations, while for-profit companies can be changed. This is the business model originally used by Signal, and it is an interesting attempt to preserve 'the best of both worlds', as one of our developer interviewees put it: allowing integration with commercial software on a case-by-case basis, while keeping the code itself free for the commons.

ENCRYPTING, DECENTRALISING AND STANDARDISING ONLINE COMMUNICATIONS IN THE GDPR ERA

So far, this chapter has drawn from our fieldwork with secure messaging developers and users to analyse the different ways in which political effects can be achieved through technological choices at the crossroads of encryption and decentralisation of digital networks, as well as the attempts to build standards in the field. This section will tie these dynamics to broader political concerns related to privacy in our present time, in particular with the advent of the General Data Protection Regulation (GDPR) as the primary and most recent supranational legal instrument aimed at securing privacy-related Internet freedoms at the European level.

In 2009, European Consumer Commissioner Meglena Kuneva acknowledged that personal data was well on its way to becoming 'the new oil of the Internet'. One decade on, the inevitable resource wars for the control of mass personal data began, with data extractivism – the strategy of the capture and refinement of personal data to sell on the world market – becoming the primary business model of Internet giants such as Google and Facebook. Public policy, meanwhile, has struggled to fully understand the value of personal data and to translate it, and a set of safeguards for it, into law. The GDPR is the most recent and comprehensive attempt by the European Commission to use legal means to ensure the 'right to a private life' in the sphere of digital data, which prompts the question whether GDPR provides an effective answer to the erosion of data sovereignty and integrity by technological platforms. While this book cannot provide a full answer to this question, it has further demonstrated that for data protection to be effective, it must *also*, if not primarily, be defended *technologically*.

As Laura DeNardis eloquently puts it, 'cyberspace now completely and often imperceptibly permeates offline spaces, blurring boundaries between material and virtual worlds' (DeNardis 2020: 3): the ubiquity of the Internet has caused the world to be enveloped in a single, data-driven, technosocial system. Faced with this rapid and all-encompassing set of evolutions, policy has frequently treated emerging technologies primarily as hostile instruments threatening a status quo, thereby creating need for legal reform (see Elkin-Koren's 2005 enlightening analysis of peer-to-peer), with, in particular, a frequent emphasis on decentralised and/or encryption technologies as enablers of crime and terrorism. In this conjuncture, any questions of data integrity, protection and control require a new approach, where rather than attempting to mandate laws that *apply* to the underlying technology, policymakers would encourage the *adoption* of technology contributing to maintain the society that they wish for. Putting rights-preserving technologies, such as 'concealing for freedom' systems, in the hands of local state actors and citizens may be the last and most effective bastion against data extractivism, especially if done in concert with the development of policies around data protection. In this sense, government-mandated organisations (such as the previously mentioned French Digital Council) have produced detailed advice on encryption technologies and have persuasively analysed why such technologies should not be banned, but encouraged. These documents establish a sort of 'philosophy' that, while it may or may not be followed in actual regulation, is interesting to assess as it takes shape.

Of course, recent (and less recent) scholarship has also analysed a number of less-than-encouraging examples of policymakers fostering the adoption of specific technologies as a tool for (co-)shaping society. Sociotechnical systems like the Chinese 'social credit system', where a single government-run platform is used to make decisions regarding nearly all aspects of their citizens lives, from education to mobility, are run in a privacy-invasive manner that disregards the fundamental rights of individuals, placing the data sovereignty of the nation over that of the individual (Chen and Cheung 2017). And, in the Western world, the inability of the United States to effectively regulate Silicon Valley platforms was a crucial shortcoming, eventually leading to the construction of extensive surveillance practices by private technical companies (Bauman et al. 2014). But precisely because technology is such an important arrangement of power – that a variety of actors seek to achieve their Internet policy objectives via choices of technical architecture and infrastructure, and specific uses of them – the building of a rights-preserving technological alternative, supported by laws that are both aware of the state-of-art of technology and co-evolve with it, seem to be an interesting way to build novel technosocial systems that preserve data integrity and sovereignty, both inside traditional national borders and across these borders.

The ability to guarantee fundamental human rights via technology – to embed rights into technology – is gaining momentum, both in the realm of law (e.g. Article 25 of the GDPR, mandating data protection by design and by default) and in the realm of technology development. In this latter regard, the work of the IRTF's Human Rights Protocol Considerations Research Group is especially interesting (see also ten Oever 2021). This research group, basing its work explicitly on the UN Human Rights Charter, attempts to undertake technical reviews of protocols so as to determine whether they are compliant with human rights. However, a shortcoming of this group's work is that the review happens after the protocol has been designed, which restricts the possibility of modifying existing protocols. One encryption-related illustration of this has been the group's support for the implementation of Encrypted SNIs (**Server Name Indication**, the indication of the one or more domain names one is connecting to via an IP address) in TLS 1.3, in order to prevent the 'breaking' of encryption by network operators in order to enable mass surveillance and censorship.

Given that standards bodies like the IETF and W3C have no legally binding regulatory power at the nation-state level (unlike, for example, the ISO), their primary role is to make recommendations, supported by the self-regulation of the industry itself. Internet governance scholars have extensively analysed the historical gap between the 'soft power' of self-regulating standards bodies like the IETF and W3C and the extent to which they respectively created most of the core standards of the Internet and Web. They have also assessed the fairly limited effectiveness of bodies such as the ISO and International Telecommunications Union (ITU), which are more closely linked to international organisations, in particular the UN system, but whose standards (and procedures to attain them) have much less endorsement from Internet technologists (see Mueller 2012; more broadly Harcourt et al. 2020).

However, the more open, 'multi-stakeholder' standards bodies, such as IETF and W3C, are not without pressure from specific groups of actors. A recent controversy illustrating this has focused on the standardisation of Encrypted Media Extensions for Digital Rights Management tools, pushed by Silicon Valley giants (Netflix and Google in particular). This took place in the face of protests by civil society groups, such as the Electronic Freedom Frontier Foundation, and objections from political figures like European Parliament representatives Julia Reda and Lucy Anderson, who were concerned about how DRM violated 'fair use' rights in Europe, as well as fundamental human rights (Reda and Anderson 2017). Tim Berners-Lee himself, the inventor of the Web, eventually yielded to powerful lobbying and supported the DRM standard, arguably to maintain the relevance of the W3C in the face of the Web's slow monopolisation (McCarthy 2017). European standardisation bodies (both national and supra-national) have also at times proved unreliable in their defence of users' fundamental rights: for example, during the aforementioned controversy over encrypted SNIs, the European Telecommunications Standards Institute (ETSI) 'forked' the IETF standard TLS 1.3 in order to create a 'backdoor' explicitly rejected by the IETF, removing the encrypted SNIs supported by human rights activists and enforcing cryptography that would allow monitoring of encrypted traffic by a 'middlebox' between a user and a website. While the ETSI justified this choice as useful for quality-of-service and monitoring enterprises, its implications for making mass surveillance easier were emphasised by commentators (Leyden 2019). Unlike other entities that are part of the Internet governance galaxy, such as the Internet Governance Forum – an arena for discussion with no decision-making power – standardisation bodies are by design not meant to include civil society at large in their discussion and consensus-making procedures. Thus, the risk exists that the governance of online privacy and surveillance, including encryption issues – and in particular the governance that includes the making of standards for this area – will become increasingly unfettered from human rights. This could override traditional forms of sovereignty and the human rights protection system of 'checks and balances', to shift towards a 'state of exception' where the private sector would hold excessive and largely unsupervised power.

To summarise, standardisation bodies are under pressure, as they are often not multi-stakeholder, and their actions can cause collateral damage in the absence of safeguards. For all these reasons, it will be increasingly difficult to maintain human rights as an important component of standards-related discussions, and there is a pressing risk that standardisation will happen without taking them into account.

The GDPR in the multi-architectural world of online communications

While the GDPR is the first global privacy framework that extends the rights of European citizens into technological platforms in other national jurisdictions – and for this reason has been hailed as a historic achievement of legislation (Gérot and Maxwell 2020) – it has been created in reference to a particular type of architectural configuration, one that is centralised and server-based, and the dominant model in the contemporary landscape of Internet-based services.

The General Data Protection Regulation is based on the core concept of informed consent, where in order to maintain user's autonomy over their data, users must be informed both about what personal data is being collected by a particular web service, called the data controller, and how this data is being processed by possible third parties, called data processors. For example, when using a service such as an online newspaper, the user must be informed of their rights and then 'opt-in' to the usage of their data and its distribution to ad networks (e.g. Google's advertisements) which are data processors. A citizen thus ideally is granted rights and control over their data in order for their digital autonomy to be maintained. However, the General Data Protection Regulation has been controversial because of what its enforcement has led to in practice. As recent studies have shown (e.g. Utz et al. 2019; Herrle and Hirsch, 2019), citizens are cognitively overwhelmed by the scope and scale of the processing of their personal data, and a gap often forms between the ground-breaking goals of the General Data Protection Regulation and its implementation. Users are confronted by endless email approvals and online forms that claim to give a data controller consent, often phrased in inscrutable ways, and often presenting a 'take it or leave it approach', leaving citizens with the impression of being forced to comply with a package of limitations in order to use the contemporary Web.

While it is out of scope for this book to comment extensively on the GDPR, we will highlight here one particular aspect: the extent to which one core hypothesis that subtended its creation may affect its effectiveness when it comes to the tools for secure communications we analyse. For, as a regulation, the GDPR is fundamentally based on the paradigm of centralised architecture: the data controllers are assumed to be large, centralised servers under the control of external entities in the 'Cloud', with any processing of data being undertaken by a discrete number of data processors, assumed to be other external third-party 'cloud' servers. Further, the assumption is both that these data processors are known in advance by the data controller and that their identity can be communicated to the user before the personal data is transferred to the data controller.

These assumptions seem problematic, though, in light of the great variety of architectural and encrypting arrangements we have examined. First, GDPR Article 24 requires controllers to implement systems capable of demonstrating that the processing of personal data is performed in accordance with the GDPR. For server-side 'cloud'-based infrastructure, this seems difficult if not impossible, as neither the user nor any legal body has insight into the data processing in the server-side cloud, which is opaque by design. The flows between data processors are thus also unknown to the user, and often processing is done in new and unforeseen ways via shadowy networks of data processors whose complexity is difficult to grasp, much less enumerate – as it is nearly impossible to prevent the copying of data. Second, although concrete measures such as data minimisation and pseudonymisation are discussed by Article 25 (centred on privacy 'by design' and 'by default' as discussed above), it is unclear how they can be assessed based on a centralised architecture. Finally, the GDPR hinges not only on the promise of the server-side data controller being transparent, but also on the assumption that consent for these increasingly opaque dataflows can be meaningfully given by the user. It appears that attempting to place these constraints on current centralised cloud-based services is quixotic, as the data protection action assumes the centralised platforms' good faith – while in many cases, such platforms' business models are based primarily on data extractivism. It is likely for this very reason that centralised platforms like Facebook and Google would rather opt to be fined by the European Commission, or specific European countries – no matter how substantial the fines are – than comply with the substance of GDPR, which would require an in-depth 're-architecturing' of their technologies.

What is in the GDPR, then, for more decentralised and federated architectures? It has been suggested that a move away from centralised platforms to alternatives based on blockchain as an architectural principle could be used to 're-architect' a new generation of platforms more in line with securing user's rights. However, scholars have argued that in its current state, blockchain technology is not mature enough to be compatible with data protection regulations (Halpin and Piekarska 2017). Institutions have mobilised on the issue as well: the European Union Blockchain Observatory and Forum has remarked that the EU's courts and data protection authorities have so far highlighted three main tensions between the distributed ledger technologies and the EU's new data protection rules, namely: the difficulties in identifying the obligations of data controllers and processors; disagreements about when personal data should be anonymised; and the difficulty of exercising new data subject rights. This includes the right to be forgotten and the possibility of erasing certain data, given that personal data shared on a blockchain prevents censorship (including changing or erasing the data by legal request of a data subject), is cryptographically intertwined into the entire blockchain by design and is public by default. As a solution, the authors propose four rule-of-thumb principles: Technologies designing systems for public usage should 'start with the big picture' and decide whether blockchain is needed and really meets their data needs; they should avoid storing personal data on blockchain and use data obfuscation and encryption techniques instead; if blockchain cannot be avoided, they should favour private, permissioned blockchain networks; and they should be transparent with users (EU Blockchain Observatory 2018).

Beyond the blockchain, decentralised networks that use end-to-end encryption and privacy enhancing-technologies, both federated and P2P, are likely to be more easily compliant with the GDPR and superior to several applications of the blockchain (e.g. from an environmental standpoint – proof of work requires substantial computing resources, and thus energy consumption). However, the challenges such technologies face both at the development stage and in relation to large-scale adoption by users are numerous and have been discussed at length in this book, especially in Chapters 3 and 4. From a theoretical standpoint, in the case of p2p networks, the user herself is the data controller, and freely chooses her own data processors and who to share data with. For federated networks, the data controller will be the entity that runs the server. If end-to-end encryption is used in both these models, then in decentralised systems the personal data are hidden from the data controller in the federated setting and from other peers in a P2P setting, and so uses of the data that are not explicitly authorised by the user are rendered technically impossible. Privacy-enhancing technologies, as we have seen throughout the more empirically oriented chapters of this book, can then be used to limit the scope of third parties from determining even the metadata of communication, rendering the data anonymised by default and so unable to be processed without consent.

Decentralised and encrypted protocols are potentially capable of providing a robust technological solution for data protection, one that is compatible with recent legislation. A marriage between these two dynamics has been identified, by the NEXTLEAP project and beyond, as a promising way forward in the quest to 'conceal for freedom'. However, as this book – and other previous and current work – has shown, 'reclaiming the Internet' (Aigrain 2010; Musiani and Méadel 2016) by fostering the coexistence of a variety of architectural, economic and governance arrangements, is a far-from-linear process: one that will include a good deal of experimentation with assemblages of human and non-human actors, rearrangements in power balances and attempts to place Internet rights and freedoms at the core of the technical development and standardisation processes.

SOCIAL STUDIES OF ENCRYPTION WITHIN INTERNET GOVERNANCE RESEARCH: MOVING FORWARD

In the final months of writing this book, two book-length contributions were published that are closely connected with the present work. Linda Monsees' *Crypto-Politics: Encryption and Democratic Practices in the Digital Era* (2019) explores the post-Snowden debates on digital encryption in Germany and the United States, showing how discussions about the value of privacy and the legitimacy of surveillance practices have closely merged with controversies around encryption technologies, making encryption a subject of technopolitical contestation within multiple expert circles. Philip DiSalvo's *Digital Whistleblowing Platforms for Journalism: Encrypting Leaks* (2020) delves into whistleblowing platforms as an increasingly important phenomenon for journalism in the post-Snowden era, as safer solutions for communicating with whistleblowers and obtaining leaks; DiSalvo explores the potentials of, and needs for, encryption for journalistic purposes, together with the perils of surveillance.

Together with the kind of work we propose in this book, with our investigation of the development and user appropriation of encrypted secure messaging tools, these recent works reaffirm the importance of encryption as an issue worthy of investigation via methods and concepts derived from STS. With this book, we have followed developers as they interact with other stakeholders and with the technical artefacts they design – with a core common objective of creating tools that 'conceal for freedom', while differing in their intended technical architectures, their targeted user publics and the underlying values and business models. Together, these stories flesh out the *experience* of encryption in the variety of secure messaging protocols and tools existing today, and its implications for the 'making of' digital liberties. Collectively, our book and these other recent works show how encryption takes shape both in visions for online freedoms and in very concrete, and diverse, sets of implementations – and how this is a core issue of Internet governance.

Internet governance, as a recent and increasingly dynamic body of work suggests, is as much about the work of institutions, and about legislative processes, as it is about the 'mundane practices' and the agency of technology designers, developers, hackers, maintainers and users as they interact, in a distributed fashion, with technologies, rules and regulations, leading to both intended and unintended consequences with systemic effects (Epstein, Katzenbach and Musiani 2016). STS approaches such as those we have adopted in this book can help in empirically analysing the diverse forms of decision-making and coordination activities that take place beyond formal and well-defined boundaries (van Eeten and Mueller 2013).

Such an approach is especially relevant at a time when online surveillance and privacy, and the technological and legal means to limit the former and protect the latter, are being identified (e.g. by Mueller and Badiei 2020) as the pre-eminent Internet governance-related issue of the last decade. It is an issue that has been catalysed by the Snowden revelations, but that has its roots in longstanding debates about personal data, identity on the Internet and cryptology. Arguably, the era ushered in by the Snowden revelations is one where the world took full measure of the extent of the United States' *de facto* global authority 'by infrastructure' on the Internet and became aware of the depth of the US government's 'dangerous liaisons' with private intermediaries (Musiani 2013). This opened up a major crisis of legitimacy for the US to keep on acting as the foremost actor in Internet governance, and arguably – even if the process was, slowly but surely, already underway before Snowden – contributed to the so-called 'IANA transition', the process through which the US relinquished their control of the Domain Name System root, and which led to substantial reforms in the accountability mechanisms used in managing it by the Internet Corporation for Assigned Names and Numbers (ICANN).

In parallel, recent years have also witnessed the rise of new 'superpowers' in Internet governance, most notably Russia and China (see e.g. Litvinenko 2020 and Negro 2017), whose predominant strategy has been to achieve 'digital sovereignty'. This is the idea that states should reassert their authority over the Internet and protect their nation's self-determination in the digital sphere, not by means of supranational alliances or international instruments, but by increasing their independence and autonomy at various technical, economic and political levels.

In this multi-faceted contemporary Internet governance scenario, encryption is becoming a central issue. As scholars of encryption grounded in the social sciences, we examine the variety of ways in which journalists and activists choose and use encrypted tools to communicate with their sources and explore the numerous arenas where technopolitical controversies about encryption happen. In the present work, we have analysed secure messaging protocols and applications as they are developed and made their own by different groups of pioneer users, and we shed light on the manifold ways in which the 'making, governing and using' of encryption in online communications unfolds; in doing so we have contributed to articulating and solidifying the study of the 'mundane practices' of Internet governance. At the same time, we have explored how these practices cannot do without a constant entwining with the institutional arenas in which political narratives and agendas about encryption unfold – an aspect which has been the focus of this concluding chapter. Indeed, institutions of Internet governance can and should be analysed with the help of the STS toolbox, understanding their authority not as a *fait accompli*, but as a result of their ability to renegotiate and reconfigure themselves in moments of controversy and destabilisation, in order to maintain momentum and legitimacy (see Flyverbom 2011 and Pohle 2016).

We also contribute to conceptualising encryption as a fully interdisciplinary subject of study, one that is as much the prerogative of social sciences as of computer science and legal studies, by unveiling the 'informal' dimensions of power arrangements surrounding it. Informal they may be, but they are no less crucial than institutional debates and decision-making processes in co-shaping our rights and freedoms – as citizens of online communications, and as stakeholders of how the Internet is governed today and will be governed tomorrow.

NOTES

1 The HADOPI (quasi-acronym, in French, of Haute Autorité pour la Diffusion des Œuvres et la Protection des droits d'auteur sur Internet) law, or 'Creation and Internet' law, was a law introduced in 2009 in France, mandating the so-called 'graduated response' or 'three-strikes procedure' that could eventually allow a user's Internet connection to be terminated in case of repeated offense (even though enforcement in practice never reached this final and drastic step because of widespread controversy and eventual abrogation of the law).

2 See Chapter 3 and, in particular, the discussions concerning the implementation of Briar's group chat.

3 One being ClaimChain, a protocol developed by the NEXTLEAP project.

4 Examples are the DECODE project, which has a decentralisation dimension in addition to an open-source one, and in France, the Territoire Apprenant Contributif (TAC) experiment in Plaine Commune, Ile-de-France, which aims to propose an innovative appropriation of digital technologies by the territory to test new economic and social models, through the implementation of a new distributed network architecture, https://recherchecontributive.org.

5 Recent history is again useful here, in recalling that, in an infamous case of subversion of a standards body, the Dual EC pseudorandom number generator (used to generate keys), ratified by the US standards agency NIST, had a backdoor placed in it by the NSA; this backdoor was placed in Juniper routers, and was later exploited by a yet-unknown actor to compromise these routers and then install their own backdoor to decrypt network traffic (Checkoway et al. 2016).

6 https://irtf.org/cfrg.

7 An Act of the Parliament in the United Kingdom (approved in 2016) that sets out and expands the electronic surveillance powers of the country's intelligence services and law enforcement agencies.

8 https://www.fsf.org/about.

9 https://www.gnu.org/licenses/gpl-3.0.en.html.

10 https://www.gnu.org/licenses/agpl-3.0.en.html.

BIBLIOGRAPHY

Abelson, H., and others, 'Keys Under Doormats: Mandating Insecurity by Requiring Government Access to all Data and Communications', MIT CSAIL Technical Report, July 2015 <http://dspace.mit.edu/bitstream/handle/1721.1/97690/MIT-CSAIL-TR-2015-026.pdf> [accessed 21 June 2021].

Abu-Salma, R., K. Krol, S. Parkin, and others, 'The Security Blanket of the Chat World: A Usability Evaluation and User Study of Telegram', in *Proceedings of the 2nd European Workshop on Usable Security (EuroUSEC)*, Paris, France, 2017a.

Abu-Salma, R., J. Bonneau, and others, 'Obstacles to the Adoption of Secure Communication Tools', in *Proceedings of the 38th IEEE Symposium on Security and Privacy*, San Jose, CA, USA, 2017b <https://doi.org/10.1109/SP.2017.65> [accessed 21 June 2021].

Aigrain, P., 'Declouding Freedom: Reclaiming Servers, Services and Data', in *2020 FLOSS roadmap*, Third edition, 2010, formerly at <https://flossroadmap.co-ment.com/text/NUFVxf6wwK2/view/> [now unavailable online, originally accessed 15 October 2012].

Agre, P., 'Peer-to-Peer and the Promise of Internet Equality', *Communications of the ACM*, 46.2 (2003), 39–42.

Aouragh, M., and others, 'Let's First Get Things Done! On Division of Labour and Techno-Political Practices of Delegation in Times of Crisis', *The Fibreculture Journal*, 26 (2015) <https://doi.org/10.15307/fcj.26.196.2015> [accessed 21 June 2021].

Arnold, M. A., E. Darmon, S. Dejean, and T. Penard, 'Graduated Response Policy and the Behavior of Digital Pirates: Evidence from the French Three-Strike (HADOPI) Law'. Working Paper <https://papers.ssrn.com/sol3/papers.cfm?abstract_id=2380522> [accessed 21 June 2021].

Assal, H., S. Hurtado, A. Imran, and S. Chiasson, 'What's the Deal with Privacy Apps?: A Comprehensive Exploration of User Perception and Usability', in *Proceedings of the 14th International Conference on Mobile and Ubiquitous Multimedia*, November 2015, pp. 25–36.

Badouard, R., *Le désenchantement de l'internet. Désinformation, rumeur et propagande* (Limoges, France: FYP éditions, 2017).

Ballve, M., 'Messaging Apps Are Overtaking Social Networks to Become the Dominant Platforms on Phones', *Business Insider*, 10 April 2015 <http://www.businessinsider.com/messaging-apps-have-completely-overtaken-social-networks-to-become-the-dominant-platforms-on-phones-2015-4> [accessed 21 June 2021].

Barbosa, S., and S. Milan, 'Do Not Harm in Private Chat Apps: Ethical Issues for Research on and with WhatsApp', *Westminster Papers in Communication and Culture*, 14.1 (2019), 49–65 <http://doi.org/10.16997/wpcc.313> [accessed 21 June 2021].

Barr, A. C. 'Guardians of Your Galaxy S7: Encryption Backdoors and the First Amendment', *Minnesota Law Review*, 101 (2016), 301.

Bauman, Z., and others, 'After Snowden: Rethinking the Impact of Surveillance', *International Political Sociology*, 8. 2 (2014), 121–44.

Becker, H. S., *Doing Things Together: Selected Papers* (Evanston, IL: Northwestern University Press, 1986).

Bendrath, R. and M. Mueller, 'The End of the Net as We Know It? Deep Packet Inspection and Internet Governance', *New Media & Society*, 13.7 (2011), 1142–60.

Benkler, Y., *The Wealth of Networks: How Social Production Transforms Markets and Freedom* (New Haven, CT: Yale University Press, 2006).

Berners-Lee, T., and H. Halpin, 'Defend the Web', in J. Bus and others, eds, *Digital Enlightenment Yearbook* (IOS Press, 2003), pp. 3–7.

Besen, S. M., and J. Farrell, 'Choosing How to Compete: Strategies and Tactics in Standardization', *The Journal of Economic Perspectives*, 8.2 (1994), 117–31.

Birkinbine, B. J., *Incorporating the Digital Commons: Corporate Involvement in Free and Open Source Software* (London: University of Westminster Press, 2020) <https://doi.org/10.16997/book39> [accessed 21 June 2021].

Borisov, N., I. Goldberg, and E. Brewer, 'Off-the-Record Communication, or, Why Not to Use PGP', in *Proceedings of the 2004 ACM Workshop on Privacy in the Electronic Society* <https://otr.cypherpunks.ca/otr-wpes.pdf> [accessed 21 June 2021].

Bortzmeyer, S., *Cyberstructure: L'Internet, un espace politique* (Caen, France: C & F Éditions, 2019).

Borup, M., N. Brown, K. Konrad, and H. Van Lente, 'The Sociology of Expectations in Science and Technology', *Technology Analysis & Strategic Management*, 18.3–4 (2006), 285–98.

Bowker, G. C., and S. L. Star, *Sorting Things Out: Classification and Its Consequences* (Cambridge, MA: The MIT Press, 1999).

Braman, S., 'Instability and Internet Design', *Internet Policy Review*, 5.3 (2016) <https://doi.org/10.14763/2016.3.429> [accessed 21 June 2021].

Brekke, J. K., and M. Isaakidis, 'Principles for Decentralized Protocol Design', NEXTLEAP Project Deliverable 2.5., 2019.

Brown, N., and M. Michael, 'A Sociology of Expectations: Retrospecting Prospects and Prospecting Retrospects', *Technology Analysis & Strategic Management*, 15.1 (2003), 3–18.

Brunton, F., *Digital Cash: The Unknown History of the Anarchists, Utopians, and Technologists Who Created Cryptocurrency* (Princeton: Princeton University Press, 2019).

Brunton, F., and H. Nissenbaum, *Obfuscation: A User's Guide for Privacy and Protest* (Cambridge, MA: The MIT Press, 2015).

Busch, L., *Standards: Recipe for Reality* (Cambridge, MA: The MIT Press, 2011).

Callon, M., 'Elaborating the Notion of Performativity', *Le Libellio d'Aegis*, 5.1 (2009), 18–29.

——, 'The Sociology of an Actor-Network: The Case of the Electric Vehicle', in M. Callon, J. Law and A. Rip, eds, *Mapping the Dynamics of Science and Technology: Sociology of Science in the Real World* (London, Macmillan Press, 1986), pp. 19–34.

Campbell-Verduyn, M., ed., *Bitcoin and Beyond: Cryptocurrencies, Blockchains, and Global Governance* (London: Routledge, 2017).

Cardozo, N., G. Gebhart, and E. Portnoy, 'Secure Messaging? More Like a Secure Mess', *EFF Deeplinks*, 26 March 2018 <https://www.eff.org/deeplinks/2018/03/secure-messaging-more-secure-mess> [accessed 21 June 2021].

Carey, S. 'The Snooper's Charter Still Has an Encryption Problem: Parliament Continues to Grapple with End-to-End Encryption in the Investigatory Powers Bill', *Computerworld*, 19 July 2016 <https://www.computerworld.com/article/3427168/the-snooper-s-charter-still-has-an-encryption-problem--parliament-continues-to-grapple-with-end-to-e.html> [accessed 21 June 2021].

Casilli, A., 'Quatre thèses sur la surveillance numérique de masse et la négociation de la vie privée', in *Rapport du Conseil d'Etat de 2015*, (2015), 423–34.

Cerf, V., 'Internet Access is Not a Human Right', *The New York Times*, Opinion, 4 January 2012 <https://www.nytimes.com/2012/01/05/opinion/internet-access-is-not-a-human-right.html> [accessed 21 June 2021].

Chapman, C., 'Mozilla Pens Open Letter to German Policymakers Over Planned Encryption Law', *The Daily Swig*, 14 June 2019 <https://portswigger.net/daily-swig/mozilla-pens-open-letter-to-german-policymakers-over-planned-encryption-law> [accessed 21 June 2021].

Checkoway, S., and others, 'A Systematic Analysis of the Juniper Dual EC incident', in *Proceedings of the 2016 ACM SIGSAC Conference on Computer and Communications Security*, 2016 (pp. 468–79) <https://dl.acm.org/doi/abs/10.1145/2976749.2978395> [accessed 21 June 2021].

Chen, Y. and A. S. Y. Cheung, 'The Transparent Self Under Big Data Profiling: Privacy and Chinese Legislation on the Social Credit System', *The Journal of Comparative Law*, 12.2 (2017), 356–78 <http://dx.doi.org/10.2139/ssrn.2992537> [accessed 21 June 2021].

CNNum (*Conseil national du numérique*, the French Digital Council), 'Prédictions, chiffrement et libertés', Report, September 2017 <https://cnnumerique.fr/files/2017-10/CNNum_avis_prédiction_chiffrement_libertés_sept2017.pdf> [accessed 21 June 2021].

Cohn-Gordon, K., C. Cremers, and L. Garratt, 'On Post-Compromise Security', in Proceedings of the Computer Security Foundations Symposium (CSF), 2016, pp. 164–78.

Cole, M., *Cultural Psychology: A Once and Future Discipline* (Cambridge, MA: Harvard University Press, 1996).

Coleman, E. G., *Coding Freedom: The Ethics and Aesthetics of Hacking.* (Princeton and Oxford: Princeton University Press, 2013) <https://gabriellacoleman.org/Coleman-Coding-Freedom.pdf> [accessed 21 June 2021].

——, *The Social Construction of Freedom in Free and Open Source Software: Hackers, Ethics, and the Liberal Tradition* (PhD Thesis, Chicago, IL: The University of Chicago, 2005).

——, 'Anonymous: From lulz to Collective Action', *MediaCommons*, 6 April 2011 <http://mediacommons.futureofthebook.org/tne/pieces/anonymous-lulz-collective-action> [accessed 21 June 2021].

Coleman, E. G., and A. Golub, 'Hacker Practice: Moral Genres and the Cultural Articulation of Liberalism', *Anthropological Theory*, 8.3 (2008), 255–77.

Conger, J. A., *The Charismatic Leader: Behind the Mystique of Exceptional Leadership* (Jossey-Bass, 1989).

Cranor, L. F. and S. Garfinkel, *Security and Usability: Designing Secure Systems That People Can Use* (New York: O'Reilly Media, 2005).

David, P. A., 'Clio and the Economics of QWERTY', *The American Economic Review*, 75.2 (1985), 332–37.

De Goede, M., E. Bosma, and P. Pallister-Wilkins, eds, *Secrecy and Methods in Security Research: A Guide to Qualitative Fieldwork* (London: Routledge, 2019).

Deibert, R. J., and M. Crete-Nishihata, 'Global Governance and the Spread of Cyberspace Controls', *Global Governance: A Review of Multilateralism and International Organizations*, 18.3 (2012), 339–61.

Dechand, S., A. Naiakshina, A. Danilova, and M. Smith, 'In Encryption We Don't Trust: The Effect of End-to-End Encryption to the Masses on User Perception', in *Proceedings of the 2019 IEEE European Symposium on Security and Privacy (EuroS&P)*, June 2019 (pp. 401–15).

DeNardis, L., *The Internet in Everything: Freedom and Security in a World with No Off Switch* (New Haven, CT: Yale University Press, 2020).

———, *The Global War for Internet Governance* (New Haven, CT: Yale University Press, 2014).

———, *Protocol Politics: The Globalization of Internet Governance* (Cambridge, MA: The MIT Press, 2009).

DeNardis, L., and A. M. Hackl, 'Internet Governance by Social Media Platforms', *Telecommunications Policy*, 2015 <https://doi.org/10.1016/j.telpol.2015.04.003> [accessed 21 June 2021].

DeNardis, L., and F. Musiani, 'Introduction: Governance by Infrastructure', in F. Musiani, D. L. Cogburn, L. DeNardis, & N. S. Levinson, eds, *The Turn to Infrastructure in Internet Governance* (New York: Palgrave Macmillan, 2016), pp. 3–21.

Denis, J., 'Les nouveaux visages de la performativité', *Études de communication*, 29 (2006), 8–24.

Denis, J., and D. Pontille, 'Material Ordering and the Care of Things', *Science, Technology, & Human Values*, 40.3 (2015), 338–67.

DiSalvo, P., *Digital Whistleblowing Platforms for Journalism: Encrypting Leaks*, London: Palgrave/Macmillan, 2020.

Douglas, M., and A. Wildavsky, *Risk and Culture* (Berkeley, University of California Press, 1982).

Dourish, P., and K. Anderson, 'Collective Information Practice: Exploring Privacy and Security as Social and Cultural Phenomena', *Human-Computer Interaction*, 21.3 (2006), 319–42.

Ducklin, P., 'Signal Secure Messaging Can Now Identify You Without a Phone Number', *Naked Security*, 22 May 2020 <https://nakedsecurity.sophos.com/2020/05/22/signal-secure-messaging-can-now-identify-you-without-a-phone-number> [accessed 21 June 2021].

Eckersley, P., 'What Makes a Good Security Audit?', *EFF Deeplinks*, 8 November 2014 <https://www.eff.org/deeplinks/2014/11/what-makes-good-security-audit> [accessed 21 June 2021].

EDRi, 'Encryption Workarounds. A Digital Rights Perspective', Position Paper, 2017 <https://edri.org/files/encryption/workarounds_edriposition_20170912.pdf> [accessed 21 June 2021].

Edwards, P., and others, *Understanding Infrastructure: Dynamics, Tensions, and Design*, Report of a Workshop on 'History & Theory of Infrastructure: Lessons for New Scientific Cyberinfrastructures', 2007 <https://deepblue.lib.umich.edu/bitstream/handle/2027.42/49353/UnderstandingInfrastructure2007.pdf> [accessed 21 June 2021].

Elkin-Koren, N., 'Making Technology Visible: Liability of Internet Service Providers for Peer-to-Peer Traffic', *New York University Journal of Legislation & Public Policy*, 9.15 (2005), 15–76.

eMarketer, 'Are We Watching the Death of SMS?', eMarketer, 2 March 2015 <http://www.emarketer.com/Article/Watching-Death-of-SMS/1012124> [accessed 21 June 2021].

Epstein, D., C. Katzenbach, and F. Musiani, *Doing Internet Governance: Practices, Controversies, Infrastructures, and Institutions*, special issue, *Internet Policy Review*, 5.3 (2016) <https://doi.org/10.14763/2016.3.435> [accessed 21 June 2021].

Ermoshina, K., *Au code, citoyens: Mise en technologie de problèmes publics*, (Unpublished PhD dissertation, MINES ParisTech, 2016).

Ermoshina, K., and F. Musiani, '"Standardising by Running Code": The Signal Protocol and De Facto Standardisation in End-to-End Encrypted Messaging', *Internet Histories*, 3.3–4 (2019), 343–63.

Ermoshina, K., F. Musiani, and H. Halpin, 'End-to-End Encrypted Messaging Protocols: An Overview', in F. Bagnoli, and others, eds, *Proceedings of the Internet Science Third International Conference*, INSCI 2016, Florence, Italy, 12–14 September, Berlin, Springer, 2016, pp. 244–254 <https://doi.org/10.1007/978-3-319-45982-0_22>.

European Commission, *Resilience, Deterrence and Defence: Building Strong Cybersecurity for the EU*, Report, 13 September 2017 <https://ec.europa.eu/transparency/regdoc/rep/10101/2017/EN/JOIN-2017-450-F1-EN-MAIN-PART-1.PDF> [accessed 21 June 2021].

European Union Blockchain Observatory and Forum, *Blockchain and the GDPR*, Thematic report, 2018 <https://www.eublockchainforum.eu/sites/default/files/reports/20181016_report_gdpr.pdf> [accessed 21 June 2021].

Fischer, C., 'The Revolution in Rural Telephony', *Journal of Social History*, 21 (1987), 5–26.

Flyverbom, M., *The Power of Networks: Organizing the Global Politics of the Internet*. (Cheltenham, UK: Edward Elgar Publishing, 2011).

Flyverbom, M., P. M. Leonardi, C. Stohl, and M. Stohl, 'The Management of Visibilities in the Digital Age', *International Journal of Communication*, 10 (2016), 98–109.

Frosch, T., and others, 'How Secure is TextSecure?', in *Proceedings of the European Symposium on Security and Privacy* (EuroS&P), 2016, pp. 457–72.

Gangneux, J., 'Book Review: Hintz, A., Dencik, L., & Wahl-Jorgensen, K. (2018). *Digital Citizenship in a Datafied Society*. Cambridge, UK: Polity Press', *Information, Communication and Society*, 22.14 (2019), 2211–13.

Gérot, M., and W. Maxwell, 'Will the GDPR Frustrate Europe's Plans for AI?', 16 March 2020, *isBuzznews* <https://www.informationsecuritybuzz.com/articles/will-the-gdpr-frustrate-europes-plans-for-ai/> [accessed 21 June 2021].

Gill, L., T. Israel, and C. Parsons, 'Shining a Light on the Encryption Debate: A Canadian Field Guide', Report by the Citizen Lab and the Samuelson-Glushko Canadian Internet Policy and Public Interest Clinic, 2018 <https://citizenlab.ca/wp-content/uploads/2018/05/Shining-A-Light-Encryption-CitLab-CIPPIC.pdf> [accessed 21 June 2021].

Goody, J., *The Domestication of the Savage Mind* (Cambridge: Cambridge University Press, 1977).

Goodwin, C., 'Practices of Color Classification', *Cognitive Studies: Bulletin of the Japanese Cognitive Science Society*, 3.2 (1996), 62–82.

Greenemeier, L., 'NSA Efforts to Evade Encryption Technology Damaged U.S. Cryptography Standard', *Scientific American*, 18 September 2013 <https://www.scientificamerican.com/article/nsa-nist-encryption-scandal/> [accessed 21 June 2021].

Haggerty, K. D., and R. D. Ericson, 'The Surveillant Assemblage', *British Journal of Sociology*, 51.4 (2000), 605–22.

Halpin, H., and M. Piekarska, M., 'Introduction to Security and Privacy on the Blockchain', in *Proceedings of the 2017 IEEE European Symposium on Security and Privacy Workshops (EuroS&PW)*, April 2017, pp. 1–3 <https://ieeexplore.ieee.org/abstract/document/7966963> [accessed 21 June 2021].

Harcourt, A., G. Christou, and S. Simpson, *Global Standard Setting in Internet Governance* (Oxford: Oxford University Press, 2020).

Hatmaker, T., 'Tor Node Operator Arrested in Russia Will be Held on Terrorism Charges Until June Trial', *TechCrunch*, 25 April 2017 <https://techcrunch.com/2017/04/24/dmitry-bogatov-tor-russia/> [accessed 21 June 2021].

Healy, C. M., 'A Tech Individualist for a Post-Snowden World', *Dazed*, 2 April 2015 <https://www.dazeddigital.com/artsandculture/article/24279/1/pavel-durov> [accessed 21 June 2021].

Hellegren, Z. I., 'A History of Crypto-Discourse: Encryption as a Site of Struggles to Define Internet Freedom', *Internet Histories*, 1.4 (2017), 285–311.

Herpig, S., and S. Heumann, 'The Encryption Debate in Germany', International Encryption Brief, Carnegie Endowment for International Peace, 30 May 2019 <https://carnegieendowment.org/2019/05/30/encryption-debate-in-germany-pub-79215> [accessed 21 June 2021].

Herrle, J., and J. Hirsh, 'The Peril and Potential of the GDPR', Centre for International Governance Innovation, Opinion, 9 July 2019 <https://www.cigionline.org/articles/peril-and-potential-gdpr> [accessed 21 June 2021].

Hintz, A., and L. Dencik, 'The Politics of Surveillance Policy: UK Regulatory Dynamics after Snowden', *Internet Policy Review*, 5.3 (2017) <https://doi.org/10.14763/2016.3.424> [accessed 21 June 2021].

Hintz, A., L. Dencik, and K. Wahl-Jorgensen, *Digital Citizenship in a Datafied Society* (Cambridge, UK: Polity Press, 2018).

Hodgson, M., 'Matrix and Riot Confirmed as the Basis for France's Secure Instant Messenger app', *Matrix.org Blog*, 26 April 2018 <https://matrix.org/blog/2018/04/26/matrix-and-riot-confirmed-as-the-basis-for-frances-secure-instant-messenger-app/> [accessed 21 June 2021].

Hodson, D., and M. Jones, 'EFF secure messaging scorecard review', *ELTTAM blog*, 11 August 2016 <https://www.elttam.com.au/blog/a-review-of-the-eff-secure-messaging-scorecard-pt2/> [accessed 21 June 2021].

Hong, S.-H, 'Criticising Surveillance and Surveillance Critique: Why Privacy and Humanism are Necessary but Insufficient', *Surveillance & Society*, 15.2 (2017), 187–203.

Howard, P. N., 'Testing the Leap-Frog Hypothesis: The Impact of Existing Infrastructure and Telecommunications Policy on the Global Digital Divide', *Information, Community and Society*, 10.2 (2007), 133–57.

Huysmans, J., *Security Unbound: Enacting Democratic Limits. Critical Issues in Global Politics* (London and New York: Routledge, 2014).

IFEX, 'HRC 36: Secure Digital Communications are Essential for Human Rights', 19 September 2017 <https://www.ifex.org/turkey/2017/09/19/apc_ifex_hrc36_4_statement/> [accessed 21 June 2021].

Internet Without Borders, 'Brazil, Elections 2018: The Risk of an Internet Shutdown Must Be Taken Seriously', *IWB blog*, 2018 <https://internetwithoutborders.org/brazil-elections-2018-the-risk-of-an-internet-shutdown-must-be-taken-seriously/> [accessed 21 June 2021].

Introna, L., and H. Nissenbaum, 'Shaping the Web: Why the Politics of Online Search Engines Matter', *The Information Society*, 16.3 (2006), 169–85.

Izal, M., and others, 'Dissecting Bittorrent: Five Months in a Torrent's Lifetime', in *Proceedings of the International Workshop on Passive and Active Network Measurement* (Berlin, Heidelberg: Springer, 2004).

Jakobsen, J. and C. Orlandi, 'On the CCA (In)Security of MTProto', in *Proceedings of the ACM Workshop on Security and Privacy in Smartphones and Mobile Devices*, 2016, pp. 113–16.

Jeditobe, 'Delta Chat, a Decentralized Messenger of Top of Email', Habr.com, 2019, <https://habr.com/ru/post/442266/> [accessed 21 June 2021].

Jouët, J., 'Retour critique sur la sociologie des usages', *Réseaux*, 18.100 (2000), 487–521.

Kaye, D., *Report of the Special Rapporteur on the Promotion and Protection of the Right to Freedom of Opinion and Expression, David Kaye*, 22 May 2015.

Kazansky, B., 'Privacy, Responsibility, and Human Rights Activism', *The Fibreculture*

Journal, 26 (2015) <https://doi.org/10.15307/fcj.26.195.2015> [accessed 21 June 2021].

Kent, D., 'Why is Having Multiple Messaging Platforms "Bad" in 2019', Dispatch, 2019 <https://dispatch.m.io/multiple-messaging-platforms-bad/> [accessed 21 June 2021].

Kockelman, P., 'The Anthropology of an Equation. Sieves, Spam Filters, Agentive Algorithms, and Ontologies of Transformation', *HAU: Journal of Ethnographic Theory*, 3.3 (2013), 33–61.

Ku, R. S. R., 'The Creative Destruction of Copyright: Napster and the New Economics of Digital Technology', in *Copyright Law* (London: Routledge, 2017), pp. 207–68.

Lave, J., and E. Wenger, *Situated Learning: Legitimate Peripheral Participation* (Cambridge: Cambridge University Press, 1991).

Levine, Y., 'Spy-Funded Privacy Tools (Like Signal and Tor) Are Not Going to Protect Us from President Trump', *The Surveillance Valley Blog*, 2016 <https://surveillancevalley.com/blog/government-backed-privacy-tools-are-not-going-to-protect-us-from-president-trump>

Leyden, J., 'EFF Condemns Financial Think-Tank for Promoting 'Weaker' Crypto', *The Daily Swig*, 28 February 2019 <https://portswigger.net/daily-swig/eff-condemns-financial-think-tank-for-promoting-weaker-crypto> [accessed 21 June 2021].

Loconto, A., and L. Busch, 'Standards, Techno-Economic Networks, and Playing Fields: Performing the Global Market Economy', *Review of International Political Economy*, 17.3 (2010), 507–36.

Mager, A., 'Algorithmic Ideology: How Capitalist Society Shapes Search Engines', *Information, Communication & Society*, 15.5 (2012), 769–87.

Manils, P., and others, 'Compromising Tor Anonymity Exploiting P2P Information Leakage', *arXiv preprint*, 2010 <https://arxiv.org/abs/1004.1461> [accessed 21 June 2021].

Marcus, G. E., 'Multi-Sited Ethnography: Five or Six Things I Know about It Now', in *Multi-Sited ethnography* (London: Routledge, 2012), pp. 24–40.

Marlinspike, M., 'Reflections: The Ecosystem Is Moving', *Signal Blog*, 10 May 2016 <https://signal.org/blog/the-ecosystem-is-moving/> [accessed 21 June 2021].

——, 'The Difficult of Private Contact Discovery', *Signal Blog*, 3 January 2014 <https://signal.org/blog/contact-discovery/> [accessed 21 June 2021].

——, 'Advanced Cryptographic Ratcheting', OpenWhisperSystems blog, 26 November 2013 <https://whispersystems.org/blog/advanced-ratcheting> [accessed 21 June 2021].

Marsden, C. T., *Network Neutrality: From Policy to Law to Regulation* (Manchester: Manchester University Press, 2017).

Martin, A., R. van Brakel, and D. Bernhard, 'Understanding Resistance to Digital Surveillance: Towards a Multi-Disciplinary, Multi-Actor Framework', *Surveillance & Society*, 6.3 (2009), 213–32.

McCarthy, K., 'Sir Tim Berners-Lee Refuses to Be King Canute, Approves DRM as Web Standard', The Register, 6 March 2017 <https://www.theregister.co.uk/2017/03/06/berners_lee_web_drm_w3c/> [accessed 21 June 2021].

Méadel, C., and F. Musiani, eds, *Abécédaire des architectures distribuées* (Paris, France: Presses des Mines, 2015).

Meier-Hahn, U., 'Internet Interconnection: Networking in Uncertain Terrain', Blog of the *RIPE Labs*, 5 February 2015 <https://labs.ripe.net/Members/uta_meier_hahn/internet-interconnection-networking-in-uncertain-terrain> [accessed 21 June 2021].

Metz, C., 'Forget Apple vs the FBI: WhatsApp Just Switched on Encryption for a Billion People', *Wired*, 4 May 2016 <https://www.wired.com/2016/04/forget-apple-vs-fbi-whatsapp-just-switched-encryption-billion-people/> [accessed 21 June 2021].

Milan, S., *Social Movements and Their Technologies: Wiring Social Change* (Berlin: Springer, 2013)

Milan, S., and N. ten Oever, 'Coding and Encoding Rights in Internet Infrastructure', *Internet Policy Review*, 6.1 (2017), https://doi.org/10.14763/2017.1.442 [accessed 21 June 2021].

Milan, S., and L. van der Velden, 'Reversing Data Politics: An Introduction to the Special Issue', *Krisis: Journal for Contemporary Philosophy*, 1 (2018), 1–3.

Minar, N., and M. Hedlund, 'A Network of Peers – Peer-to-Peer Models through the History of the Internet', in A. Oram, ed., *Peer-to-Peer: Harnessing the Power of Disruptive Technologies* (Sebastopol, CA: O'Reilly, 2001), pp. 9–20.

Monsees, L., *Crypto-Politics. Encryption and Democratic Practices in the Digital Era* (Abingdon and New York: Routledge, 2019).

Mueller, M. L., 'ITU Phobia: Why WCIT was Derailed', *Internet Governance Project, Georgia Tech School of Public Policy*, 18 December 2012 <https://www.internetgovernance.org/2012/12/18/itu-phobia-why-wcit-was-derailed/> [accessed 21 June 2021].

Mueller, M. L., and F. Badiei, 'Inventing Internet Governance: The Historical Trajectory of the Phenomenon and the Field', in L. DeNardis, D. Cogburn, N. S. Levinson and F. Musiani, eds, *Researching Internet Governance: Methods, Frameworks, Futures* (Cambridge, MA: The MIT Press, 2020), pp. 59–83.

Mueller, M. L., A. Kuehn, and S. M. Santoso, 'Policing the Network: Using DPI for Copyright Enforcement', *Surveillance & Society*, 9.4 (2012), 348–64.

Muir, S., 'Multisited Ethnography', in D. Southerton, ed., *Encyclopedia of Consumer Culture* (London: Sage, 2011) <http://dx.doi.org/10.4135/9781412994248. n375> [accessed 21 June 2021].

Musiani, F., 'Gaps in Peer Design', in M. O'Neil, C. Pentzold and S. Toupin, eds, *Handbook of Peer Production* (Wiley-Blackwell, 2021), pp. 334–46.

——, 'Walled Gardens or a Global Network? Tensions, (De-)Centralizations, and Pluralities of the Internet Model', in J. Kulesza and R. Balleste, eds, *Cybersecurity and Human Rights in the Age of Cyberveillance* (London: Rowman & Littlefield, 2016), pp. 129–46.

——, 'Practice, Plurality, Performativity and Plumbing: Internet Governance Research Meets Science and Technology Studies', *Science, Technology and Human Values*, 40.2 (2015a), 272–86.

——, *Nains sans géants: Architecture décentralisée et services Internet.* (Paris: Presses des Mines, 2015b).

——, 'Dangerous Liaisons? Governments, Companies and Internet Governance', *Internet Policy Review*, 2.1 (2013) <https://doi.org/10.14763/2013.1.108> [accessed 21 June 2021].

——, 'Caring About the Plumbing: On the Importance of Architectures in Social Studies of (Peer-to-Peer) Technology', *Journal of Peer Production*, 1 (2012) <http://hal-ensmp.archives-ouvertes.fr/hal-00771863> [accessed 21 June 2021].

——, 'When Social Links are Network Links: The Dawn of Peer-to-Peer Social Networks and Its Implications for Privacy', *Observatorio (OBS)*, 4.3 (2010), 185–207.

Musiani, F., D. L. Cogburn, L. DeNardis, and N. S. Levinson, eds, *The Turn to Infrastructure in Internet Governance* (New York: Palgrave/Macmillan, 2016).

Musiani, F., and K. Ermoshina, 'What is a Good Secure Messaging Tool? The EFF Secure Messaging Scorecard and the Shaping of Digital (Usable) Security', *Westminster Papers in Communication and Culture*, 12.3 (2017), 51–71.

Musiani, F., and C. Méadel, 'Reclaiming the Internet' with Distributed Architectures: An Introduction', *First Monday*, 21.12 (2016) <http://firstmonday.org/ojs/index.php/fm/article/view/7101> [accessed 21 June 2021].

Myers West, S., 'Cryptographic Imaginaries and the Networked Public', *Internet Policy Review*, 7.2 (2018) <https://doi.org/10.14763/2018.2.792> [accessed 21 June 2021].

Nocetti, J., 'Russia's "Dictatorship-of-the-Law" Approach to Internet Policy', *Internet Policy Review*, 4.4 (2015) <https://doi.org/10.14763/2015.4.380> [accessed 21 June 2021].

Norman, D. A., 'When Security Gets in the Way', *interactions*, 16.6 (2009), 60–3.

Nyman, L., *Understanding Code Forking in Open Source Software: An Examination of Code Forking, Its Effect on Open Source Software, and How It Is Viewed and Practiced by Developers* (PhD dissertation, Hanken School of Economics, Finland, 2015) <https://helda.helsinki.fi/bitstream/handle/10138/153135/287_978-952-232-275-3-1_v2.pdf?sequence=5&isAllowed=y> [accessed 21 June 2021].

Nyman, L., and J. Lindman, 'Code Forking, Governance, and Sustainability in Open Source Software', *Technology Innovation Management Review*, 3.1 (2013), 7–12 <https://timreview.ca/sites/default/files/article_PDF/NymanLindman_TIMReview_January2013.pdf> [accessed 21 June 2021].

Oladimeji, E. A., S. Supakkul, and L. Chung, 'Security Threat Modeling and Analysis: A Goal-Oriented Approach', in *Proceedings of the 10th IASTED International Conference on Software Engineering and Applications (SEA)*, 2006, pp. 13–15.

O'Neil, M., L. Muselli, M. Raissi, and S. Zacchiroli, '"Open Source Has Won and Lost the War": Legitimising Commercial–Communal Hybridisation in a FOSS project', *New Media & Society*, 23.5 (2021), 1157–80.

Oram, A., ed., *Peer-to-peer: Harnessing the Power of Disruptive Technologies* (Sebastopol, CA: O'Reilly, 2001).

Oudshoorn, N., and T. Pinch, *How Users Matter: The Co-Construction of Users and Technology* (Cambridge, MA: The MIT Press, 2005).

Paloque-Bergès, C., 'Usenet as a Web Archive: Multi-layered Archives of Computer-Mediated-Communication', in N. Brugger, ed., *Web 25: Histories from the First 25 Years of the World Wide Web* (London: Peter Lang Publishing, 2017), pp. 227–50.

Piscitello, D., 'Metadata Collection and Controversy', ICANN Blog, 27 June 2016 <https://www.icann.org/news/blog/metadata-collection-and-controversy> [accessed 21 June 2021].

Pohle, J., 'Multistakeholder Governance Processes as Production Sites: Enhanced Cooperation "in the Making"', *Internet Policy Review*, 5.3 (2016) <https://doi.org/10.14763/2016.3.432> [accessed 21 June 2021].

Pohle, J., and L. Van Audenhove, 'Post-Snowden Internet Policy: Between Public Outrage, Resistance and Policy Change', *Media and Communication*, 5.1 (2017), 1–6.

Ponterotto, J. G., 'Brief Note on the Origins, Evolution, and Meaning of the Qualitative Research Concept Thick Description', *The Qualitative Report*, 11.3 (2006), 538–49.

Porter, T. M., *Trust in Numbers: The Pursuit of Objectivity in Science and Public Life* (Princeton, NJ: Princeton University Press, 1995).

Pouwelse, J. A., and others, 'Tribler: A Social-Based Peer-to-Peer System', *Concurrency and Computation: Practice & Experience*, 20.2 (2006), 127–38.

Powell, A., 'Democratizing Production through Open Source Knowledge: From Open Software to Open Hardware', *Media, Culture & Society*, 34.6 (2012), 691–708.

Pozen, D. E., 'The Mosaic Theory, National Security, and the Freedom of Information Act', *The Yale Law Journal*, 115.3 (2005), 628–79.

Raman, A., S. Joglekar, E. D. Cristofaro, N. Sastry, and G. Tyson, 'Challenges in the Decentralised Web: The Mastodon Case', in *Proceedings of the ACM Internet Measurement Conference*, October 2019 (pp. 217–29).

randall-signal, 'Introducing Signal PINs', *Signal Blog*, 19 May 2020 <https://signal.org/blog/signal-pins/> [accessed 21 June 2021].

Raymond, E., 'Homesteading the Noosphere', Working Paper <http://catb.org/~esr/writings/homesteading/homesteading/> [accessed 21 June 2021].

Reda, J., and L. Anderson, 'Open Letter to the European Commission on Encrypted Media Extensions', April 2017 <https://juliareda.eu/2017/04/open-letter-to-the-european-commission-on-encrypted-media-extensions/ > [accessed 21 June 2021].

Riordan, J., *The Liability of Internet Intermediaries* (Oxford: Oxford University Press, 2016).

Rivest, R. L., 'The Case Against Regulating Encryption Technology', *Scientific American*, 279.4 (1998), 88–9.

Rochko, E., 'The Mastodon Project', 14 November 2018 <https://joinmastodon.org>

Rogaway, P., 'The Moral Character of Cryptographic Work', IACR Distinguished Lecture at Asiacrypt 2015 <http://web.cs.ucdavis.edu/~rogaway/papers/moral.pdf> [accessed 21 June 2021].

Rowe, A., 'Everything You Need to Know about the Decentralized Internet', *Tech.co*, 23 February 2018 <https://tech.co/news/decentralized-internet-guide-2018-02> [accessed 21 June 2021].

Ryan, P. 'ISO Leadership Encourages Rejection of OOXML Appeal', *Ars Technica*, 7 October 2008 <https://arstechnica.com/information-technology/2008/07/iso-leadership-encourages-rejection-of-ooxml-appeal/> [accessed 21 June 2021].

Sanger, D., and N. Perlroth, 'Encrypted Messaging Apps Face New Scrutiny Over Possible Role in Paris Attacks', *New York Times*, 17 November 2015 <http://www.nytimes.com/2015/11/17/world/europe/encrypted-messaging-apps-face-new-scrutiny-over-possible-role-in-paris-attacks.html> [accessed 21 June 2021].

Schmitt, C., *The Nomos of the Earth* (New York: Telos Press, 2003).

Schneider, A., 'Decentralization: Conceptualization and Measurement', *Studies in Comparative International Development*, 38.3 (2003), 32–56 <https://doi.org/10.1007/BF02686198> [accessed 21 June 2021].

Schneider, N., 'Decentralization: An Incomplete Ambition', *Journal of Cultural Economy*, 12.4 (2019), 265–85.

Schulze, M., 'Clipper Meets Apple vs FBI: A Comparison of the Cryptography Discourses from 1993 and 2016', *Media and Communication*, 5.1 (2017), 54–62.

Simcoe, T., 'Open Standards and Intellectual Property Rights', in H. Chesbrough, W. Vanhaverbeke and J. West, eds, *Open Innovation Researching a New Paradigm* (Oxford: Oxford University Press, 2006), pp. 161–83.

Snowden, E., 'Without Encryption, We Lose All Privacy. This Is Our New Battleground', *The Guardian*, 15 October 2019 (2019a) <https://www.theguardian.com/commentisfree/2019/oct/15/encryption-lose-privacy-us-uk-australia-facebook> [accessed 21 June 2021].

——, *Permanent Record* (Henry Holt and Company, 2019b).

Soghoian, C., 'Caught in the Cloud: Privacy, Encryption, and Government Back Doors in the Web 2.0 Era', *Journal on Telecommunications and High Technology*, 8 (2010), 359.

Solove, D. J., 'A Taxonomy of Privacy', *University of Pennsylvania Law Review*, 154.3 (2006), 477–560.

Sparrow, E., and H. Halpin, 'LEAP: The LEAP Encryption Access Project', in *Reforming European Data Protection Law* (Dordrecht: Springer, 2015), pp. 367–83.

Star, S. L., and M. Lampland, 'Reckoning with Standards', in M. Lampland, and S. L. Star, eds, *Standards and Their Stories: How Quantifying, Classifying, and Formalizing Practices Shape Everyday Life* (Ithaca, NY: Cornell University Press, 2009), pp. 3–24.

Tänzer, M., 'The Influence of Architectural Styles on Security, Using the Example of a Certification Authority', arXiv preprint, 2014 <https://arxiv.org/abs/1408.2758> [accessed 21 June 2021].

ten Oever, N., "This Is Not How We Imagined It': Technological Affordances, Economic Drivers and the Internet Architecture Imaginary', *New Media and Society*, 23.2 (2021), 344–62.

Tilly, C., 'Models and Realities of Popular Collective Action', *Social Research*, 52 (1985), 717–47.

Trienes, J., A. T. Cano, and D. Hiemstra, 'Recommending Users: Whom to Follow on Federated Social Networks', arXiv preprint, 2018 <https://arxiv.org/abs/1811.09292> [accessed 21 June 2021].

Torr, P., 'Demystifying the Threat Modeling Process', *IEEE Security & Privacy*, 3.5 (2005), 66–70.

Turner, F., *From Counterculture to Cyberculture: Stewart Brand, the Whole Earth Network, and the Rise of Digital Utopianism* (Chicago, IL: University of Chicago Press, 2010).

Unknown, 'We Have Discovered and Addressed a Security Breach. (Updated 4 December 2019)', Matrix.org Blog, 28 November 2019 <https://matrix.org/blog/2019/04/11/we-have-discovered-and-addressed-a-security-breach-updated-2019-04-12/> [accessed 21 June 2021].

———, 'Decentralize or Perish: Making Network Architecture Political', Chapsterhood, 28 November 2019 <https://www.chapsterhood.com/2019/03/09/decentralize-or-perish/> [accessed 21 June 2021].

Utz, C., M. Degeling, S. Fahl, F. Schaub, and T. Holz, '(Un)Informed Consent: Studying GDPR Consent Notices in the Field', in *Proceedings of the 2019 ACM SIGSAC Conference on Computer and Communications Security* (pp. 973–90) <https://dl.acm.org/doi/abs/10.1145/3319535.3354212> [accessed 21 June 2021].

Van den Hooff, L., and others, 'Vuvuzela: Scalable Private Messaging Resistant to Traffic Analysis', in *Proceedings of the 25th ACL Symposium on Operating Systems Principles*, 2015 <http://dx.doi.org/10.1145/2815400.2815417> [accessed 21 June 2021].

Van Eeten, M., and M. Mueller, 'Where Is the Governance in Internet Governance?', *New Media & Society*, 15.5 (2013), 720–36.

Vargas-Leon, P., 'Tracking Internet Shutdown Practices: Democracies and Hybrid Regimes', in F. Musiani and others, *The Turn to Infrastructure in Internet Governance* (New York: Palgrave Macmillan, 2016), pp. 167–88.

Vaz, P., and F. Bruno, 'Types of Self-Surveillance: From Abnormality to Individuals "at Risk"', *Surveillance and Society*, 1.3 (2003), 272–91.

von Hippel, E., 'Lead Users: A Source of Novel Product Concepts', *Management Science*, 32.7 (1986), 791–806.

Walker, S., D. Mercea, and M. Bastos, 'The Disinformation Landscape and the Lockdown of Social Platforms', *Information, Communication & Society*, 22.11 (2019), 1531–43.

Weinberger, M., 'Matrix Wants to Smash the Walled Gardens of Messaging', *ComputerWorld*, 16 September 2014 <https://www.computerworld.com/article/2694500/matrix-wants-to-smash-the-walled-gardens-of-messaging.html> [accessed 21 June 2021].

Winter, P., and S. Lindskog, 'How China is Blocking Tor', arXiv preprint, 2012 <https://arxiv.org/pdf/1204.0447.pdf> [accessed 21 June 2021].

Wire, 'Product Design Decisions for Secure Messengers', *Medium*, 19 May 2017 (2017a), https://medium.com/@wireapp/product-design-decisions-for-secure-messengers-e8a5e7d1a373 [accessed 21 June 2021].

———, 'The road to a more private and secure calling protocol', *Medium*, 17 March 2017 (2017b), https://medium.com/@wireapp/the-road-to-a-more-private-and-secure-calling-protocol-a8f22d23f112 [accessed 21 June 2021].

Yee, K. P., 'Aligning Security and Usability', *IEEE Security & Privacy*, 2.5 (2004), 48–55.

Ziewitz, M., 'Governing Algorithms: Myth, Mess, and Methods', *Science, Technology and Human Values*, 41.1 (2016), 3–16.

Zorz, Z., 'How the EFF was Pushed to Rethink Its Secure Messaging Scorecard', HelpNetSecurity, 11 August 2016 <https://www.helpnetsecurity.com/2016/08/11/eff-secure-messaging-scorecard/> [accessed 21 June 2021].

Zhang, C. B., Y. N. Li, B. Wu, and D. J. Li, 'How WeChat Can Retain Users: Roles of Network Externalities, Social Interaction Ties, and Perceived Values in Building Continuance Intention', *Computers in Human Behavior*, 69 (2017), 284–93.

APPENDIX

INTERVIEW SELECTION PROCESS AND ETHICAL GUIDELINES

INTERVIEW SUBJECTS WHO WERE ALSO DEVELOPERS WERE SELECTED ACCORD-
ing to pre-existing personal relationships that researchers had with the cryptographic research community of NEXTLEAP research team members. Although
this does result in some bias, we believe it is countered by the large number of
interviews we have undertaken. The relatively small size of the global developer
community might also be considered in mitigation. We also reached out to some
developers via the GitLab and GitHub pages of projects to which we did not
have personal connections (e.g. Ricochet, Conversations).

In contrast, user studies were undertaken with individuals who were selected
more by chance. Some attended training events in their local environments
(both high-risk, in the case of Ukraine and Russia, and low risk in the case of
France, Germany, Austria and the United Kingdom). Some attended conferences in pre-selected venues that were determined by us to be likely to attract
high-risk users who lived in areas that, due to the level of repression they were
likely experiencing, would make it difficult if not impossible to interview them
in their local environment, or would make it such that they could not speak
openly in their native environment. This was the case for users from Egypt,
Turkey, Kenya and Iran, where the interviews took place in March 2017 at
the Internet Freedom Festival and at RightsCon. A total of 54 interviews were
completed in a first phase of fieldwork between autumn 2016 and spring 2017.
We interviewed developers (17), experts from NGOs focused on privacy and

security, such as EFF, Tactical Tech and Privacy International (5), and everyday users (32). Developers from LEAP and Pixelated (PGP), ChatSecure (OTR), Signal protocol and its implementations and forks (including Wire and Conversations (OMEMO)) were interviewed, as well as developers from Tor, Briar and Ricochet that use their own custom protocols.

Within user groups we distinguish between high-risk users (14) and users (including researchers and students) from low-risk countries (18). The developers were all from the USA/Western Europe, and the high-risk users included users from Ukraine, Russia, Egypt, Lebanon, Kenya and Iran. Some high-risk users, due to the conditions in their country, had left (4) or maintained dual residency (2) between their high-risk environment and a low-risk environment. The 'users' category also includes a subset (18) of security trainers, for example users involved in organising seminars on security, disseminating privacy-enhancing technologies, practices and knowledge. We interviewed trainers from both high-risk (9) and low-risk countries (9).

A second round of interviews (28) took place in 2018. It focused in particular on aspects of project governance, and as such mostly developers (14) and corporate users (8) were interviewed, in addition to other users living in high-risk environments (6).

A specific protocol was developed in order to protect the privacy of our respondents: if they wished to complete the interview online, we let users and developers suggest a tool of communication of their choice to us. These tools ranged from PGP to Signal, meet.jitsi, Wire and WhatsApp. If an 'in person' interview was preferred, the interview was recorded with an audio recorder isolated from the Internet. We use a dedicated encrypted hard drive to store the interviews. Before the interview we asked our respondents to carefully read two user-consent forms related to the study and ask any questions they might have regarding their privacy, their rights and our methodology. The two forms were written in collaboration with UCL usability researchers and were based on the European General Data Protection Regulation. The documents included an Information Sheet and an Informed Consent Form. The first document explained the purpose of the interview, described the research project and clearly mentioned the sources of funding for the project. It also provided information about the length of the interview, as well as information about the researcher, including her email, full name, academic affiliation and the address of the research institution. The second form described the data processing procedures and the period and conditions of data storage; it emphasised the right of the interviewees to demand, at any moment, to withdraw their data from the research. A copy of each document was given to the interviewee. Different forms were used for users and developers.

Additional measures have been taken to ensure enhanced privacy for our interviewees. Thus, the name of the interviewee was not mentioned during the recording. We also adapted some questions to withdraw any elements of context (such as the country or the city, the precise social movement or affinity group a user was involved in and so on), if interviewees asked for this. We respected the right of our interviewees to refuse to answer a specific question. However, our questions were specifically designed to focus on digital tools, with no biographical questions included. The names of both developers and users are mentioned in this book only when a user gave us permission to do so; otherwise, users remain anonymised and we instead use qualifying labels such as 'lead developer of…' or 'high-risk user from…'.

GLOSSARY

Build: In software development, the term may refer either to the process by which source code is converted into a stand-alone form that can be run on a computer, or to the form itself. One of the most important steps of a software build is the compilation process, where source code files are converted into executable code. See also https://www.techopedia.com/definition/3759/build

Chat-over-email: An approach to designing instant messaging applications using email transfer protocols, such as SMTP and IMAP, often with an implementation of PGP on top, to offer end-to-end encryption. The most well-known projects of a chat-over-email app are Delta Chat, COI, Spike and MailTime.

Client-server: Computer networking model where the machines that communicate are not equivalent: one is a server, permanently on and waiting for connections, the others are clients, who connect when they have something to ask.

Client-side implementation: 'Client-side' means that the action takes place on the user's (the client's) computer, as opposed to 'server-side' which means that the action takes place on a web server.

Constant bit rate encoding: In telecommunications, the term indicates a situation in which the rate at which data is consumed by a codec (a device that encodes or decodes a data stream) is constant.

(Cryptographic) deniability: Encryption technique that allows 'denying' the existence of an encrypted file or message, in the sense that an adversary is unable to prove that the associated data exists.

Double Ratchet: Key management algorithm developed by the creators of Signal (Trevor Perrin and Moxie Marlinspike) in 2013, which manages the ongoing renewal and maintenance of short-lived session keys after a first key exchange. It is a 'double' ratchet because it combines a cryptographic component with a key derivation function.

End-to-end encryption: Only the communicating parties can read the message, which is encrypted in transit *and* on users' terminals.

Ephemeral key exchange: See **key exchange**. With ephemeral methods, a different key is used for each connection.

Ephemeral (or disappearing) messaging: Mobile-to-mobile transmission of multimedia messages that automatically disappear from the recipient's screen after the message has been viewed. See also https://searchcio. techtarget.com/definition/ephemeral-messaging

Forking: Forking a piece of software during its development process means that developers take a copy of its source code and start independent development on it, creating a separate piece of software. An act of forking is generally not merely a technical issue, but involves a (governance/organisational) change, possibly conflictual, in the developer community.

Forward/future secrecy: A cryptographic feature of the last generation of instant messaging apps, ensuring that a user's **session keys** will not be compromised even if the private key of the server *is* compromised. In particular, it is meant to protect past sessions against future compromises of secret keys or passwords.

F/OSS (Free and Open-Source Software): Software that anyone is freely licensed to use, copy, study and change in any way, and whose source code is openly shared so that people are encouraged to voluntarily improve the design of the software.

Gossiping/gossip protocol: A process of peer-to-peer communication between computers which ensures that data is disseminated to all members of a group; in the absence of a central registry, the only way to spread data is to rely on each member to pass it along to their neighbours. Thus, gossip protocols are based on the way epidemics spread, and are also called epidemic protocols.

Group messaging: Holding a conversation via a messaging application between two or more people.

Hash: A function that converts an input of letters and numbers into an encrypted output of a fixed length.

Header (email): A code snippet in an HTML email, which precedes the body of the email and contains information about the sender, recipient, the email's route to get to the inbox and a number of authentication details. See https://sendpulse.com/support/glossary/email-header

Interoperability: The ability of programs (messaging apps or any kind of software) to exchange data and communicate smoothly with each other.

IP address: A numerical label assigned to each device connected to a computer network that uses the Internet Protocol for communication. An IP address has the two main functions of acting as a host or network interface identifier and providing location addressing.

IPv6: The most recent version of the Internet Protocol, the communications protocol that provides an identification and location system for computers on networks and routes traffic across the Internet.

Key exchange (v. key discovery): In **public key cryptography**, key exchange is the method by which cryptographic keys are exchanged between two parties; key verification is any way that lets you match a key to a person, making sure that it is indeed that person who uses the key (see e.g. https://ssd.eff.org/en/glossary/key-verification)

Key management: All operations related to the management of cryptographic keys in an encrypted system, including their generation, exchange, storage, use, destruction and replacement.

Latency: In engineering, latency is the time interval between a stimulation and a response, or, from a more general point of view, a time delay between the cause and the effect of some change in the system being observed.

MAC (media access control) address: A unique identifier assigned to a network interface controller (a hardware component connecting a computer to a network) to use as an address in a communication.

Mail User Agent: a computer application that allows a user to send and retrieve email – colloquially called an email program.

Man-in-the-middle attack: In computer security, MITM is an attack where the attacker secretly relays and possibly alters the communications between two parties who believe that they are directly communicating with each other.

Mesh networks: A network model in which the infrastructure nodes connect directly, dynamically and non-hierarchically to as many other nodes as possible and cooperate with one another to efficiently route data.

Metadata: Succinctly defined as 'information about information', the data providing information about one or more aspects of the data itself. Metadata is used to summarise basic information about data, which can make tracking and working with specific data easier.

Mixnet (mix network): Routing protocols that create hard-to-trace communications by using a chain of servers known as *mixes,* which take in messages from multiple senders, shuffle them and send them back out in random order to the next destination. *De facto*, this breaks the link between the source of the request and the destination, making it harder for third parties to trace end-to-end communications.

Network-layer protection: The network interface layer is the physical interface between the host system and the network hardware, which defines how data packets should be formatted for transmission and routings. This layer has several security vulnerabilities unique to it, needing specific protection responses.

Non-repudiation: Assurance that someone cannot deny the validity of a particular operation; in cryptography, the concept refers to a service that is able to provide proof of the origin of data as well as their integrity.

OMEMO: stands for 'OMEMO Multi-End Message and Object Encryption', an encryption protocol developed to solve specific limitations and problems that existed both in OpenPGP and in OTR. It provides future and forward secrecy and deniability and gives the possibility of message synchronisation and offline delivery.

Open standards and protocols: non-proprietary, open source, well-documented protocols that have been standardised by relevant institutions and are available to be reused and shared by the wider developer community. Open standards are usually believed to ensure better **interoperability** and improve further collaboration between projects based on open standards.

Out of band (data): The data transferred through a stream that is independent from the main data stream ('in band'). An out-of-band data mechanism provides a conceptually independent channel, which allows any data sent via that mechanism to be kept separate from in-band data.

OTR (Off-the-Record Messaging): A cryptographic protocol that provides encryption for instant messaging conversations. In addition to authentication and encryption, OTR provides **forward secrecy**. Version 4 of the protocol (OTRv4) is currently being designed by a team led by Sofía Celi and reviewed by Nik Unger and Ian Goldberg.

Passive attack: An attack on a network in which the attacker does not – as it cannot – interact with any of the parties involved, thus attempting to break the system solely based upon observed data.

Pastebin: A type of online content hosting service where users can store plain text.

Patent disclosure: A public claim of data about an invention; more generally, any part of a patenting process in which data regarding an invention is disclosed to the public. A patent disclosure is used by individuals such as inventors and attorneys, seeking to prepare a patent application. A patent disclosure provides information on the invention and its originality/uniqueness. See also https://www.upcounsel.com/patent-disclosure.

Peer-to-peer (p2p): Computer networking model where two machines or two humans communicate directly to exchange messages, files, or other data.

Primitive (cryptographic): Well-established, low-level cryptographic algorithms, frequently used as a basis to build cryptographic protocols.

Protocol: Referring to the Internet, this word indicates a set of criteria and procedures that provide the conceptual model of the network of networks, as well as the set of specifications that explain how data should be regrouped into packets, addressed, transmitted, routed and received.

Public-key (or asymmetric) cryptography: Cryptographic system that uses pairs of keys: public keys which may be disseminated widely, and private keys known only to the owner.

Public-key infrastructure: The set of roles, policies and procedures needed to create, manage, distribute and use public-key cryptography.

Pull request: In software development, a pull request is a method of submitting contributions to an open development project, which occurs when a developer (or an expert user) asks for changes committed to an external repository to be considered for inclusion in a project's main repository.

PGP (Pretty Good Privacy): An encryption programme that provides privacy and authentication for online communications. PGP is used for signing, encrypting and decrypting texts, e-mails, files, directories and disk partitions, as well as increasing the security of e-mail communications.

Security vs Usability: A widely discussed hypothesis according to which it is extremely hard to design truly secure communication systems and still keep them user-friendly.

Server Name Indication (SNI): An extension to the Transport Layer Security (TLS) computer networking protocol by which a client indicates which hostname it is attempting to connect to at the start of the handshaking process.

Server-side archives: When an e-mail program uses this option, the mail server archives to the mail server itself, or to another server designated as the archive server. This is opposed to client-based archiving, when the individual workstations process mail file archiving. Mail is archived either to the mail server, a designated server, or to its local workstations.

Server-side encryption: Data is encrypted on the server (of the company providing the messaging services).

Social graph: A graph (representation of a structure) representing social relations between a set of entities, e.g. individuals.

TLS (Transport Layer Security): Cryptographic protocol designed to provide communications security over a computer network. TLS aims primarily to provide data integrity and privacy between two or more communicating computer applications.

Two-factor authentication: In an Internet-based service, this is a method of confirming users' claimed identities by using a combination of *two* among these different factors: (1) something they know, (2) something they have, or (3) something they are.

XMPP: Extensible Messaging and Presence Protocol, originally named Jabber and created by the eponymous community, is a communication protocol based on XML (Extensible Markup Language). Unlike most instant messaging protocols, XMPP is defined in an open standard and uses an open systems approach for its development and application. https://xmpp.org/

UI/UX design: User experience design is the process of influencing user behaviour by acting upon some features of a product, such as usability and accessibility. User interface design is the design of the graphical layout of an application – all the items the user interacts with. The two processes are generally considered as part of a whole.

Untrusted server problem: Being able to provide security even in the event of a 'worst case scenario' server breach, where an attacker has full control of server resources, including the ability to read and modify back-end application code and data and remain undetected for at least some time.

Upcycling (of protocols): An approach to designing instant messaging applications by reusing existing open standards and protocols, instead of creating new ones. This approach is said to increase interoperability and help engage bigger communities of developers, as it is based on open standards or well documented protocols.

Usable security: The interdisciplinary research field that addresses the usability of secure communication technologies.

MATTERING PRESS TITLES

Engineering the Climate: Science, Politics and Visions of Control
JULIA SCHUBERT

With Microbes
EDITED BY CHARLOTTE BRIVES, MATTHÄUS REST AND SALLA SARIOLA

Environmental Alterities
EDITED BY CRISTÓBAL BONELLI AND ANTONIA WALFORD

Sensing In/Security
EDITED BY NINA KLIMBURG-WITJES, NIKOLAUS POECHHACKER & GEOFFREY C. BOWKER

Energy Worlds in Experiment
EDITED BY JAMES MAGUIRE, LAURA WATTS AND BRITT ROSS WINTHEREIK

Boxes: A Field Guide
EDITED BY SUSANNE BAUER, MARTINA SCHLÜNDER AND MARIA RENTETZI

An Anthropology of Common Ground: Awkward Encounters in Heritage Work
NATHALIA SOFIE BRICHET

Ghost-Managed Medicine: Big Pharma's Invisible Hands
SERGIO SISMONDO

Inventing the Social
EDITED BY NOORTJE MARRES, MICHAEL GUGGENHEIM, ALEX WILKIE

Energy Babble
ANDY BOUCHER, BILL GAVER, TOBIE KERRIDGE, MIKE MICHAEL, LILIANA OVALLE, MATTHEW PLUMMER-FERNANDEZ AND ALEX WILKIE

The Ethnographic Case
EDITED BY EMILY YATES-DOERR AND CHRISTINE LABUSKI

On Curiosity: The Art of Market Seduction
FRANCK COCHOY

Practising Comparison: Logics, Relations, Collaborations
EDITED BY JOE DEVILLE, MICHAEL GUGGENHEIM AND ZUZANA HRDLIČKOVÁ

Modes of Knowing: Resources from the Baroque
EDITED BY JOHN LAW AND EVELYN RUPPERT

Imagining Classrooms: Stories of Children, Teaching and Ethnography
VICKI MACKNIGHT

www.ingramcontent.com/pod-product-compliance
Lightning Source LLC
Chambersburg PA
CBHW032346280326
41935CB00008B/468